GARCÍA MÁRQUEZ

Stephen Minta

GARCÍA MÁRQUEZ

Writer of Colombia

1817

HARPER & ROW, PUBLISHERS, New York
Cambridge, Philadelphia, San Francisco, Washington
London, Mexico City, São Paulo, Singapore, Sydney

GARCÍA MÁRQUEZ: WRITER OF COLOMBIA. Copyright © 1987 by Stephen Minta. All rights reserved. Printed in the United States of America. No part of this book may be used or reproduced in any manner whatsoever without written permission except in the case of brief quotations embodied in critical articles and reviews. For information address Harper & Row, Publishers, Inc., 10 East 53rd Street, New York, N.Y. 10022.

FIRST U.S. EDITION

Index by Sylvia Farrington

Library of Congress Cataloging-in-Publication Data

Minta, Stephen.
    García Márquez, writer of Colombia.

    Bibliography: p.
    Includes index.
    1. García Márquez, Gabriel, 1928 —Criticism and interpretation. I. Title.
PQ8180.17.A73Z74 1987   863   86-45671
ISBN 0-06-435755-4   87 88 89 90 91 10 HC 9 8 7 6 5 4 3 2 1
ISBN 0-06-430166-4 (pbk.)   87 88 89 90 91 10 HC 9 8 7 6 5 4 3 2 1

To the memory of
DINOS PATRIDES,
colleague, friend and
scholar

Contents

Acknowledgments

I could never have completed this book in its present form without the help and encouragement of David Skidmore, of the Politics Department in the University of York: I owe him a great deal, and am very happy to be able to record my gratitude here. My thanks go also to Anthony Goff, of David Higham Associates; to Ray Yu and Peggy Barth, for providing some valuable material; to the staff of the Taylor Institution Library in the University of Oxford; and to Sal Brabyn, for much help in the final stages.

S. M.

I

Colombia

For Europeans, South America is a man with a moustache, a guitar, and a revolver.' The words are those of one of the characters in García Márquez's long short story *No One Writes to the Colonel*, a work written during a period of self-imposed exile in Paris in the 1950s. Although since then Latin America has come to figure more prominently in European eyes, with wide media coverage of events in Chile and Argentina in the 1970s and in Central America in the 1980s, such stereotypes still retain something of their deceptive power. In North America, too, the image of the ever-smiling, half-crazed, and free-shooting Mexican who, in the popular imagination, stands for all of Latin America, is one that is taking a long time to die. This is despite the fact that in some of the larger cities the image has inevitably been modified by direct contact with Latin Americans, or, more truthfully perhaps, by fear of such contact.

Now García Márquez does not systematically require a deep knowledge of Latin American history and culture from his readers; millions of people have obviously read and enjoyed his books without the benefit of such knowledge. Nevertheless he is a writer who is profoundly concerned with the past of his continent, and, more specifically, with the history of his native land, Colombia. Accordingly this chapter will concentrate on Colombia's past and present in order to give access to aspects of García Márquez's work which often remain concealed. I hope particularly that, in this way, the broader implications of the solitude which is the subject of his most important novel to date, and which is implicit in much of his writing, may become apparent. The term 'magical realism' has frequently been applied to books like *One Hundred Years of*

Solitude, and the following pages are certainly not intended to deny the importance of the imagination, of myth and magic and wonder, in such a work. They should, however, provide the basis for an understanding of something which is also important, and to which García Márquez has drawn attention many times over the years, often in the face of disbelief or incomprehension: 'every single line . . . in all my books', he has said, 'has a starting point in reality'.

All nations strive to maintain or to resist certain images of themselves, and it has always been one aspect of a writer's task to explore and to challenge such images. Within the circles of its élite, Colombia has long retained a pride in the high quality of its spoken Spanish, a concern for the values of cultural distinction, and a feeling for the uniqueness of its 'Athenian' democracy. Among specialists in politics and sociology, it is a country which has attracted much attention because of the high levels of political violence to which it has been subject over long periods, and because it exhibits some curiously archaic features of social and political organization. Political figures in North America often single out Colombia, with some relief, as one of Latin America's few regularly functioning democracies. For those working in the field of human rights, however, the contradictions within Colombian democracy are also very much in evidence; the title of an Americas Watch report of October 1982, *Human Rights in the Two Colombias: Functioning Democracy, Militarized Society*, clearly underlines this. Finally, in the minds of many people in the United States, Colombia has, over the past decade or so, become almost synonymous with the drug trade. It is the world's largest exporter of cocaine, the source, until very recently, of perhaps 80 per cent of both the cocaine and the marijuana consumed in North America, and one of those rare countries whose major export does not appear anywhere in the official statistics.

Colombia also reveals, as one would expect, numerous features which are characteristic of a large number of other Latin American countries. It has experienced very high birth rates: an average annual growth of 3 per cent throughout the 1960s; and a high rate of urbanization: the percentage of the population described as urban has risen from 48 per cent in 1960 to 70 per cent in 1980. It maintains extreme differences of wealth and poverty, and marked inequalities in all important areas of life. Illiteracy is high in rural areas, and the pattern of landholding is characterized by the alternation of a limited number of very large farms and numerous smallholdings which barely admit subsistence. In his book on the agrarian question in Colombia, published in 1974, Pierre Gilhodes provides figures which show that approximately 63 per cent of Colombian farms collectively occupied less than 4 per cent of the country's cultivated land; such unequal distribution is found all over Latin America, from El Salvador to Chile. Levels of unemployment or underemployment are high, both in rural and urban areas, and access to sanitation facilities, safe water, electricity, and medical care is very unequally distributed. The consequences of such a situation are easily predicted. One study in 1977 showed that at least 90 per cent of all children admitted to hospitals showed signs of undernourishment. Nearly 50 per cent of families receive less than the recommended level of calories and proteins. As a counterpart to that, René Dumont, in a book published in 1981, noted that the national budget for the coercive forces of the state – the army and police – exceeded that for education, health, and agriculture combined.

The last point should not, however, be taken to imply that Colombia is yet another Latin American country ruled by endless military figures in dark glasses. The military remain an important, if somewhat unquantifiable, influence in Colombian politics, but only on rare occasions have they intervened directly in the political process. When García Márquez was writing his dictator novel, *The Autumn of the Patriarch*, he chose to move to Franco's Spain in order to gain some sense of what life under a classic dictator was really like.

There are a number of other respects in which Colombia fails to match the stereotype of Latin American repressive regimes. There has been relative freedom for political parties to organize and for newspapers to publish. There has never been anything like the persecution of writers and intellectuals on the scale which countries such as Argentina and Uruguay have experienced. Moreover, it has never been accurate to describe Colombia as a banana republic, in the sense that the term might fairly be applied to Honduras. This is true even given the fact – and it is a fact of particular significance for García Márquez's work – that by the mid-1920s Colombia had become the largest exporter of bananas in the world. Foreign intervention in the Colombian economy has never been comparable to that experienced in Chile or Venezuela or pre-revolutionary Cuba. So Colombia retains, for all that it shares in the contemporary plight of most Latin American countries, some important features which are the product of a distinctive historical development.

So far I have spoken as if Colombia were a single nation and this is, inevitably, misleading. The country is nominally and uniformly Catholic, but, in many important respects, the original hazards of nature which, for a long time, acted as a barrier to communication within the country have maintained a decisive and divisive influence. As far as the work of García Márquez is concerned, it is important to recognize that there is a crucial difference between the culture of the tropical, Caribbean zone of Colombia on the one hand, and the high-Andean interior culture associated with the nation's capital Bogotá on the other. The population of the former zone is of mixed African, Indian, and Spanish descent; in the interior the legacy of Spanish colonialism is stronger and, though there has been considerable racial mixing, the social advantages of a white face are much more in evidence.

A study of Colombian immigrants in Chicago showed, interestingly enough, that those from the Caribbean zone tended to socialize with each other and with Cubans, but not with their 'Spanish' compatriots from the interior of the country, thus clearly reproducing the racial and regional distinctions of Colombian society. García Márquez is unreservedly the representative of the Caribbean zone in which he was born and brought up and he has spoken often of the characteristics of the Afro-American culture which he sees as the shared inheritance of all Caribbean people, as well as of his sense of alienation in the face of the interior culture of his own country. He has placed nearly all his work to date in the tropical zone, a world of drama, movement, and light, of endless, and frequently oppressive, heat; and the 'cold culture' of the interior rarely intrudes except in the colours of mournful resignation or dull political reaction.

García Márquez first went to Bogotá in January 1943, at the age of fourteen, and in 1981 he recalled his initial impressions in the following terms: 'Bogotá was . . . a remote and mournful city, where a cold drizzle had been falling since the beginning of the sixteenth century. I suffered its bitterness for the first time one ill-fated afternoon in January, the saddest of my life, when I arrived from the coast . . .' Since that first experience his attitude has never really altered. Bogotá is a city 8,600 feet above sea-level, in the eastern cordillera of the Andes. Its mean annual temperature is around 58°F and the average temperature varies by only a degree or so throughout the year, the only real difference in climate being between rainy months and less rainy months. The description of Fernanda, one of the characters in *One Hundred Years of Solitude*, clearly reveals García Márquez's feelings towards this Andean world. She is an intruder from the interior into the tropical zone in which the novel is set: 'Fernanda was a woman lost to the world. She had been born and brought up a thousand kilometres from the sea, in a mournful city where, on ghostly nights, the carriages of the viceroys still rattled through the narrow, stone streets.' The reference to the viceroys recalls the fact that Bogotá, in the period of Spanish colonial domination before Colombian independence in 1819, was the capital of the viceroyalty of New Granada and occupied an influential position within the centralized and absolutist political system of the Spanish empire.

How different was the impression which the Nicaraguan writer Rubén Darío retained of Bogotá. Darío (1867–1916), the effective founder of the modernist movement in Latin American poetry, a highly influential figure who makes a significant appearance in *The Autumn of the Patriarch*, admired the attention to cultural distinction which he found in Colombia's capital; he valued its traditions, its long-enjoyed reputation as the Athens of Latin America. It was, he wrote, 'a paradise for the spirit', a city which cared about literature, a place 'long since famous for its cultivation of intellectual disciplines, a city of Greek and Latin . . .' García Márquez is certainly aware of the cultural importance of Bogotá in the history of Colombia, but the kind of culture which it represents is one with which he is wholly out of sympathy.

Perhaps the single most important aspect of Colombian history since the country gained independence from Spain has been the nature and extent of the political violence it has experienced. As James Payne puts it, 'On a scale of political deaths per generation,

Colombia has one of the highest levels of political conflict in the world.' The intensity of such conflict is the more bewildering in that the neighbouring countries of Panama, Ecuador, and Venezuela, which historically were closely linked with Colombia, have not suffered political violence to anything like the same degree. Payne writes further that 'perhaps the most perplexing aspect . . . is that political conflict has never been low. One cannot say that politics has ever been "tranquil" or "harmonious" in Colombia.' This may be somewhat exaggerated, in that there have been some quite long periods of relative peace in Colombia, most notably, perhaps, the peace of exhaustion which followed the civil war of 1899–1902. Nevertheless, in the first century of its independence Colombia went through thirteen periods of violent political strife, some of them lasting for four or five years at a time. From around 1946 to 1966, it experienced a conflict so intense and so protracted that Colombians call it simply *la violencia*. The civil war of 1899–1902 caused perhaps 100,000 deaths, in a country whose total population at that time was probably less than four million; while the *violencia*, which has been described by R.W. Ramsey as 'the western hemisphere's largest internal war in the twentieth century', led to an estimated quarter of a million deaths, including around 112,000 between 1948 and 1950. Both conflicts find their reflection in the writings of García Márquez, and the implicit links between them are, as I shall show, of considerable significance.

To explain something of the origins of the political violence in Colombia it is necessary to look at the history of the two major Colombian political parties, the Liberals and the Conservatives. The competition for state power between the élites of those two parties has, until recent times, been almost uniquely responsible for the high levels of violence. The two parties have dominated the politics of post-independence Colombia, and though there have been occasional challenges to that domination – a military dictatorship in the 1950s, for example, which had some populist aspirations, or the rise of the ANAPO party in the 1960s – the two major parties have always to date been able to defeat such challenges. It is interesting to note that, before the Colombian presidential elections of 1978, García Márquez and others prominent on the Colombian left urged the adoption of a single left-wing candidate to stand against the Liberal and Conservative nominees. No agreement on a single candidate was forthcoming, and the left-wing candidates between them eventually took less than 3 per cent of the total vote. This demonstrated, besides the persistent factionalism on the Colombian left, the firm control which the two major parties still exercised over Colombian politics. It points to the enormous difficulties facing anyone active on the left in Colombia, and helps to explain the importance which García Márquez has always attached to history and to political education in its broadest sense. His concern has been expressed not only in the writing of novels, but in his work as a journalist and in his life-long interest in the creation of alternative sources of information, through the establishment of new newspapers and magazines, in an attempt to broaden the base of Colombian political opinion.

In passing, it is worth noting two further features of the 1978 presidential elections which throw light on the general state of Colombian politics. If one test of a democratic society is the holding of elections, then Colombia passes with ease, for it has a long electoral tradition. It also has a long tradition of voter abstention, as the 1978 elections confirmed. Exact figures are always difficult to obtain, and are subject to varying degrees of manipulation, but abstention rates of 60 per cent in presidential elections and 70 per cent in congressional contests do not seem to have been uncommon. The phenomenon is not, of course, confined to Colombia. In the United States, for example, abstention rates of over 40 per cent in presidential elections have been recorded in recent times. The second interesting element in the 1978 Colombian elections concerns the possibility of fraud. Charges of fraud and intimidation have marked most electoral contests there, though once again the exact dimensions of the problem are hard to establish. In 1978, the Conservative candidate, Belisario Betancur, who had unsuccessfully contested the presidency in 1970 and was to be finally elected to the post in 1982, refused to concede defeat when it was announced that his Liberal opponent, Julio César Turbay Ayala, had won. Betancur alleged fraud and his supporters took to the streets. A re-count was then organized, the Liberal candidate, of whom García Márquez had written ironically that he had to his credit 'twenty years of personal sacrifices in the name of all the commonplaces of the class in power', was once again declared the winner, and Betancur finally conceded.

The details of the incident are of passing concern, but the suspicion of fraud, or the real existence of it, points to a perennial tension within the Colombian political system. So intense has been the struggle for power between Liberals and Conservatives, so much is at stake for the élites of both parties in Colombian elections, that there has been a marked tendency throughout post-independence history for the party in power to seek to retain that power by any available means. Political violence and electoral fraud are two sides of a single problem. The resources available to the party in power are such that, as Robert Dix notes, 'in Colombia the governing party, when unified, has practically always been able to control the outcome of elections.' In all of Colombia's history between independence and the institution of the National Front in 1958, there was only one occasion − and that was in 1861 − when power changed hands other than as a result of a split within the governing party. The consequences of this for the functioning of a democratic system of government are not difficult to grasp.

It is less easy, however, to convey a sense of just how and why the two-party system functions as it does and of the importance of party identification in Colombia. In the United States or Great Britain, the democratic process rests firmly on the assumption that voters can be relied upon, from time to time, to change their party allegiance. Of course some will remain Democratic or Labour party voters all their lives, and would never consider voting any other way, but enough people will change their minds over the years to ensure an alternating system of government. In Colombia, the lack of such a political mentality has been striking. Eduardo Santa, a prominent Colombian intellectual, wrote in 1962 that: 'We could almost say that in Colombia a person is born with a political identity card ('carnet político') tied to the umbilical cord.' The overwhelming majority of Colombians have traditionally identified with one of the two main parties, and have retained this identification throughout their lives. 'To change one's party loyalty', as Dix states, 'is to be considered an apostate and a traitor,' and he notes further that 'any change in political identification requires corresponding changes in one's closest social and personal relationships.'

As we have seen, the strength of party identification does not necessarily mean that people will turn out to vote; marking a cross is only one way in which such identification may be expressed. But the extremely polarized situation can, in fact, be seen in some remarkable voting patterns. Dix gives the example of one town in the department of Antioquia which, in the elections of March 1962, recorded 5,683 votes for the Conservative party and 11 votes for the Liberals, and he comments that such voting patterns 'are by no means uncommon'. Traditionally, there has been very little middle ground in Colombian politics, very few voters occupying a neutral position, waiting to be persuaded by the force of one side's policies or candidates.

This degree of polarization, so foreign to the practice of the democratic systems in Europe or the United States, has sometimes been compared with the present situation in Northern Ireland, where religious identification is strong and where, in the minds of many people in the rest of the United Kingdom, Catholics and Protestants seem to have been eternally locked within the violence of their historic hatreds. Such a comparison gives some sense of the forms and extremities of partisan violence, and throws some light on the inevitable problems which successive British governments have encountered in their search for the middle ground in Northern Ireland. However, the comparison fails to highlight a crucial difference between the kind of polarization experienced in Colombia and that experienced in Northern Ireland. In the latter case, there is fairly general agreement that, historically, one side has consistently exercised power at the expense of the other. The Catholics collectively, that is to say, have always occupied an inferior position in relation to the Protestants. However random the violence in Northern Ireland may sometimes appear to outside observers, it obeys a grim logic and is the direct and predictable legacy of an unequal historical relationship. The same cannot be said of the situation in Colombia. There both major parties have always been under the control of élite elements, and the problem has been to understand the logic of a more or less continuous conflict which has drawn large numbers of Colombians of all classes into violent confrontation in the name of élite power politics with which they might have been expected to have little sense of identification. There is a widespread assumption in democratic countries that different parties stand for different sets of policies, and although experience may tend to suggest that there is, in fact, a constant blurring in areas of policy (this is obviously true, for example, in the case of the Democratic and Republican parties in the United States), nevertheless to identify with one party or another is, by implication, to adhere − however imprecisely or even subconsciously − to a particular set of attitudes, beliefs, or political principles. The bankruptcy of Colombian politics in this respect, the apparent lack of any substantive ideological differences between the two parties, coupled with the ability of the party élites to mobilize large sections of the population in support of their struggles for power and their ability to limit the development of alternative sources of political expression, all these have been important factors in the formation of García Márquez's own political viewpoint.

In this process of political bankruptcy, the civil war of 1899–1902, known in Colombia as the War of a Thousand Days, together with the preceding periods of civil conflict which affected Colombia intermittently from 1875 onwards, seem to have played an important role. Dix writes: 'The frequency of civil wars and the party struggles they represented − characteristics less true of most other Latin American nations − cemented the cohesion of particular communities around one of the political contenders.' While Paul Oquist comments that: 'The final ossification of party identification would appear to have occurred as a result of the War of a Thousand Days . . . From then until the 1960s there was extremely little change in family-based party identification and practically none in the partisan orientations of party factions.' The fact that nineteenth-century landowners had the power to enlist their agricultural workers on behalf of the political party of their allegiance did much to attach the loyalties of the peasantry firmly to one side or the other. Charles Bergquist quotes from the writings of a Colombian who witnessed the War of a Thousand Days as a young man, and who recalled that neither the Liberal nor the Conservative rank and file had any clear idea as to why they were fighting, and yet killed each other 'with a dull, savage hatred'. Gilhodes notes how the political leaders in Colombia have studiously kept alive the memory of such hatreds as one means of mobilizing partisan loyalties among the peasantry, and this goes some way towards explaining the involvement of the Colombian peasantry in the political violence of the twentieth century.

One figure more than any other in García Márquez's work allows us imaginative access to the hollowness of the Liberal-Conservative conflicts, and that is Colonel Aureliano Buendía in *One Hundred Years of Solitude*. His military exploits in the novel are to be located within the period of the War of a Thousand Days and the twenty or so years of civil conflict which preceded it. He conducts his endless campaigns on behalf of the Liberals, but he comes to understand that the civil war is nothing but a naked struggle for power, to which political or ideological issues are irrelevant. At one point in the novel he receives a delegation of lawyers from the Liberal director-ate. The war has reached a position of stalemate, and he is asked, for allegedly tactical reasons, to abandon some of the key principles for which he has ostensibly been fighting:

'That means', said Colonel Aureliano Buendía, smiling . . . 'that all we're fighting for is power.'

'They're tactical reforms,' replied one of the delegates. 'For now, the essential thing is to broaden the popular base of the war. After that, we'll see.'

One of Colonel Aureliano Buendía's political advisers hastened to intervene.

'It's a contradiction,' he said. 'If these reforms are good, it means that the Conservative regime is good. If, by adopting them, we manage to broaden the popular base of the war, as you say, it means the regime has a broad popular base. It means, in short, that for nearly twenty years we have been fighting against the sentiments of the nation.'

Later in the novel, Aureliano Buendía's mother, Úrsula, comes to recognize the hollowness of her son's heroic reputation:

She sensed that he had not fought so many wars out of idealism, as everyone thought, nor given up out of fatigue on the brink of victory, as everyone thought, but that he had won and lost for the same motive, pure and sinful pride.

The Liberal and Conservative parties in Colombia emerged out of the political conflicts of the post-independence period. Freedom from Spanish domination meant that political power devolved to the local *criollo* oligarchy, a group of wealthy landowners, mer-chants, and high-clergy who had long occupied key economic positions in the state, but who, having been born in Spanish

America rather than in Spain, had been discriminated against socially in colonial times and largely excluded from positions in government. The fundamental question in the post-independence period was whether and how the inherited socio-economic structure was to be modified. Those who became Liberals saw their interests best served by reform; they supported free trade, a federal system of government, freedom of religion, civil marriage, secular education, and the separation of church and state. Merchants, financiers, and lawyers were prominent in this group. The Conservatives favoured the preservation of the traditional order, sought protectionist trade policies, a centralized system of government, and a close relationship between church and state. Among their group were numbered most of the traditional landowners and the clergy. After 1850, the Liberals were in the ascendancy and they consolidated their power through the civil wars of 1858–63. The Conservatives won control in 1885 and held it until 1930, whereupon the Liberals returned to office, only to lose power again in 1946, as a result of a split in their ranks. Colombia then entered upon the long period of the *violencia*, from around 1946 to 1966, during which time the country experienced a military dictatorship (1953–7), followed by the institution of the National Front (1958), a belated, and in some ways successful, attempt by the élites of the two parties to suspend their traditional antagonisms in the face of growing non-partisan violence among other sections of the population.

Long before this point, however, the early philosophical and policy distinctions between the two parties had become blurred, to the point that they hardly seemed significant any longer. Both post-independence political groupings had developed into mass parties, in the sense that they could command the allegiance of large numbers of people from all classes in the Colombian population. Factionalism became an increasingly prominent feature within each of the two parties from the 1860s onwards, and it remains important today; so that conflicts between different factions within the same party have frequently been as bitter as those between the different parties. However, one problem has remained dominant in Colombian politics through nearly all its modern history, which is that the two main parties have maintained their control over the distribution of power within the state, and that the manner in which such control has been exercised has led over and over again to conflict.

The key to control in Colombia has almost invariably been exclusion. Before 1958, whichever party was in power generally excluded the other completely from access to the benefits of that power. Parties were therefore able to retain control for long periods, and elections consequently often led to violence. Oquist writes: 'The group that did not control the state could expect only discrimination from it, whereas those persons politically connected with the party in power could expect to monopolize state decision making and the benefits to be derived from state power.' Dix, similarly, writes: 'Colombia's centralized and unitary form of government has meant that the party which captured the national administration was able to dictate the appointments of such officials as mayors, police chiefs, district judges, and even teachers in the public school system.' He quotes a highly illustrative extract from an article which appeared in the Bogotá weekly *Semana* in 1958:

> To lose power . . . meant that the mayor of the town would turn into a dangerous enemy, that the official of the branch of the Agrarian Bank would refuse the loan, that the new teacher would look with disfavour on one's child attending school, that the official of the Department of Health would first attend his fellow partisan of the other party . . . and that it was necessary to remain at a prudent distance from the local police.

Simply to ensure the preservation of life and property during the worst years of the *violencia*, Conservative and Liberal peasants frequently depended on the local defence capabilities of their respective parties.

These remarks give some idea of the political situation underlying such works as *No One Writes to the Colonel* and *In Evil Hour*. Both books are set during the *violencia*, and the connexions between that period and the time of the civil wars of 1899–1902 will by now, I hope, be clear. Both were periods of extremely violent civil strife, and both were intimately connected with the struggle for state power on the part of the two Colombian élites, a struggle in the cause of which they enlisted large numbers of Colombians whose ultimate interests they had no claim or desire to represent.

Rafael Uribe Uribe and the War of a Thousand Days

The most notable figure in the War of a Thousand Days was Rafael Uribe Uribe, a general on the Liberal side. He is, as far as I know, the only important figure from Colombian history whom García Márquez has acknowledged to be a direct model for one of the characters in his books. García Márquez's grandfather fought under Uribe Uribe during that war and it was shortly after the end of it that he moved to Aracataca, in the department of Magdalena, where García Márquez was born and spent his early years. García Márquez has described his grandfather as 'the most important figure in my life', and his grandfather's past, dramatic and expansive in more ways than one, provided the substance of many of the stories García Márquez heard as a boy.

Perhaps the strangest aspect of Uribe Uribe's life and military career was the way in which he was able to preserve a glorious reputation unscathed through a wealth of defeats. This alone gives a clue to the identity of his literary counterpart, Aureliano Buendía in *One Hundred Years of Solitude*, who 'promoted thirty-two armed uprisings and lost them all.' Not only did Uribe Uribe fail to achieve anything for the Liberal party in the course of his various military campaigns, but shortly after the end of the war he accepted a diplomatic posting from the Conservative government, a Conservative government, moreover, whose president Rafael Reyes had, by that time, assumed quasi-dictatorial powers. Uribe Uribe's dissident faction of the Liberal party backed the Reyes administration throughout its term of office, and then, later, united with the Conservatives in 1914 to defeat the official Liberal candidate for the presidency and ensure the election of an orthodox Conservative. Yet Uribe Uribe retained considerable popularity among large numbers of Colombians. Dix quotes from the preface to the *History of the Colombian Liberal Party*, by Milton Puentes, published in Bogotá in 1942, in which the author recalls the death of Uribe Uribe, who was murdered by two newly unemployed labourers on 15 October 1914:

> When they assassinated Uribe Uribe . . . I was a child of nine, but I recall that when in my distant home in the department of Boyacá my mother read me, with a barely audible voice

tremulous through her tears, the stories of the dastardly crime which the newspapers of the day carried, I cried with her, chilled by the fearful drama. As for my father, his eyes still cloud with tears . . . when he speaks to me of the . . . heroic times of his adored Liberal party.

This is not an isolated testimony. On 12 April 1959, the centenary of Uribe Uribe's birth was marked by a ceremony before his grave in Bogotá. The speech given on that occasion, by Eduardo Santa, has been published under the title *Rafael Uribe Uribe: Portrait of a Great Patriot*. Its language, even allowing for the spectral gravity of the occasion and the Athenian rhetoric beloved of so many Colombian intellectuals, is still remarkable. The published speech is preceded by a quotation from Uribe Uribe himself, in which the defeated Liberal general declares: 'I have given up, once and for all . . . being a revolutionary under arms, but I have not given up being a revolutionary and an agitator in the realm of ideas.' The following speech takes up the high tone:

The story of this apostle is nothing but a ceaseless struggle against the destiny (*fatum*) of his own existence. It seemed as if a blind force . . . dogged his steps minute by minute, to pluck victories out of his hands, to close off all doors to success, to cripple his heart, and to ruin all his plans . . . He loved liberty and, in order to defend it for himself and for those on his side, he was reduced on more than one occasion to the dark and narrow world of the prison cell . . . he was a committed pacifist, but the circumstances of despair through which his party was living made him take up arms and contribute to the shedding of the blood of the Fatherland . . . Everything was against him. But his romantic figure grew in adversity, like the cactus in the sand of the desert.

Among other things, García Márquez is seeking, through his depiction of Aureliano Buendía in *One Hundred Years of Solitude*, to rewrite the fabled history of Uribe Uribe, and to redress a balance long overdue.

Uribe Uribe: lawyer, and at one time teacher of law and political economy, agent of the New York Life Insurance Company, owner of one of the largest coffee plantations in the department of

Antioquia, and Liberal general. He began his military career at the age of seventeen, fighting on behalf of the Liberal government of the time against a Conservative rebellion in 1876. In 1885, he served as a colonel in an insurrection which brought one faction of the Liberal party into armed conflict with a Liberal-Conservative coalition. Following the defeat of the insurrection, he was jailed, released the following year, and then returned to private life. He moved to Bogotá in the early 1890s, and took an active part in national Liberal politics. He was involved in another failed rebellion against the government in 1895, was again imprisoned, and subsequently emerged as a hero of his party. In the highly polarized congressional elections of 1896, he was one of only two Liberals to be elected to the House of Representatives − no Liberals at all reached the Senate − and the only Liberal to take his seat. In 1897, as part of the Liberal preparations for war, he travelled to Central America in an attempt to enlist, though with little success, the support of the Liberal governments of Nicaragua and Guatemala. This episode is reflected in the lines from *One Hundred Years of Solitude* where Aureliano Buendía is discovered to have been pursuing his idea for 'the unification of the federalist forces of Central America, in order to sweep away Conservative regimes from Alaska to Patagonia'.

Important elements within the Liberal party sought to avert war, partly because they recognized that the resources on the Liberal side were markedly inferior and partly because, as Oquist points out, there had been an increasing tendency in recent periods of civil war to expropriate the conquered enemy's goods and property. Official Liberal policy, indeed, remained opposed to renewed fighting. Uribe Uribe, however, quickly rose to a dominant position within the war faction of the Liberals, and in February 1899 the war faction met to plan the strategy for a full-scale rebellion. In July 1899, Uribe Uribe and others prominent in the war group were arrested, paraded through the streets of Bogotá, and temporarily imprisoned. However, the drift towards violent confrontation was inexorable, and the War of a Thousand Days began in October 1899. As so often in the history of warfare, there was a general expectation that the fighting would be of short duration. None the less, divisions within both the Conservative and Liberal parties, as well as the development of a highly lucrative speculative business within the war economy, led to a protracted and terrible campaign. As we have seen, it is the political bankruptcy of the war which features so prominently in the account which García Márquez provides in *One Hundred Years of Solitude*, and this aspect is brought home to the reader in a number of different ways. It is reflected, for example, in the curious friendship between Aureliano Buendía and his Conservative opponent, José Raquel Moncada, a friendship which is paralleled by Uribe Uribe's close ties with the Conservative general, Pedro Nel Ospina. Vargas Llosa, in his book on García Márquez, quotes from a letter which Uribe Uribe sent to his Conservative opponent in November 1900, on being forced to withdraw from the town of Corozal in northern Colombia. Uribe Uribe acknowledges defeat in the most affectionate terms, enquiring after the health of his opponent's wife and children, and signing himself 'tu condiscípulo y amigo: Rafael Uribe Uribe'.

The Liberals had a few early successes in the War of a Thousand Days, but, as both sides dug in for a long campaign, the inherent superiority of Conservative resources was bound to prove eventually decisive. In May 1900, the defeat of the Liberals at Palonegro, 'the longest and bloodiest battle ever fought on Colombian soil' (Bergquist), effectively sealed the fate of the Liberal cause, and by the end of 1900 Uribe Uribe, along with the other Liberal generals, had been forced to leave Colombia in order to seek support abroad. For the remaining two and a half years of the war, the Liberals largely abandoned conventional warfare in favour of guerrilla tactics. This threatened to prolong the conflict indefinitely and led to a degree of savagery and social dislocation which greatly alarmed traditional leaders on both sides of the political divide. Increasingly, attempts were made to bring the war to a close. Uribe Uribe, unable to secure enough aid to launch a further invasion of Colombia, and opposed to the adoption of guerrilla tactics, issued a call for peace from New York in April 1901, but his failure to persuade the Liberal guerrilla forces to lay down their arms simply confirmed the degree to which the situation was moving beyond the control of traditional political elements.

Uribe Uribe did return to fight in Colombia, and to be defeated, to leave again, and to return. By September 1902, he was operating on the Atlantic coast, and it was there, in a battle for the town of Ciénaga, which lies to the north of García Márquez's birthplace in the department of Magdalena, that he finally gave up. Ciénaga, by coincidence, was to be the scene, twenty-six years later, of the massacre of striking workers from the banana plantations, an episode which figures prominently towards the end of *One Hundred Years of Solitude*. Uribe Uribe capitulated, and, on 24 October 1902, he signed the Treaty of Neerlandia, an event recorded both in *One Hundred Years of Solitude* and in *No One Writes to the Colonel*. In José María Valdeblánquez's *History of the Department of Magdalena*, there is a somewhat indecipherable photograph of the area where the signing took place. Neerlandia was the name of a banana plantation which belonged to a Dutch owner. The house has now gone, and all that remains is the almond tree which once graced the patio, and which, in the two works by García Márquez mentioned above, appears as a gigantic ceiba (silk-cotton) tree.

On 21 November 1902, the Liberal general Herrera signed his own treaty of capitulation with the Conservative forces, and the War of a Thousand Days was effectively brought to an end. This treaty is known, somewhat curiously, as the Treaty of Wisconsin, having been signed aboard the United States warship of that name, and the symbolism of name and venue is striking. The United States had come to take a considerable interest in Colombia, and that interest was to have important repercussions in the years to come. In 1903, the department of Panama, which had until then been an integral part of Colombia, seceded, with the backing of the United States, and in 1904 work began on the building of the Panama canal, a chain of events which Theodore Roosevelt was later to summarize succinctly: 'I took the Canal Zone and let Congress debate.' As far as the Colombian Liberal party was concerned, it ended the war in near total disarray, but the victors were careful not to deprive the vanquished of their property. Uribe Uribe spent some time in Brazil, and gave much thought to the workings of the Brazilian coffee industry. After his assassination in 1914 he was given a state funeral, a dramatic and myth-provoking end of the kind which García Márquez firmly denies Aureliano Buendía, who dies unnoticed and miserably alone. The War of a Thousand Days had brought the Liberal party nothing in political terms; the Conservatives were to retain power for nearly thirty more years. About 100,000 Colombians had been killed, the majority of them peasants: Conservative peasants press-ganged into the government forces, with the spiritual encouragement of the Church, Liberal peasants volunteered into service on the rebel side by those upon whom their precarious existence depended. One list of Liberal prisoners who were captured in December 1900 showed that more than 11 per cent of the group were fourteen years old or less. Such were the conditions in which the War of a Thousand Days was fought. In the following years, at least, Colombia was to enjoy a period of relatively peaceful exhaustion.

The *Violencia*

The long period of violence in Colombia which is known simply as the *violencia* took place between about 1946 and 1966. The precise dating of the period, its causes, development, and subsequent influence on Colombian history remain a source of controversy, as, inevitably, does any attempt to attribute responsibility. The events have been the object of intense scrutiny by sociologists, political scientists, and military analysts, both inside and outside Colombia. There is general agreement, at least, that the period was one of exceptional and prolonged savagery.

The War of a Thousand Days represented the last attempt by one side or other of the Colombian political divide to win power through the conventional nineteenth-century tradition of the battlefield. In such conflicts, the armies of both sides were generally under the command, not of professional military men, but of civilians who, like Uribe Uribe, took to the battlefield when other methods of achieving power proved fruitless. The rank and file were seldom professionals either, but men drafted into service under forced or semi-forced conditions. In the years after the War of a Thousand Days, however, the situation changed considerably. The Colombian armed forces became professionalized, and began to acquire modern military technology. As Oquist puts it: 'Armed conflict in Colombia ceased to be a matter of ill-equipped rebel armies of peasants confronting ill-equipped government armies of peasants.' He adds: 'The new military circumstances gave great advantages to the groups in power. Under these conditions, partisan violence in the twentieth century assumed the forms of street riots, isolated clashes between civilians and government authorities, local violence between civilians, *coup d'état* attempts, and guerrilla warfare.' Even during the War of a Thousand Days we have seen that the uneven distribution of resources tended to encourage the adoption of guerrilla tactics, and in the twentieth century violent conflict between the parties came more and more to be expressed in forms we are accustomed to prejudging as random, gratuitous, and anarchic. The Conservative party retained power until 1930, when, as a result of divisions within their ranks, they presented two candidates at the presidential elections, thus allowing the Liberal nominee to take office. The transfer of power was a peaceful one, but over the next two years, as the Liberal party strove to consolidate its hold and to 'liberalize' the public administration, incidents of violence proliferated. The potential for violent conflict had been increased by the fact that non-élite groups were now also competing for power and influence; the strike among the workers on the banana plantations in 1928 was but one sign of the growing organization of the Colombian working class. In the face of growing pressure from non-élite groups, reformist elements within the Liberal party secured the passage of some important pieces of social legislation, particularly in the period 1934–8, and this raised opposition among the traditional landowning class and in the Church.

Then, in 1946, a split in the Liberal ranks led the party to commit the same mistake as the Conservatives had made in 1930. Two Liberals stood at the presidential elections, the Conservative candidate was elected as a result, and the new Conservative administration embarked on the inevitable struggle to secure its position in the country and to reverse the policies of the previous Liberal governments. In 1977, García Márquez published an interesting article on the two failed Liberal candidates of the 1946 elections. It is entitled 'Only for Those Under 30 Years Old', and is an attempt to convey some sense of the political situation at a vital point in Colombian history to those too young to have had any direct experience of it. One of the candidates in 1946 was Gabriel Turbay; he was backed by most elements within the official Liberal party apparatus. He was, as García Márquez puts it, 'a perfect oligarch of the kind you don't see any more', a distinguished doctor, who had been Colombian ambassador to Washington and who had, according to rumour, been secretly involved with the actress Joan Crawford. He was to die shortly after his electoral defeat, in Suite 302 of the Hôtel George V in Paris, a fitting end, as García Márquez observes, for a man of his class.

The other Liberal candidate in 1946 was an altogether different proposition. His name was Jorge Eliécer Gaitán, and he was one of the most interesting and controversial political figures Colombia has yet produced. Dix, writing in 1967, said: 'What is truly significant about the rise of Gaitán was that to date he has been the only Colombian to have attained major political stature by challenging the position of the élite and appealing to the Colombian masses.' The judgment remains true today. García Márquez notes how both the Liberal and Conservative élites despised Gaitán, because he was not of their class, and he adds: 'The only new thing that Gaitán had to say was a very old truth that nobody dared to speak: "The Liberal peasant and the Conservative peasant are exploited equally by the Liberal oligarchy and the Conservative oligarchy".' Gaitán had made his initial political reputation through his investigation of the circumstances surrounding the massacre of the striking banana-plantation workers in 1928. By June 1947, with the resolution of the differences within the Liberal camp, he had become undisputed party leader. It was a critical time. The Conservative victory of 1946 and its aftermath had led to increasing acts of violence, and by the beginning of 1948 Colombia was once again moving into a state of civil war.

On 9 April 1948, Gaitán was assassinated in the centre of Bogotá. The circumstances have never been clarified, but the immediate effect was to unleash a full-scale urban insurrection. Several thousand deaths occurred in the three days following the assassination, and large parts of the city were devastated, with members of the police force, which at that time was still largely Liberal, often intervening on the side of the rioters. US Secretary of State Marshall, who was in Bogotá for the ninth Pan-American conference, argued that the violence was the work of 'international communism', and he linked it, somewhat randomly, with recent strikes in France and Italy. Speaking on 12 April, he said: 'In the actions we take here in regard to the present situation we must have clearly in mind that this is a world affair, and not merely Colombian or Latin American.' On 4 May 1948, after what it described as 'deep and thoughtful study', the Colombian government broke off diplomatic relations with the Soviet Union, and relations were to remain severed for the next twenty years. No serious evidence was ever produced to suggest that the violence was anything but the result of purely internal Colombian pressures, but allegations of outside interference are common enough in such situations; they are frequently heard today in connexion with the conflicts in Central America. At all events, following what is still known in Colombia simply as the *Nueve de abril* (Ninth of April), the country entered upon the most savage phase of the *violencia*, a phase which was to last until 1953. In Bogotá itself, order was restored by the army, the political élites closed ranks in the face of the obvious threats posed by the situation and signed a formal political truce on 18 April. Matters grew rapidly worse in the countryside, however, as violence spread throughout the central zone of Colombia. By 1949, organized guerrilla forces were in action, the attempts at bipartisan solidarity on the part of the political élites foundered, the president closed the Liberal-controlled Congress, and a state of siege was declared. Indeed from then on, at least until 1982, states of siege were the norm in Colombia.

In 1953, in a *coup d'état* supported by nearly all the national political groups in Colombia, the Army Commander, General Gustavo Rojas Pinilla, took power. An amnesty was offered to those involved in the violence, and the scale of the conflict was drastically reduced. The relief was short-lived, however; from late 1954, the violence once again began to reach high levels, and the army instituted a systematic repression of both Liberals and Conservatives. In this second period of the *violencia*, traditional partisan rivalries tended to become secondary, as the political parties strove to unite against the threat posed by the military government, and as socio-economic issues came to play a more significant role. Rojas Pinilla was brought down in May 1957, and gradually, between 1958 and 1966, order was, in a relative sense, restored, though some areas of Colombia remain outside full state control to this day. What had begun in the late 1940s as a prolongation of traditional partisan conflict had developed, by the mid-1950s, into a highly complex situation in which different sources of violence, deriving from a range of political and socio-economic issues, found their expression through a number of different agencies: the army, the police, paramilitary groups, terror squads, Liberal and Communist guerrilla bands, and semi-organized bandit gangs which simply took advantage of the general breakdown in public order. It was not always easy to distinguish between the activities of these various agencies, but, as always, it was the Colombian peasantry that suffered the worst excesses of the violence, largely, in this case, because the breakdown of public order was substantially more serious in the countryside than in the towns. All the horrors of the conflict were minutely charted by the National Investigating Commission on the Present Causes of the Violence, which was sponsored by the government, and which reported its findings in 1962–4.

The long-term effects of the *violencia* on modern Colombia have been much debated. Oquist suggests that, in a very real sense, the *violencia* 'survives today in the common violent crime that affects most Colombian cities'. As the Colombian countryside was gradually pacified, a process which was itself characterized by much violence on the part of the police and armed forces, the remnants of the bandit gangs which had operated there moved into the towns. Then, too, the rise of revolutionary guerrilla groups in the 1960s has obvious links with the conditions prevalent during the late *violencia*. There are currently four main guerrilla groups in Colombia, and their existence has served as the pretext for the militarization of large areas of the state, a process which has led to further violence in the Colombian countryside.

The *violencia* naturally exercised an important influence on Colombian writers of the period, and R. W. Ramsey's *Survey and Bibliography* of it contains an interesting section devoted to the fictional literature of the conflict. He lists twenty-three separate items, and includes, too, Harold Robbins's *The Adventurers*, several chapters of which, he says, 'are valid portraits of the Colombian *violencia*'. And Lucila Inés Mena's annotated bibliography of the literature of the *violencia*, published in 1978, lists seventy-four novels, dating from between 1951 and 1972. García Márquez's attitude towards this literary production is interestingly ambiguous. In an article which first appeared in 1960, he argued that, as a genre, the 'novel of the *violencia*' was significant, in that it marked a clear recognition on the part of Colombian writers that here was an issue of profound national importance; and he compares that act of recognition favourably with the inability or unwillingness of Colombian writers in the late nineteenth century to deal with the issues raised by the civil wars of that time. The novel of the *violencia*, he says, constitutes 'the only literary explosion of a genuinely national character that we have had in our history'. At the same time, he argues that, because Colombia is a country which has produced a few isolated great works of literature, rather than a significant and coherent literary tradition, attempts by writers to convey the drama of the *violencia* in fictional terms were almost bound to be unsuccessful. 'In reality', García Márquez says, 'Colombia was not sufficiently mature culturally for the political and social tragedy of the past few years to have left us with anything more than fifty or so crude pieces of testimony.'

This is a literary area in which García Márquez was, of course, involved personally, though the point does not emerge from his article of 1960. In an interview which he gave ten years later, however, he spoke at length about his own response, as a writer, to the period of the *violencia*. He looks back to the worst years of the conflict, around 1950, and he says:

At that time I was twenty-two or twenty-three, I had written *Leaf Storm* [his first novel], I had in my head the glimmerings of *One Hundred Years of Solitude*, and I said to myself: 'How can I keep on working in this mythical field and with this poetical style, in the circumstances that we're living through? It seems like an evasion'. It was a political decision, a mistaken one, I now think. I decided to come nearer to the actuality of the Colombian experience and I wrote *No One Writes to the Colonel* and *In Evil Hour*. I didn't exactly write what you could call a novel of the *violencia*, for two reasons: one, because I hadn't experienced the *violencia* directly, I lived in the cities; and two, because I considered that the important thing, in terms of literature, was not the inventory of deaths and the description of the methods of violence − which was what the other writers were doing − but what mattered to me, which was the root of that violence, the motives . . . and, above all, the consequences of that violence for the survivors. That's why you find that in *In Evil Hour* there aren't any killings. The critical period of the *violencia* is practically over, but what you do see in the book is that the moment of respite hangs by a thread, and that the *violencia* will return, that it is a kind of constant, that we haven't finished with it because we haven't finished with its causes.

García Márquez suggests, then, that, as a result of his political commitment, he made the wrong choice as a writer when he consciously decided to turn away from the direction he had taken with *Leaf Storm* in order to try to deal with the issues raised by the *violencia*. He says later in the interview that he came to believe that his primary concern with the myths and legends of the Colombian people did not necessarily involve an abdication of political responsibility; so then, retracing his steps, he began to work on *One Hundred Years of Solitude*.

García Márquez also says in the interview that he did not experience the *violencia* directly, because he was living in the cities at the time, and not in the countryside. It is true, as we have seen, that the worst areas of the *violencia* lay outside the urban zones, but there is another point to be made. When Gaitán was assassinated, García Márquez was in Bogotá, as a student at the National University, but, following the violence of 9 April 1948, the University was closed and he returned to his Caribbean homeland. The Caribbean coastal region as a whole was much less affected by the *violencia* than most parts of Colombia, and that is one reason why *No One Writes to the Colonel* and *In Evil Hour* are set further south towards the *violencia* zones, whereas *Leaf Storm* and *One Hundred Years of Solitude* are firmly located in the Caribbean world of Macondo.

Following the experience of the worst years of the *violencia*, and then of the military dictatorship which governed the country from 1953 to 1957, the Colombian political élites drew together, realizing that continued inter-party struggle could only threaten their collective hold on power. An agreement was reached to form a kind of Liberal-Conservative coalition government, and the terms of that agreement were ratified in a national plebiscite in December 1957. Thus came into being what was known as the National Front. Dix suggests that many people who voted in the plebiscite probably did not understand what they were voting for. If this were the case, it would not have been altogether surprising, for Colombia was about to embark on one of the strangest experiments in democratic government that have been tried anywhere. Basically, the two parties agreed that elections would continue to be held, but that the competitive element which had led to so much violence at election time would be removed by deciding the results in advance. Only the two main parties were to be involved in the political process, all others being legally excluded, and, however the votes were cast, the two parties agreed to split them evenly. So, at the national level, Conservatives and Liberals would have equal representation in the two Houses of Congress, and, at the local level, parity in all departmental assemblies and municipal councils. There was to be an equal division of ministerial positions and governorships, while the presidency would alternate between the two parties every four years. The principle of equal representation was to be applied to all areas under government control, so that, for example, there would be equal numbers of Liberals and Conservatives in the judiciary and the civil service. Just how far the principle was extended can be deduced from the following telegram, which appeared in the Bogotá Liberal newspaper *El Espectador* on 22 July 1963, and in which the local Liberal office in the town of Socorro, in the department of Santander, appealed to the national Liberal office for the rectification of some anomalies:

> The Liberal Directorate of Socorro requests the National Liberal Directorate and [Liberal] Congressmen to intervene directly with the Minister of Communications and the Minister of Justice to the end of the fulfilment of parity in this city where in the circuit jail there are nineteen Liberal [employees] to thirty-two Conservatives and in the telegraph office eighteen Conservatives to five Liberals.
>
> (Quoted in R.H. Dix, *Colombia: the Political Dimensions of Change*)

The National Front experiment was scheduled to last from 1958 until 1974, with variations according to the particular offices and assemblies concerned. This, along with the developments which took place following the assassination of Gaitán, meant that there were no competitive elections in Colombia from 1949 until the mid-1970s. Indeed, after the expiry of the agreement in 1974, vestiges of the parity arrangement have survived to the present day. The National Front has been described as 'the world's first attempt at a two-party dictatorship', while Oquist accurately summarizes its workings as follows: 'Instead of representing the political hegemony of the Liberals *or* the Conservatives, the Frente Nacional [National Front] was the exclusivistic hegemony of the Liberals *and* the Conservatives.' It is easy to deride the experiment, and it certainly stretches the definition of a 'functioning democracy', but within the context of Colombian politics it was not entirely absurd. In so far as the violence in Colombia continued to derive from inter-party competition, the National Front did contribute to its diminution, though the persistence of the *violencia* into the mid-1960s suggests that other sources of violence had become important by that time. The arrangement was also less monolithic than might appear, for the persistent factionalism which has characterized Colombian politics led rapidly to the proliferation of dissident groups within the National Front, and there was also some judicious bending of the rules to allow the return to politics of the former dictator Rojas Pinilla, whose ANAPO party developed at first within the National Front, but later constituted itself as a separate entity.

Developments in Colombia following the end of the National Front experiment are still too recent to assess with any assurance. Aureliano Babilonia's ability, at the end of *One Hundred Years of Solitude*, to decipher the moment as it is lived, is one that is rare outside the closed and pre-determined world of fiction. The applicability of what I have written of Colombian history to the Colombia of the 1980s may be challenged, but my aim has been primarily to give some sense of the developments during the period in which García Márquez's political attitudes were formed, so that his preoccupations in the novels may be more clearly understood. Certainly, Colombia has experienced a period of rapid change over the last twenty years. The high rate of urbanization has affected many areas of life, and has clearly had an influence on the patterns of political identification, given that partisan loyalties have traditionally been more tenacious in the countryside than in the cities. At the same time, however, it is doubtful whether much has changed in terms of the political expectations of the majority of the Colombian people. Since the death of Gaitán, there have been few attempts to broaden the base of Colombian political life, and such attempts as have been made have, to date, been successfully contained by the two party élites. In 1967, echoing a phrase from one of Gaitán's biographers, Dix wrote that the rural masses of Colombia 'do, in a sense . . . participate in politics, but only as fodder for the cannon or the ballot box', and the observation retains much of its force. Progress in such areas as land reform has been slow, largely for reasons one would expect in a country where wealthy landowners exercise a great deal of political power; and many have been forced off the land into the cities, where they maintain, at best, a precarious existence.

One of the most negative developments in Colombia in recent years would seem to have been the expansion of the illegal drug trade, involving both home-grown marijuana and cocaine, which is processed in Colombia largely from coca paste imported from Peru and Bolivia. There are interesting similarities between this narcotics bonanza and the 'banana fever' which affected Colombia in the early decades of the twentieth century. Both have involved substantial transformations within the rural economy to adapt to the demands of a largely North American consumer market; both have generated very large sums of money which have been very unevenly distributed; both have caused serious social dislocation in rural areas; and both have been a source of violent conflict in one form or another. We shall look at the phenomenon of the banana fever in later chapters, for its influence on García Márquez's work is considerable. As far as the drug trade is concerned, its effects on Colombian society have been uniformly disastrous, except for the relatively few people in whose hands the vast wealth derived from the trade has been concentrated. Increasing numbers of peasants have been evicted from their land, as agricultural production has been switched from crops that could be eaten to the cultivation of marijuana, a crop which is more profitable and less demanding of labour. The inflow of large untaxed funds from the drug trade has inevitably created distortions within the Colombian economy, and has contributed significantly to inflationary pressures, and the levels of crime and corruption associated with the drug trade in other countries have been clearly reproduced. A study in the late 1970s by the US House of Representatives select committee on narcotics abuse and control found, inevitably, that there was evidence of 'official complicity' against attempts to halt the drug traffic in Colombia, and in 1978 the Minister of

Labour resigned amid allegations that his department was involved in drug smuggling.

Of all these problems, perhaps the most serious is the contribution which the drug trade has made to the incidence of violence in Colombian society. We have seen that the level of traditional partisan violence declined markedly during the years of the late *violencia*. None the less, Colombia has remained one of the more violent countries of the world, as conflicts deriving from other sources have become prominent. Recent drug-related violence has not only proved a serious problem in itself, but its existence enabled Liberal governments in the late 1970s to adopt wide-ranging powers in the name of a crusade against the drug trade, powers which simultaneously furnished a context for the repression of all forms of radical political protest. Two security measures taken in 1978 illustrate the problem. One, adopted without parliamentary consultation, exempted the police and armed forces from all responsibility before the law for actions taken against violence and drug-trafficking, and also authorized the use of arms by civilians involved in similar circumstances. The other provided for terms of imprisonment of up to five years for 'disturbing public order', up to one year without trial for the possession of subversive literature, and for trial by summary court martial, with limited right of defence and appeal, for offences such as painting slogans.

Particularly disturbing has been the recent emergence of paramilitary death squads, financed by the drug trade, and apparently enjoying some degree of official complicity. The most widely publicized of these, known as MAS (*Muerte a secuestradores*/Death to Kidnappers), appeared in October 1981. It was formed ostensibly as a response to the activities of guerrilla groups which kidnap the wealthy in order to raise funds for their operations. However, the principal victims of MAS have been the same as those of death squads elsewhere in Latin America: trade unionists, peasant leaders, left-wing lawyers, and the like. In addition to the violence associated in these various ways with the drug trade, violence in a number of different forms continues as one of the most distinguishing marks of contemporary Colombian society. The existence of revolutionary guerrilla forces has led to the militarization of large parts of the country, and to increasingly numerous signs that the army is conducting a campaign of terror against the peasant population in those areas. Behind it all, apparently divorced from human agency, is the conspicuous violence of underdevelopment that prevails throughout much of Latin America, the violence of malnutrition, poverty, and disease, squalid housing, and unemployment.

This apparently endless cycle has been one of the central pre-occupations in nearly all of García Márquez's works to date: the violence of civil war and of economic exploitation in *One Hundred Years of Solitude*; the violence of partisan political hatreds in *No One Writes to the Colonel* and *In Evil Hour*; the structural violence of dictatorship in *The Autumn of the Patriarch*; the sexual violence of a repressive rural society in *Chronicle of a Death Foretold*. García Márquez's concerns in this area have rarely, however, had to do with the outward forms of violence, with the sort of grotesque details of torture and murder that, appropriately, characterize human rights reports. His concerns are, rather, with the origins of violence, and with the effects that it has on the society in which people have to live. He is thus, inevitably, concerned with the whole history of his country and continent, and, both as a writer of novels and as a journalist, he has constantly laid stress on the importance of developing alternative sources of history as a challenge to the status of conventional ones.

Fernando Cardenal, the co-ordinator of the literacy crusade which was launched in Nicaragua in the aftermath of the revolution of 1979, has written:

> Only through knowing their past and their present, only through understanding and analysing their reality can people choose their future. Only in that process can people fulfil their human destiny as makers of history and commit themselves to transforming their reality.

This view of the dynamic importance of history is one which García Márquez shares, and it is one which has an immediate relevance to the theme of solitude that pervades so much of his work. He is clearly fascinated by the individual psychology of solitude, and that is an aspect which all readers can understand from personal experience; but solitude also fascinates him as an expression of the collective isolation of Latin American people, a people for whom history has seemed a process to be endured rather than created, a people divorced from a sense of history because theirs has been written by outsiders, a people condemned to a peripheral role in relation to a greater world whose limits have been defined elsewhere. 'For Europeans, South America is a man with a moustache, a guitar, and a revolver.'

But the sense of solitude is more pervasive yet. For not only has Latin America seemed isolated from the creative forces of world history, ignored by the rest of the world except as a convenient source of raw materials, or a certain transitory exoticism, the isolation has also been internal. It has been a continent in which things have happened of which history might have been made, but those things have too often remained unknown to the majority of the people, or have not been understood, or not acknowledged. In *One Hundred Years of Solitude*, José Arcadio Segundo actually sees the massacre of the banana-plantation workers, but when he tries to talk about it afterwards, no one is prepared to accept that a massacre has taken place. Non-fictional parallels in modern Colombia are not hard to find. When the first volume of the official report on the *violencia* appeared in 1962, it created an uproar in literate urban circles, revealing that there was widespread ignorance about the full horrors of the civil war. It may seem strange to an outsider that this could be so, and no doubt some of the ignorance was wilful. However, it is important to remember that Colombia is a large country, with a surface area equal to that of France, Spain, and Portugal combined, that its geography has always acted as a barrier to communication, and that, above all, the general conditions of underdevelopment − poverty, illiteracy, and the unequal distribution of central government's bureaucratic authority − are a relentless source of isolation. Extraordinary things can happen, and yet easily fail to achieve significance, or even recognition.

The point is further illustrated in an article by Geoffrey Matthews, entitled 'Colombia's Own Savage El Salvador', which appeared in *The Times* (London) of 5 September 1983. The article describes the violence which has recently affected the Magdalena Medio region of Central Colombia, and which is one of the main concerns of those currently working in the field of human rights in Colombia. The violence seems to be the result of death-squad activity directed against presumed guerrilla sympathizers, and it has led to the abandonment of villages, the closing of schools, and widespread accounts of massacres and terrifying savagery. Geoffrey Matthews reports that 'it has taken months for the full horror of what is happening in Magdalena Medio, only four hours by road from Bogotá, to be understood in the capital'. It is situations such as these, such crises of ignorance, that help to explain the urgency of much of García Márquez's fiction, along with his continual search for a form and a language in which the apparently endless cycle of Colombia's violent history can be creatively explored and understood.

II

Gabriel García Márquez

'Go to the tropics boy, the glorious tropics,
where the sun is supreme, and never shares
his dominion with blue-nosed, leaden-
coloured, rheumy-eyed frost-gods; go there,
and catch the matchless tints of the skies,
the living emerald of the forests, and the
light-giving azure of the waters; go where
the birds are rainbow-hued, and the very
fish are golden . . .' (Samuel A. Bard, *alias*
Ephraim George Squier, *Waikna*, 1855)

Gabriel García Márquez was born in Aracataca, in the Colombian
department of Magdalena, on 6 March 1928. That, at least, is the
date favoured by most critics, and, usually, by García Márquez
himself. His father, in the course of an interview in 1977, said he was
sure the year was 1927, but on this, as on other more serious
matters, the opinion of the son has generally prevailed. Aracataca,
now a town of some twenty thousand people, lies to the south of the
capital of the Magdalena department, Santa Marta, on the railway
line which connects Santa Marta with the Colombian interior. It is
an area of sultry heat and torrential rains, with the Caribbean some
fifty miles to the north, and, to the east, the high peaks of the Sierra
Nevada de Santa Marta, rising in places to nearly 19,000 feet. The
city of Santa Marta has been an important one in Colombian
history; founded on 29 July 1525, it is, in fact, the oldest city in
Colombia, and it was on the outskirts of the city that Simón Bolívar,
one of the heroes in the struggle for Latin American independence,
died in 1830. Aracataca, however, has only been briefly touched by
history, emerging at the end of the nineteenth century with the
development of the banana industry in the area, and, thereafter,
dependent on political and economic fluctuations over which its
inhabitants had no control. It flourished, in a certain sense, in the

early decades of the twentieth century, but the town into which García Márquez was born was one from which the wider world was already in retreat. The 'banana fever' had subsided, and a community that had, until recently, been alive, vigorous, and apparently prosperous, was now returning to the timeless insularity from which it had been so unexpectedly drawn.

García Márquez, like James Joyce, was one of a large and somewhat indeterminate number of children. His father acknowledges a total of fifteen or sixteen, including three from the days before he was married. In the event, however, García Márquez's early upbringing was that of an only child, for he spent the first eight years of his life, not with his parents, but in the house of his grandparents. In later years that house came to acquire the emotional and literary status of a lost childhood world, a place of magic and mystery, of sombre and brooding decline. His grandparents' house is the model for the colonel's house in *Leaf Storm*, his first novel, as it is for the house of the Buendías in *One Hundred Years of Solitude*, and it comes to stand as the private, familial representation of the larger process of disintegration which carries Aracataca, or Macondo, out of history and back into the endless cycle of mythological time. As early as June 1950, García Márquez published a fragment entitled *The House of the Buendías (Notes for a Novel)*, and the dominant tone here is already one of nostalgia, of loss and decay, linked, significantly, with the return of Aureliano Buendía at the end of the nineteenth-century civil wars. García Márquez remembers his grandparents' house as a dwelling place of the dead, rather than of the living:

> In that house there was an empty room where Aunt Petra had died. There was an empty room where Uncle Lazarus had died. And so, at night, you couldn't walk in that house, because the dead outnumbered the living. They would sit me down, at six in the evening, in a corner, and they would say to me: 'Don't move from here, because, if you do, Aunt Petra, who is in her room, will come, or Uncle Lazarus . . .' I always stayed sitting . . . In my first novel, *Leaf Storm*, one of the characters is a boy of seven who, all through the novel, is sitting in a small chair. Now I realize that there was something of me in that boy, sitting in that small chair, in a house full of fears.

There was, however, another side to life in Aracataca, though it may have been less productive in literary terms. García Márquez's grandparents were influential people in the local community, and their house, for all its nocturnal horrors, attracted a large number of visitors. His grandfather had settled in Aracataca at the end of the War of a Thousand Days, in which, as we have seen, he fought under the Liberal general Rafael Uribe Uribe, and he was clearly a man of enormous presence and vitality. Indeed, his influence was of a kind which García Márquez has almost never attempted to render into fiction; of all the characters in his books, he has said, there is only one who resembles his grandfather, and that is the nameless colonel in *Leaf Storm*. This is not surprising, given the psychological division within García Márquez's fictional world, a world in which strength of character is generally the prerogative of women, while the power men seek to yield is invariably found to be illusory. Nevertheless, details from his grandfather's life, applied to very different sorts of characters, do recur in many of García Márquez's novels. An obvious example is the record of his service in the civil wars; another is his long period of waiting for a war-pension, after the civil wars were over, an attribute which is transferred to the central figure in *No One Writes to the Colonel*. His grandfather, García Márquez has said, was 'the biggest eater I can remember and the most outrageous fornicator', both qualities which added to his prestige as a war veteran in the context of traditional Colombian society, and his aggressive sexuality, which expressed itself in the fathering of numerous illegitimate children, finds a reflection in the career of Aureliano Buendía in *One Hundred Years of Solitude*. His grandfather's open and expansive personality, however, has nothing in common with the aloofness and austerity of Aureliano, and García Márquez pays his grandfather a lasting tribute in the following words: 'Throughout my adult life, whenever something happens to me, above all whenever something good comes my way, I feel that the only thing I need in order for my happiness to be complete, is that my grandfather should know about it.'

García Márquez's grandfather came from the town of Riohacha, situated on the Caribbean coast of Colombia, and now in the department of La Guajira; and, appropriately, it is in Riohacha that the story of *One Hundred Years of Solitude* begins. Riohacha is another of Colombia's oldest cities; it was founded in 1545, twenty years after the founding of Santa Marta, and it was once famous for its pearl industry. In 1595, it was sacked by the English pirate Francis Drake, an incident that is recorded with ironic amusement in the early pages of *One Hundred Years of Solitude*: Úrsula's great-great-grandmother, terrified by the noise of the English assault, loses her nerve, and, as a result, sits down on a lighted stove; this makes her a permanent invalid, she withdraws from the world, and she and her husband move away from Riohacha to live in a village far from the sea. There her husband builds her a bedroom without windows, so that the pirates who haunt her nightmares will be unable to gain access. In the small village to which they move, in the foothills of the Sierra, there lives a tobacco-planter, Don José Arcadio Buendía, with whom Úrsula's great-great-grandfather goes into partnership, and this provides the initial, and fatal, link between the two sides of the Buendía dynasty. As a result, centuries later, whenever Úrsula found herself driven to distraction by the follies of her husband, 'she would leap back over three hundred years of chance events ('casualidades'), and curse the hour when Francis Drake attacked Riohacha'. There is a comic insight here into the way people seek refuge in family traditions as a means of dealing with the inexplicable vagaries of family life, a comic contrast between the apparently assured significance of a major historical event and the endless, uncharted circles of family psychological warfare. However, there is also, in the context of a novel in which everything will turn out to have been rigidly determined, a reflection that the comic exaggeration contains an element of truth. To seek to read a pattern in the 'chance events' of three hundred years may possibly be futile, but it is not necessarily absurd: English piracy does set the family saga in motion, as the economic exploitation of a United States banana-company will act to bring the story to a close.

García Márquez's grandfather and grandmother, like Úrsula Iguarán and José Arcadio Buendía in *One Hundred Years of Solitude*, were cousins. His grandmother, through her beliefs as through her behaviour, belonged to a world of myth, magic, and superstition. As García Márquez recalls, 'my grandfather . . . was for me an absolute security within the uncertain world of my grandmother', and it is to his grandmother that he traces his fascination for what, in literary terms, has been called 'magical realism'. He has spoken often of the way his grandmother could tell the story of an event, or provide an explanation for something which had happened, in a way that carried complete conviction, and seemed to obey some internal logic, and yet which was, from an objective point of view, beyond all reason, fantastic. 'It's possible to get away with *anything*', he has said, 'as long as you make it believable. That is something my grandmother taught me.' Behind this apparently casual remark, there is a long-held belief that the world is open to other forms of knowing and understanding than those sanctioned by a rational consciousness, and that the writer has as much of a responsibility towards such forms of knowledge as towards the revelations of a more purely analytical enquiry. The problem for a writer in Latin America, García Márquez has often observed, lies not in finding a subject, but in ensuring credibility, in making the reader understand that the sense of wonder and infinite strangeness which emerges from much Latin American writing is a true reflection of the complex realities of Latin American experience, not merely the product of a feverish, literary imagination.

The reasons why García Márquez spent his early years with his maternal grandparents are uncertain. He himself has never attached any particular significance to the situation, given the extended nature of traditional Colombian families, but, at the same time, it is clear that relations between his father and his grandparents were problematic. His father was an outsider; he came from farther south, from the town of Sincé, at that time in the department of Bolívar, now in the department of Sucre. He was, moreover, a Conservative, whereas Aracataca was a Liberal stronghold. He had spent some years studying medicine at the University of Cartagena, on the Caribbean coast, but was forced to abandon his career for lack of money, and he came to Aracataca in the 1920s, when the banana fever had made it a boom town. He worked as a telegraph operator. The well-established families of Aracataca, of which García Márquez's grandparents were one of the most eminent representatives, inevitably looked with disfavour on the invasion of fortune-seeking outsiders. This invasion, which brought people into the area from all over Colombia and from many other parts of the world, was termed 'la hojarasca', and that is the title which García Márquez gave to his first novel. It is a word which means literally 'dead leaves', 'fallen leaves', and, by extension, 'trash', 'rubbish';

the English translation of the novel is entitled *Leaf Storm*, which is an attempt to preserve both the idea of foliage and that of a whirlwind invasion, but fails to capture the sense of worthlessness which the expression implies. That an outsider, one of the 'hojarasca', should seek to marry their daughter seems to have appeared quite inadmissible to García Márquez's grandparents, and, according to Vargas Llosa, they eventually consented to the marriage only on condition that the couple did not live in Aracataca. García Márquez's parents set up house in Riohacha, returning to Aracataca for the birth of their first child, Gabriel, in March 1928. They subsequently returned to Riohacha, leaving the child behind to spend the first eight years of his life in his grandparents' house.

García Márquez came to know his mother for the first time when he was five or six years old. His relationship with her has always been an important one, characterized, he says, by a high seriousness, 'perhaps the most serious relationship that I have had in my life'; she appears as herself, the mother of the narrator, and with her own name, Luisa Santiaga, in *Chronicle of a Death Foretold*. His father, however, remains a shadowy and distant figure, and García Márquez has said little about him, except to acknowledge that he never knew him well. His father worked for a time as a medical pharmacologist in the town of Barranquilla, on the Caribbean coast; the family then moved to the inland river port of Sucre, where they spent some twelve years, from around 1940 to 1952, after which they went to live in Cartagena. The family often experienced material difficulties in these years, though were never, in the context of their society, impoverished. After the death of his grandfather, García Márquez moved from Aracataca to live with his parents, though he was sent away for much of his schooling. From 1940 to 1942, he attended a Jesuit college in Barranquilla, and from there he went on to a school in Zipaquirá, some thirty miles north of the Colombian capital Bogotá, to complete his secondary education.

The move to Zipaquirá gave García Márquez his first experience of the interior culture of his country, and his memories of it remain sharp:

Of all the cities I know in the world . . . none has made such an impression on me as Bogotá. I arrived from Barranquilla in

1943 at five o'clock in the afternoon . . . and that was the most terrible experience in the whole of my youth. Bogotá was dismal, smelling of soot, and the drizzle fell unceasingly, and men dressed in black, with black hats, went stumbling through the streets . . . You only saw a woman occasionally, since they were not allowed in the majority of public places. At that time, Colombia looked more like Bolivia.

He also says that, for those who, like himself, had come from the Caribbean zone of Colombia, there was an instant recognition that here, in Bogotá, was the source of an oppressive power: 'in that remote and unreal city was the centre of gravity of the power which had been imposed upon us since our earliest times.' The school in Zipaquirá was, however, one that offered a broad range of educational experience. On the one hand, he says, the school was a refuge for poor students from all over Colombia. On the other, it had at that time, due to a series of developments within the Colombian political and educational system, a large number of teachers who were familiar with Marxist theory. As a result of the years he spent in Zipaquirá, between 1943 and 1946, the lines of his future career were, he suggests, firmly established: 'When I left there, I wanted to be a journalist, I wanted to write novels, and I wanted to do something for a more just society. The three things, I now think, were inseparable.'

García Márquez graduated from his secondary school in Zipaquirá in December 1946, and returned to the family home in Sucre. Sucre was the town which provided the setting for *No One Writes to the Colonel* and *In Evil Hour*, his two major pieces on the Colombian *violencia*, and also for *Chronicle of a Death Foretold*. It was also in Sucre that he met his future wife, Mercedes. She appears in the closing pages of *One Hundred Years of Solitude* as 'Mercedes, the secret girlfriend of Gabriel', and she is also the 'cocodrilo sagrado' ('sacred crocodile') to whom the stories of *Big Mama's Funeral* are dedicated, a nickname reflecting her Egyptian ancestry. In February 1947, García Márquez enrolled at the National University of Bogotá, at the beginning of a half-hearted attempt to read for a degree in law. A fellow-student at that time was Camilo Torres, who was to become one of the most famous of the militant priests who emerged throughout Latin America in the 1960s.

Camilo Torres was also to be one of the founders of the first faculty of sociology at the National University, and one of the University's chaplains. In 1959, he baptized García Márquez's first son. Because of his political commitment to a socialist future for Colombia, he was forced to abandon the priesthood in 1965, following which he joined the guerrilla forces of the Army of National Liberation, and was subsequently killed in a clash with the Colombian armed forces in February 1966.

García Márquez was in the second year of his university career when, on 9 April 1948, the assassination of the populist Liberal leader Jorge Eliécer Gaitán precipitated Colombia into the worst phase of the *violencia*. The National University was closed down, and García Márquez returned to the Caribbean zone, going first to Barranquilla, where the university was also closed, and then on to Cartagena, where, from 1948 to 1949, he continued his law studies. He thus spent the worst years of the *violencia* in the relative peace of the Caribbean coastal region. Conditions there remained better than almost anywhere else in Colombia, and Paul Oquist suggests the likely reason for this, noting that both in the Caribbean zone and in another area of similar relative calm, the department of Nariño in the far south-west of Colombia, 'it would appear that the regional power structure maintained its coherence. The local Liberal and Conservative political élites actively worked to remain united despite the breakdown in political relations at the national level'. Whatever the reasons, the Caribbean coastal zone was a favoured area in the Colombia of the late 1940s and early 1950s.

While studying in Cartagena, García Márquez began to write for a Liberal newspaper, *El Universal*, and his first article appeared there on 21 May 1948, just two months after the founding of the paper. This was the beginning of a long journalistic career which García Márquez continues to pursue to the present day, a career which has provided both material support and a forum for the expression and discussion of his political views. When he announced, after the publication of *The Autumn of the Patriarch* in 1975, that he would publish no more works of fiction and would devote himself entirely to journalism as long as the Pinochet regime remained in power in Chile, it came as a surprise to some people, but there was nothing inherently illogical about the gesture. The decision was, of course, an act of political protest, a reflection that,

in circumstances as horrifying as those which followed the overthrow of democracy in Chile in 1973, a writer could not, in honesty,
sit quietly at his desk creating fictions; but it also reflected a view,
which García Márquez has held with varying degrees of intensity
over the years, that journalism is a more powerful, because more
immediate, weapon of education and persuasion than literature. In
the event, García Márquez broke his literary silence in 1981, with
the publication of *Chronicle of a Death Foretold*, but that subsequent action does not completely invalidate either the force or the
logic of the initial response. García Márquez's early journalism,
dating from the years 1948 to 1960, has recently been published in
four volumes, edited by Jacques Gilard. Little of it would ever be
read today, were it not for García Márquez's literary status, and a
great deal of it was clearly constrained by the fact that he began his
newspaper career as a columnist, not as a reporter. The daily search
for a subject, the frequent necessity of writing about nothing, or
almost nothing, he obviously found limiting, but, at the same time,
the early experience in Cartagena, followed by a period in Barranquilla where, from 1950 to 1952, he wrote for another Liberal
newspaper, *El Heraldo*, was of critical importance in determining
the future direction of his career.

García Márquez has often spoken of the stylistic lessons he
learned from journalism, more particularly from the time when he
began to work as an investigative reporter in 1954. He believes that
what he learned, essentially, were the literary equivalents of the
oral techniques of story-telling which people like his grandmother
possessed in such high degree: the 'tricks you need to transform
something which appears fantastic, unbelievable into something
plausible, credible, those I learned from journalism,' he once said,
adding, a trifle disingenuously, 'the key is to tell it straight. It is done
by reporters and by country folk.' During his early days as a
journalist, in Barranquilla, García Márquez also came into contact
with a number of literary and intellectual figures whose influence
and friendship were to be of considerable importance. The so-called
'Barranquilla group', which was never more than a loose and
shifting network of people with common interests, included the
Catalan poet and dramatist Ramón Vinyes, Germán Vargas, a
literary critic, Alfonso Fuenmayor, a journalist and son of a prominent Colombian novelist, and Álvaro Cepeda Samudio, who was

later to write a novel about the 1928 massacre of the Colombian banana-plantation workers, and who, shortly before his death in 1972, gave García Márquez the details which provide the extraordinary conclusion to *Chronicle of a Death Foretold*. All these figures were to be written into the final pages of *One Hundred Years of Solitude*, at the point when the mythological world of Macondo is finally brought into contact with the real world of its creator. Ramón Vinyes appears as the 'wise Catalan' who owns a bookshop in Macondo, while the 'fictional' Aureliano is introduced to the 'real' characters 'Álvaro, Germán, Alfonso, and Gabriel, the first and last friends he had in his life'.

The influence of the 'wise Catalan' is of particular significance for the closing pages of *One Hundred Years of Solitude*, though quite how far that influence can be traced to the Catalan whom García Márquez knew in Barranquilla is a question unlikely to be resolved. Alfonso Fuenmayor, for example, has cast doubts on the veracity of the portrait given in the novel, but there are a number of interesting points of contact between fact and fiction. Ramón Vinyes spent a life divided between Colombia and his native Catalonia, the region of north-eastern Spain whose capital is Barcelona. At one time, long before García Márquez knew him, he had owned a bookshop in Barranquilla; it was destroyed by fire in June 1923. At the time of the Spanish Civil War, he was in Catalonia, and he escaped from Barcelona into France in 1939, shortly before Franco's victorious fascist troops entered the city. García Márquez met him for the first time in April 1949, and knew him for about a year. At the age of sixty-four, in April 1950, Ramón Vinyes made his final return to Barcelona, and, on 5 May 1952, he died. On 13 April 1950, García Márquez published an open letter to 'Don Ramón' in *El Heraldo*, lamenting his departure from Barranquilla, and reflecting on all that his friends had learnt from him, including the daily lesson 'not to take life seriously, as the best means of triumphing over death'. Two years later, after hearing of the death of Vinyes, García Márquez wrote another article for *El Heraldo*, in which he recalled their first meeting and then the sudden, disorganized way in which Vinyes had finally left for home.

The 'wise Catalan' of *One Hundred Years of Solitude* is a complex and moving figure. He first appears in the book as a man who holds the key, though perhaps unknowingly, to the whole story of the

Buendía clan. That story, foreseen in its every detail by the gypsy sage Melquíades, and written down by him in an unknown language which cannot be deciphered until one hundred years have passed, will eventually be understood by Aureliano in the final paragraphs of the novel. In the course of his attempts at decipherment, Aureliano receives a visitation from Melquíades, who confirms his supposition that the language in which the story has been written down is Sanskrit, and who tells him that, in the bookshop owned by the wise Catalan, there is a Sanskrit Primer which will help him on towards his final goal. So the wise Catalan acts, in a way, as a traditional fountain of knowledge within the book, and he stands in general for all that is best and most attractive in the imaginative and creative aspirations of the human mind. He is also, and just as importantly, the book's firmest critic of the dangerous deceptions to which those same aspirations may give rise, one who understands how easily people may be duped by the power of their own imaginative gifts, how readily they may confuse the brilliance of their creative fictions with the realities of the world. It is he who, more than anyone else in the novel, acts as the critic of the fictions that have so magically involved the reader in the course of the unfolding of the Buendía story; it is he who lies behind Álvaro's demonstration that 'literature was the best plaything that had ever been invented in order to make fun of people'; and it is he who, as the source of all wisdom, rails against the futility of knowledge divorced from reality, one for whom, as Aureliano discovers, 'wisdom was worth nothing unless it could be used to invent a new way of preparing chick-peas'.

The wise Catalan leaves Macondo, in the same precipitate and disorganized way that Ramón Vinyes left Barranquilla, and he goes home to his 'native village' on the Mediterranean; from there he keeps up a correspondence with Germán and Aureliano, as Vinyes did from Barcelona with Germán Vargas. On his journey home from Macondo, he takes with him three boxes containing his own writing, work which he has composed in the back of his shop during the long years of exile, but the exact nature of which is never disclosed. He insists that his writing should go along with him, for, as he puts it, 'the world will be finally screwed up . . . on the day that men travel first class and literature goes as freight'. However, his attitude towards his own writing is, in fact, as ambiguous as his attitude towards literature in general, 'an interweaving of solemn respect and gossiping irreverence'. The night before he leaves Macondo, he points to the piles of books from his shop which have sustained him over the years, and, turning towards his friends 'with a kind of impudent benediction', he says: 'All that shit there I leave to you!' His death in the novel is recorded only obliquely, without the pain of direct confirmation: a letter arrives from Barcelona which 'was clearly not from the wise Catalan', addressed in conventional blue ink and in an official hand, a letter which 'had the innocent and impersonal look of hostile messages', and which Aureliano leaves unread, because he does not want to have to accept its contents.

By the end of his life, the wise Catalan has become a highly disillusioned sage. Indeed, he is able to play the role of mediator between the deceptive attractions of the world of fiction and the superior demands of the real world precisely because he is shown to be one of the primary victims of the creative power of the imagination. This is brought out in the passage dealing with his departure from Macondo and the return to his native land. For when he is in Macondo, lost in a tropical world that has no seasons as Europeans know them, he longs to go home, 'overcome by the longing for an everlasting springtime'. After his return to Europe, he finds that he cannot escape a nostalgia for the world he has left behind, and so lives on, bewildered and disillusioned, inexorably trapped between two irresistible images of his own making. Having taught his friends so much about the world, about literature and the human heart, he finally calls on them to forget it all, and to reject for ever the duplicitous claims of the imagination to recover the true nature of past experience:

> On winter nights, while the soup was bubbling on the hearth, he longed for the heat in the back room of his shop, the buzzing of the sun in the dusty almond trees, the whistle of the train in the drowsiness of siesta time, just as in Macondo he longed for the winter soup on the hearth, the street cries of the coffee-seller and the fleeting larks of springtime. Bewildered by two nostalgias facing each other like two mirrors, he lost his marvellous sense of unreality, so that he ended by recommending to all of them that they should leave Macondo, that they

should forget all he had taught them about the world and the human heart, that they should shit on Horace, and that, wherever they might be, they should always remember that the past was a lie, that memory had no ways of return, that every spring gone by was irrecoverable, and that the wildest and most tenacious love was an ephemeral truth in the end.

The wise Catalan commits the error of mythologizing both the 'mythological' world of Macondo and the 'real' world of Catalonia. Both come to occupy a favoured place within the imagination, a position which everyday experience will inevitably fail to sustain, but which the imagination will seek to defend unless opposed by the most violent and destructive means. The relationship between the process of nostalgia and the creation of the literary work is clear: both nostalgia and literature involve an imaginative selection from the details of past experience, and our perception of the truth of both depends ultimately, not on the 'representative' nature of the details presented, but on the creative skill with which they have been assembled, and there lies the danger. The real substance of life in Macondo is not, in the end, recoverable by the evocative descriptions of the heat and the almond trees, any more than life in Catalonia by the memory of the larks in springtime. Yet it is all too easy to come to believe in the veracity of these fictional resurrections. The disillusionment of the wise Catalan is thus a critical factor in the process of awakening at the end of García Márquez's novel, where the reader is brought to recognize that what has taken place within the book *has* been a fiction, after all, that it is impossible to recover in language what has been lost in time, and that there are, in the real world outside the book, no second chances.

The influence of Ramón Vinyes and the Barranquilla group on García Márquez may be strictly unquantifiable, but it was without question of great importance. The contact with other people who were interested in writing, the possibility of regular discussion, the opportunity to discover new areas of literature, all were significant for his future development. A superficial indication of his new contacts can be seen in the adoption of the pseudonym 'Septimus' – a name taken from one of the characters in Virginia Woolf's novel *Mrs Dalloway* – for his column in *El Heraldo* from January 1950 to December 1952. He says that he first read Virginia Woolf seriously

in 1953, while he was working as a travelling bookseller in the
sweltering heat of the Guajira peninsula of Colombia, but the
impulse clearly derived from the experiences of the previous years.
Later, in 1959, when he was writing the short story 'Big Mama's
Funeral', he included an affectionate tribute to the surviving members of the Barranquilla group: in the midst of an extravagant list of
those who have come from all over northern Colombia to attend the
funeral of the 'absolute sovereign of the kingdom of Macondo', he
mentions the 'mamadores de gallo de La Cueva' ('the jokers from
La Cueva'), an allusion to the bar in Barranquilla where those who
remained of the group met in later years. The English translation of
the story, by J.S. Bernstein, renders the phrase 'mamadores de
gallo' as 'cock breeders', but this is a simple misreading of an
expression in common use along the Caribbean coast.

   During his student days in Bogotá, from 1947 to 1948, García
Márquez had published a number of short stories in the Liberal
newspaper *El Espectador*, and, in the period 1948 to 1950, he
continued writing short stories, both in Cartagena and in Barranquilla. Between June or July 1950 and the following year, he also
worked on his first novel, *Leaf Storm*; this was rejected for publication when initially offered, and remained unpublished until 1955. A
far more important event at this time was his return to Aracataca in
1950, with his mother, to sell his grandfather's house. His grandmother had died, blind and demented, while he was a student in
Zipaquirá, and a family friend, who went to visit her when she was
living alone in the house in Aracataca, has given an account of her
situation during her final years. He described her as altogether lost
in solitude, already unable to see clearly, and enveloped by the
disintegrating power of the tropics, with the almond trees around
the house eaten away by ants, the flowers gone, and the garden
shrivelled in the heat; and he contrasted his experience with the
memory of how lively the house once had been. For García Márquez, the return to Aracataca was deeply disturbing, and provided a
strong impulse to locate the nature of that disturbance in writing.
The loss of his childhood home, and the sense of the terrible
circularity which was returning Aracataca to the nothingness from
which it had come, both contributed to the desire to re-create,
however deceptively, the story of that house and of that community
in a work of fiction.

In 1950 and 1951, García Márquez became involved in the running of two new publications, *Crónica*, a weekly on which he collaborated with Alfonso Fuenmayor and in which he published six of his own short stories, and *Comprimido*, of which he was editor. So, effectively, began a life-long commitment to the development of new outlets for creative journalism in Colombia, to counteract what he has always felt to be the crippling uniformity of the established Colombian press. Nearly thirty years later, in 1979, García Márquez was to become a member of an international commission, set up by UNESCO, for the study of communications problems, while in 1982 he announced that he would be devoting most of the money from his Nobel Prize award to the founding of a new Colombian daily paper. Both these developments follow logically from his basic political and educational concerns. Of course, his early attempts in the 1950s were not quite on the same scale: *Crónica* survived for about a year, *Comprimido* for only two issues. García Márquez has always regarded the latter with particular affection, however; it was distributed free, and in its first editorial, presumably written by García Márquez himself, its modest aims were heroically stated: '*Comprimido* is not the smallest newspaper in the world, but it seeks to be so, with the same painstaking tenacity with which others seek to be the largest.' At the beginning of 1954, García Márquez went to Bogotá to work for *El Espectador*, one of the two most important Liberal daily papers in Colombia. The paper was founded in 1887, and carries on the front page the following statement of its political attitudes: 'EL ESPECTADOR will work for the good of the country with Liberal criteria, and for the good of Liberal principles with patriotic criteria.' García Márquez inaugurated a regular column in *El Espectador* as a film reviewer, and, from February 1954 until the middle of 1955, this column occupied most of his working time. He did, however, begin to do some investigative reporting, the most notable result of which was a series of interviews with a Colombian sailor, Luis Alejandro Velasco.

The Velasco affair was to have important national consequences. García Márquez first dealt with the story in an article published in March 1955; he subsequently spent many hours interviewing Velasco, and the result was a series of fourteen articles which appeared in *El Espectador* in April 1955, written by García Márquez under

Velasco's name, and entitled 'The Truth About My Adventure'. Velasco was a young sailor, serving aboard a Colombian naval vessel. In February 1955, his ship had been in Mobile, Alabama for eight months, undergoing repairs and a refit, and his adventure began in the early hours of 24 February, when the ship finally left port to return to Cartagena in Colombia. All went according to plan until 28 February; then, when the ship was just two hours sailing-time away from her destination, Velasco and a number of companions were washed overboard in a heavy sea. All were drowned, except Velasco. He managed to clamber into a life-raft, and, having failed to be picked up, went on to spend ten days on the open sea, with only the occasional scrap of food to eat and nothing but salt-water to drink. Finally, he made a landfall on the Colombian coast. He became a national hero, was decorated by the President of the Republic, secured some highly lucrative publicity arrangements for himself, and generally seemed destined for a long and happy life. His story, as it appears in *El Espectador*, is a classic adventure; dominating everything is the sense of struggle between the lone individual and a hostile environment. Velasco experiences all the agonies of hunger and thirst, all the wearisome fluctuations between hope and despair; he fights with sharks over a piece of fish, and the passing ship or aeroplane always fails to notice him, lost in his small raft on the endless sea.

The story obviously had great potential, and García Márquez tells it well, with a firm grasp of the literary techniques needed to create suspense. He has a reporter's eye for the significant, unexpected detail, and this emerges in the account of Velasco's pathetic, and rather more than sentimental, aversion to eating a small seagull that he has painstakingly captured, or in his decision, in a moment of inspiration, to chew three cardboard store-cards which he has kept in his pocket, a souvenir of a shopping expedition with his girlfriend in Mobile. All such stories of adventure are both exceptional and typical. For the survivors, the adventure will probably be the most important thing that ever happens to them in life, and may bring out qualities which perhaps they will never need to show again. For the audience in front of their morning newspaper, there is an unconscious desire for the extraordinary to be mediated in a language which relates it to their sense of the typical, so that, in the end, we read both the strange story of Velasco and also another instalment in the centuries-old genre of shipwreck tales. García Márquez was well aware of the literary quality of his account, and, at the time of the republication of the story in book form in 1970, he gave it a mock heroic title, reminiscent of the style of the Renaissance chroniclers: 'Story of a Castaway Who Was Lost at Sea for Ten Days on a Raft with Nothing to Eat or Drink, Who Was Proclaimed a National Hero, Kissed by Beauty Queens and Made Rich by Publicity, and Later Spurned by the Government and Forgotten Forever.'

As this long title suggests, the sailor Velasco's triumph was short-lived. In the course of his interviews with García Márquez, it became all too clear that the official explanation of his disappearance at sea was unsustainable. It had been declared that Velasco and his companions had been washed overboard when their ship, a Colombian naval destroyer, was struck by an unexpected storm. Velasco revealed that there had been no storm. The disaster had occurred because the destroyer had listed badly in heavy seas, and this had been due to the fact that she had been carrying an illegal cargo: contraband, in the form of domestic consumer goods, radios, refrigerators, washing machines, and the like, all lashed insecurely to the deck. The cargo had come loose, and, given the excessive load and poor distribution, it had been impossible to turn the ship round in order to rescue those who were swept away. The political dimensions of the affair swiftly unravelled. As García Márquez noted in his introduction to the 1970 edition of the story, 'it was clear that the tale, like the destroyer, also carried an ill-secured political and moral cargo which we had not foreseen'. Velasco became an embarrassment to the Colombian authorities, and the circulation of *El Espectador* soared. Despite enormous pressures and inducements, Velasco never retracted his story. He lost his status as a national hero, along with his job in the navy, and he vanished into obscurity. As a late act of reparation, García Márquez said that the royalties from the 1970 edition would go to their rightful owner, 'the anonymous compatriot who had to endure ten days on a raft without eating or drinking, in order to make this book possible'.

The government of Colombia at the time of the Velasco affair was that of the dictator Gustavo Rojas Pinilla. He had come to power in a *coup d'état* in 1953, and, by 1955, his regime was in considerable difficulties. Conflicts with the press were inevitable in such circumstances, and the revelations of the Velasco case were simply a further step in the process of a complete breakdown in relations between press and government. Of the two main Liberal daily papers, *El Tiempo* was closed down in August 1955, while *El Espectador* suspended publication in January 1956. Shortly after the Velasco affair, and possibly in part because of it, García Márquez was sent to Europe by *El Espectador* as a roving foreign correspondent. He went to Geneva in July 1955, to cover the four-power summit conference, and he was to remain in Europe until the end of 1957, visiting a number of countries on both sides of the Iron Curtain. He was in Paris early in 1956 when he read, in *Le Monde*, that *El Espectador* had ceased publication. This did not immediately affect his situation, for, soon afterwards, a new paper under the same management appeared, called *El Independiente*, for which he continued to write. The closure of this new paper in April 1956, after only two months, was, however, a moment of personal crisis; he could return home, or remain in Europe without a job. In the event, he decided to stay, and entered then on a period of great material hardship, reflected partially, no doubt, in the permeating atmosphere of hunger and general deprivation which is so characteristic a feature of *No One Writes to the Colonel*, a work he finished in Paris early in 1957.

In assessing García Márquez's attitudes towards his European experience, as they emerge from his journalistic writings between 1955 and 1957, Jacques Gilard points to an obvious contrast between his treatment of the capitalist societies of the west and the socialist states of the east. The dominant tone of the articles dealing with the countries of western Europe is one of detached, often ironic, observation. García Márquez was signally unimpressed with a civilization which seemed to him in a state of terminal decline, and, unlike so many other visitors to Europe from the American continent, he seems never to have doubted that his own cultural values were the equal of those he found in Europe, and that the world from which he came was a more vital and innovative one. His brief reference to the house in Geneva where Jean-Jacques Rousseau was born suggests something of this attitude: the house seems to him only a formal shell, 'a big old house, full of windows, which must have died a long time ago, and no one has realized', now simply a tourist attraction, devoid of the energy which made Rousseau one of the major figures of the European Enlightenment. In García Márquez's articles, western Europeans often appear as simple caricatures, and he clearly felt no need, and certainly no desire, to try to go further. This is amusingly true of a piece entitled 'A Saturday in London'. He went to London in October or November 1957, and Vargas Llosa says he spent most of his time shut up in his hotel room in South Kensington, defending himself against the cold. In his article, all the typical images of the British capital are brought together: the speakers at Hyde Park Corner, a military band, children playing hockey, a fog which is remarkable for its absence, since, of course, everyone knows that 'in normal times in London, whatever the hour, it is five o'clock in the morning'; he talks of English breakfasts and tea, the strange currency of the period, bottles of milk outside silent houses, and the immutable laws of the class system. Not least, he talks of the English character. When he first arrived in London, he says, he had the impression that English people were continually talking to themselves in the street. After a while, he comes to realize that, in fact, they are all spending their time saying 'Sorry' to each other; and he gives this picture of a normal Saturday in the British capital, with the vast crowds flowing into Piccadilly Circus, mere voices lost in the darkness: 'I used to listen to them, apologizing to each other in the half-light of noon, travelling on instruments, the way planes do, through the dark cotton wool of the fog.' Throughout the article, García Márquez plays the old role of the naïve observer, gazing through apparently innocent eyes, and, as if in spite of himself, revealing the absurdities of an alien culture.

This view of Britain as a nation locked into the circularity of its traditions, unwilling or unable to recognize the harsh reality of its recent eviction from the paradise of world-power status, corresponds fully with García Márquez's general impression of the decadence of western European culture. His view of the socialist countries to the east is altogether different. Where in the west he is generally content to observe, in the east his dominant concern is to understand. He recorded his direct experience of the socialist countries in a series of articles that were originally intended for publication in *El Independiente*. This paper, following its closure in April 1956, reappeared in February 1957, three months before the fall of the dictator Rojas Pinilla. However, it seems as if the picture which García Márquez gave of the countries of eastern Europe was too favourable to find acceptance with the editor of *El Independiente* at that time, and so the articles initially appeared in the Venezuelan review *Momento* and the Colombian review *Cromos*, between November 1957 and September 1959. They were published in book form in 1978, under the title *Travelling in the Socialist Countries: 90 Days Behind the 'Iron Curtain'*.

The title suggests a single visit to the countries of eastern Europe, but it is clear to anyone reading the articles in book form that they are not an entirely coherent sequence, and Jacques Gilard persuasively argues that they represent, in fact, the results of three separate visits to the east. The first of these, unacknowledged at the time, presumably because of the political conditions in Colombia, was to Czechoslovakia and Poland in 1955; the second, to East Germany in 1957; and the third, to the USSR and Hungary later the same year. On his visit to East Germany, García Márquez was accompanied by the Colombian writer Plinio Apuleyo Mendoza and his sister, but in his account he is careful to conceal their identities under the names Jacqueline and Franco, presumably, again, because of the political sensitivities involved. García Márquez's friendship with Plinio Apuleyo Mendoza is of long standing. They first met during García Márquez's student days in Bogotá, saw each other again in Europe in 1955, travelled together to East Germany and also to Moscow, worked together later in Venezuela, and were both involved in the early days of the Cuban press agency Prensa Latina. In 1982, a volume of conversations between the two writers appeared, translated into English a year later as *The Fragrance of Guava*.

In the course of his three trips to eastern Europe, García Márquez visited East Berlin, Leipzig, Weimar, Prague, Warsaw, Kraków, the concentration camp at Auschwitz, Moscow, and Budapest. His attitude towards the different countries is always one of interest, always questioning, willing to make allowances where necessary, but by no means uncritical. He believed then, as he has always done, that socialism is the only system capable of resolving the vastly unequal distribution of wealth that is one of the basic causes of poverty throughout Latin America, and so he went to the socialist countries of eastern Europe with a willingness to learn.

None the less, he was quite ready to point out his objections to the way he observed socialism working in practice: 'Public order in East Germany', he wrote, 'very much resembles that in Colombia in the days of political persecution. The population lives in terror of the police.' Moreover, comparing the university city of Leipzig in the east with Heidelberg in the west, his response was one of open dismay: 'For us it was incomprehensible that the people of East Germany could have seized power, the means of production, commerce, banking, communications, and yet could be a sad people, the saddest people that I had ever seen.' His general reaction to disappointments of this kind was not, however, to reject the validity of the socialist system, but to seek to understand why, in the particular case, things should have turned out as they had. He was also highly aware of the great differences between the various socialist countries, of their failure to conform to western notions of superimposed homogeneity.

His account of his visit to Hungary is of particular interest. He was there only months after the national rising of October–November 1956, which had led to the military intervention of the Soviet Union on behalf of the Kádár faction within the Hungarian Communist Party and the defeat of the reformist groups identified with the Hungarian Prime Minister Imre Nagy. The national rising was suppressed with considerable bloodshed. It led to the creation of a large refugee problem and became, for a variety of reasons, a highly emotive symbol in the west, the proof for many of the profoundly undemocratic nature of eastern-block socialism. Here again, García Márquez's method is to try to understand the position of the parties involved in the Hungarian disaster, without seeking to apportion blame, to make sense of what had happened, rather than to throw up his hands in despair. He subsequently modified this even-handed position in an article published in June 1958, after the duplicitous execution of Nagy had been made public, but he still sought to argue that the conflict in Hungary had not been a simple confrontation between communism and liberty, as the western media had generally tried to show. This desire for reasoned discussion, and for criticism based on knowledge and understanding, rather than as a reflex of propaganda, has remained central to García Márquez's attitude towards socialism. He does not seek to defend the secrecy and authoritarianism of some socialist states, still less the excesses of the Stalinist era, but he recognizes the enormous problems associated with the building of socialism. He has understood, too, that, with his increasing fame as a writer, his room for manoeuvre in political debate has been significantly reduced. He knows that any criticism he may make today of socialist states will be widely misapplied in the west, and he has, therefore, increasingly taken the view that any reservations he may have about the operation of socialism in particular circumstances should remain private. It is perhaps against this background that one should understand the continued non-appearance of a book he has been writing on Cuba.

In general, then, the experience of the socialist states of eastern Europe led to no obvious changes in García Márquez's political attitudes. He neither became a consistent apologist for what he saw of socialism in the east, nor did his reservations lead him to doubt the essential validity of socialism as a political system and as the only likely solution to the problems of his native continent. In terms of his literary career, it was perhaps the visit to Moscow which left the greatest impression. He was there four years after the death of Stalin, and the year after Khrushchev's famous attack on Stalin and the 'cult of personality' at the Twentieth Party Congress in January 1956. Stalin's embalmed body was still, at that time, in the Lenin Mausoleum in Red Square, and the sight of it was one of the first in a series of visions about power and the solitude of power which lay behind the writing of *The Autumn of the Patriarch*. García Márquez recalled the scene in one of his 'Iron Curtain' articles: he pictures Stalin 'plunged in a sleep without remorse'; and, characteristically, he notes an unexpected detail: 'Nothing made such an impression on me as the elegance of his hands, with their delicate and transparent nails. They are the hands of a woman,' a detail reflected, perhaps, in the 'manos lisas de doncella' ('smooth maiden's hands') of his dead patriarch.

García Márquez's political position is one that has inevitably brought him hostility from a number of quarters. His socialist convictions have, naturally, failed to find favour in official North American circles, and he has served his time, like many other prominent Latin American writers and intellectuals, as a prohibited visitor to the United States. An understanding of this context is essential, in order to interpret some of García Márquez's own political statements to the western press. In an interview he gave to *Playboy* magazine in February 1983, for example, he provoked the interviewer at an early stage to ask the inevitable question − 'Are you a communist?' − and he then took care to distance himself from the communist movement by replying: 'Of course not. I am not and have never been. Nor have I belonged to *any* political party.' Now this is stretching the truth, for, in fact, García Márquez was closely involved with the Colombian Communist Party in the early 1950s, both while he was working in Barranquilla and, later, in Bogotá, where he had regular contacts with the leader of the Party who was living there clandestinely. From 1954 to 1957, the Communist Party was an illegal organization in Colombia, but, while working for *El Espectador*, García Márquez continued to pay monthly contributions to Party funds, and to collect contributions from fellow journalists. Towards the end of the 1950s, he became more critical of the direction of the Colombian CP, but, in 1972, in an interview with Plinio Apuleyo Mendoza, he still defined himself as a communist, though he admitted he was uncertain about the precise direction in which he wanted to go. In the *Playboy* interview, however, García Márquez would have known that there was no room for details or subtleties of this kind, and that to identify himself in any way with the communist movement would be to lose all potential influence over a North American audience. Only in a few restricted circles in the United States is a genuine discussion about the nature and problems of socialist politics at all possible, and to be labelled a communist is, generally, to forfeit any consideration either as a writer or as a political animal.

The United States press has, on a number of occasions, offered simplified and distorted images of García Márquez's political position, and it is interesting, in this context, to compare the attitudes of the press on both sides of the Atlantic to the announcement of his Nobel Prize award in October 1982. The British press, on the whole, produced dutiful pieces stressing his literary achievements and his concern for human rights, the only exception being the *Daily Telegraph* which, obviously caught out, carried a short piece entitled ' "Unknown" Nobel Writer'. The press in the United States, on the other hand, seemed much more preoccupied with García Márquez's political activities. *Time* magazine did, it is true, carry an article with the title 'A Latin Faulkner', but the *New York*

Times offered the far more eye-catching summary 'Storyteller With Bent for Revolution', picking up on an earlier article from 1980 which was headed 'For García Márquez, Revolution is a Major Theme'. The fact is that none of García Márquez's works to date has shown much concern with revolution in any of the political senses in which the term is normally used. Indeed, he has frequently expressed grave reservations concerning traditionally 'committed' literature; 'Latin Americans', he has said, 'expect something more from a novel than the revelation of oppressions and injustices of which they are only too well aware.' However, the pattern of response in the United States press inevitably follows the trends of a general national rhetoric, which seeks to analyse all political activity in terms of right and left. It is the prevalence of such a rhetoric which enabled the *New York Times*, in an article on 4 December 1982, to define the Colombian *violencia* as 'a civil war between leftist and rightist factions'. More significantly, of course, such a rhetoric has provided a smoke-screen for widespread United States interference in the domestic affairs of a large number of Latin American countries.

If García Márquez has met with opposition from sectors of opinion hostile to his socialist convictions, he has also encountered a measure of opposition from within the socialist camp itself. The reasons for this are not hard to find. He has, in recent years, generally kept his distance from the organized political parties of Colombia. His ambiguous attitude towards the Colombian Communist Party, one of respect but not whole-hearted support, is a reflection of this. He has, therefore, left himself open to the charge of being a political dilettante. Moreover, while refusing to ally himself openly with any of the left-wing movements in Colombia, he has expressed considerable enthusiasm for a Venezuelan party, the MAS (Movimiento al Socialismo); in 1972, for example, he gave the MAS $22,000 towards the purchase of a printing press for the party newspaper, the proceeds of the Premio Rómulo Gallegos, a major Latin American literary prize which had been awarded that year to *One Hundred Years of Solitude*. In response to criticisms from the socialist camp − reminiscent, in some ways, of the criticisms once levelled at Sartre on account of his enthusiasm for the Italian Communist Party and his reservations about the French CP − García Márquez has argued that, in the first place, the

Colombian left is too fragmented to constitute a viable opposition force in its present form: 'The different groups are bogged down in a dialogue of the deaf, separated by a swamp of sectarianism'; and, in the second place, that a party like the MAS is one which is more in keeping with the needs of contemporary Latin America, less motivated by the orthodoxies of the class struggle, more concerned to find a national, Venezuelan path to socialism than to follow the example of the Soviet Union, China, or Cuba. García Márquez has also suggested that formally-constituted political parties have not been essential to the making of revolutions in Latin America, and, if one looks at the examples of Mexico in 1910, Bolivia in 1952, Cuba in 1959, or Nicaragua in 1979, the point is, at least, arguable. On western-style democracy, García Márquez has recently commented: 'Democracy in the developed countries is a product of their own development, and not vice versa. To try to introduce it in a crude form into countries with other cultures — like those of Latin America — is as mechanical and unreal as to try to introduce the Soviet system.' Behind such statements lies the fact that the trappings of western democracy, and, in particular, the regular holding of elections, have frequently served to confer apparent legitimacy on some of the most repressive regimes in Latin America. But in general, García Márquez argues, neither imported socialism, nor imported democracy, will suffice. Each country must find its own way, in the light of its own historical traditions.

García Márquez's continued residence in Europe, after the closure of *El Independiente* in April 1956, was, as I have said, a time of great material hardship. Plinio Apuleyo Mendoza, who had become editor of the Venezuelan weekly *Elite* in 1956, provided a much-needed outlet for his journalistic writings at the time, and, a year later, when he became editor of another Venezuelan weekly, *Momento*, he arranged a job for García Márquez on the paper. In this way, García Márquez's first visit to Europe was brought to a close, and he left for Caracas at the end of 1957.

As it happened, the first few months of 1958 were to be of particular importance in the history of Venezuela. In the twentieth century, Venezuela had been subject to two long periods of dictatorial rule, the first that of Juan Vicente Gómez, from 1908 to 1935, the second that of Marcos Pérez Jiménez, which had begun in 1948 and was now on the point of collapse. When García Márquez was growing up in Aracataca, he recalls, there were many Venezuelan exiles from the Gómez regime living there; now, in January 1958, he was to be present in Caracas for the fall of Pérez Jiménez. Both experiences, in different ways, played a part in the evolution of *The Autumn of the Patriarch*. Richard Nixon, in his book *Six Crises*, described Pérez Jiménez as 'probably the most hated dictator in all of Latin America', an assertion which Cubans living under Batista might have challenged, but which gives some measure of the savagery of his regime. His fall created a wild sense of jubilation in the Venezuelan capital, and led to a period of feverish political activity in which Plinio Apuleyo Mendoza and García Márquez were fully involved. As the former succinctly put it, 'it was the first time that we had witnessed the fall of a dictator in Latin America'. In March 1958, García Márquez made a brief visit to Colombia; there, on 27 March, in Barranquilla, he married Mercedes Barcha Pardo, whom he had first met, and to whom he had first proposed, many years before in Sucre. He was back in Caracas, however, for the events surrounding the visit to Venezuela, in May 1958, of the then Vice-President of the United States, Richard Nixon.

Nixon gives a colourful account of his Venezuelan experience in *Six Crises*. Certainly, his reception by large sections of the Venezuelan population was both violent and abusive. The motorcade in which he was travelling from the airport was ambushed on the outskirts of Caracas, and Nixon was probably lucky to escape death or serious injury. Considering that Pérez Jiménez and his Chief of Secret Police had only recently fled the country to take up residence in the United States, the nature of the reception was not altogether surprising, as Nixon himself recognized. Inevitably, though, he saw the effectiveness of the demonstrations against him as further proof of the influence of what he rather oddly termed 'the Communist high command in South America':

> It made me almost physically ill to see the fanatical frenzy in the eyes of teenagers — boys and girls who were very little older than my twelve-year-old daughter, Tricia. My reaction was a feeling of absolute hatred for the tough Communist agitators who were driving children to this irrational state.

Of course, had anything more serious happened to Nixon, the consequences for Venezuela might have been disastrous. As it was,

President Eisenhower ordered four companies of marines and paratroops into the Caribbean, so that they might 'be in a position to cooperate with the Venezuelan Government', an offer not to be taken lightly. The Venezuelan authorities offered apologies for the incident, and considerable concern and regret were expressed in the national press. Carlos Ramírez MacGregor, who had overall control of *Momento*, insisted that his paper, too, should carry a note of apology, whereupon both Plinio Apuleyo Mendoza and García Márquez resigned in protest. As Jacques Gilard points out, Nixon's visit to Caracas came only four years after the Eisenhower administration had contrived to bring to an end the only period of democratic government that the Central American state of Guatemala has ever had, and, in the general context of relations between the United States and Latin America, an apology for Nixon's rough handling seemed inappropriate, in both moral and political terms.

Without a job, García Márquez sought employment with a paper called *Venezuela Gráfica*, a paper whose style and aspirations were summarized by its popular nickname, *Venezuela Pornográfica*. He began work there at the end of June 1958, and was still operating in these reduced circumstances when news arrived of the success of Fidel Castro and his guerrilla fighters of the Sierra Maestra. Castro had returned secretly to Cuba from exile in 1956, with a small group of followers, including Che Guevara, in order to wage war on the corrupt and brutal regime of the dictator Batista. Finally, on 8 January 1959, Castro and his followers entered Havana in triumph, to the delight of many, and with the support of most of the countries around the world, including the United States. García Márquez's enthusiasm for the Cuban revolution has remained undiminished to the present day, and, if he has had some private reservations about the direction which the revolution has taken, he has never doubted that its achievements have been of far greater significance than its limitations. In an article published in 1977, he recalled that, when Batista was defeated, it seemed 'as if time had gone into reverse and Marcos Pérez Jiménez had been overthrown for a second time'. Both he and Plinio Apuleyo Mendoza were invited to Havana in January 1959, and, again, he compared the experience with the excitement of being in a liberated Venezuela: 'For those of us who had lived in Caracas throughout the previous year, the feverish atmosphere and the creative disorder of Havana at the beginning of

1959 were no surprise.' He contrasts his interest in post-revolutionary Cuba with his feelings about Cuba in earlier times: 'Before the Revolution, I never had the curiosity to get to know Cuba. The Latin Americans of my generation thought of Havana as a scandalous gringo brothel . . .' Those were times when, as Ernesto Cardenal notes, in his book *In Cuba*, 'businessmen would phone from New York or Miami and ask for a room with a woman'; and, indeed, Havana's reputation in the 1950s, as an extended brothel and gambling house for a largely North American clientele, was one that was soundly based in reality.

While he was in Havana, García Márquez attended the trial of one of Batista's officers, Sosa Blanco, who was subsequently condemned to death for atrocities committed against the Cuban people, and the experience of the trial provided a further element in the elaboration of *The Autumn of the Patriarch*. But it was in the field of journalism that the Cuban revolution had the most immediate effect on García Márquez's career. In the aftermath of the revolution, the Cuban press agency Prensa Latina was founded, with the aim of creating an alternative source of news about developments in Cuba, and of counteracting the influence of the existing international press agencies. It was set up by the Argentinian journalist Jorge Ricardo Masetti, a friend of Che Guevara, and he suggested to Plinio Apuleyo Mendoza and García Márquez that they should open the Bogotá office of the new agency. Thus began, for García Márquez, two years of energetic journalistic activity in defence of the Cuban revolution, which included a period as assistant bureau chief in Prensa Latina's New York office. It also included the launching of a new magazine in Bogotá, called *Acción Liberal*, an attempt to galvanize the Colombian left in the wake of the recent events in Cuba. The magazine ran to only three issues, but one of these contained an important article by García Márquez on Colombian literature, from which I quoted in the first chapter of this book, in connexion with his views on the literature of the *violencia*.

Writing in 1977 about the death of Rodolfo Walsh, another Argentinian journalist who was involved with Prensa Latina from the earliest days, García Márquez tells an interesting story about an incident which occurred in the Havana offices of the agency. Masetti had installed a special teleprinter room there, in order to monitor the large volume of material put out by the rival agencies.

One night, a message, apparently in code and emanating from Guatemala, was accidentally received on the teleprinter. Rodolfo Walsh, who had once been a writer of detective stories, decided to try to decipher the message, and, with the help of some cryptography manuals purchased from a second-hand bookshop in Havana, he succeeded. The message, according to García Márquez, was from the CIA station chief in Guatemala, and contained a detailed account of the preparations which the United States government was making at that time for an invasion of Cuba. Those preparations were to lead to the Bay of Pigs episode of 17 April 1961, when a force of Cuban exiles, backed by the CIA, landed in southern Cuba in a vain attempt to overthrow the Castro government. If the story García Márquez tells is true in detail, then the Cuban authorities would have had ample advance warning of what was to come. The two who presumably knew most about the affair are, however, both now dead. Masetti was last seen alive in 1963 in northern Argentina, where he was attempting to organize a guerrilla band, while Rodolfo Walsh was one of the thousands of victims of the Argentinian military regime's 'dirty war' of the 1970s.

The period after 1960 was one of great difficulty for the Cuban revolutionary process. As the socialist nature of its development became unmistakably apparent, it came under increasing attack from conservative and liberal elements within Cuba, and there was mounting pressure, too, from outside the country, particularly from the United States government and from Cuban exiles living in the United States. Diplomatic relations between Cuba and the United States were broken off in January 1961, and, when García Márquez was working in New York, there were constant threats against the journalists of Prensa Latina. Tensions also began to appear within the revolutionary process itself, as long-standing members of the Cuban Communist Party became engaged in a struggle for power with the supporters of Castro's '26 July Movement'. The latter dispute quickly reached Prensa Latina, threatening Masetti's position. García Márquez decided to resign from the agency, before, as he said, 'they throw me out as a counter-revolutionary'. In the face of the imminent threat of an invasion of Cuba, he withdrew his resignation, but when, some weeks later, he learnt that Masetti himself was about to resign, both he and Plinio Apuleyo Mendoza made their final decision to leave.

The years between childhood in Aracataca and the experience of the Cuban revolution were the truly formative ones for García Márquez's career, and much that he has done since that time has followed a relatively logical direction. The main areas of concern, literature, journalism, human rights, and socialist politics, have remained, and his success as a novelist has enabled him to devote considerable amounts of time and money to the pursuit of all of them. After leaving New York and Prensa Latina in 1961, he moved to Mexico, and it was there, over a period of eighteen months beginning in 1965, that he wrote *One Hundred Years of Solitude*, a book which brought him immediate financial success and an international reputation. He has subsequently led the life of a famous writer, with all that that implies in terms of the division between public and private man. He has friendships with a number of well-known political figures, including Fidel Castro and François Mitterrand, he travels widely, and lives well.

In the 1970s, he made an important contribution to Latin American journalism with the launching of a new magazine in Colombia called *Alternativa*. The function of the magazine, as ever, was to provide a different kind of news coverage, particularly in the wake of the overthrow of democracy in Chile in 1973, and to try to give some measure of cohesion to the expression of broad left-wing opinion. The paper ran to 257 issues between 1974 and 1980, and contained some journalism of a very high order, including a number of articles by García Márquez himself. None the less, the experience of *Alternativa* also revealed some major problems. In September 1974, barely six months after the first issue of the magazine, internal disputes about its political direction led to the departure of one group of journalists to start up a more radical version entitled *Alternativa del Pueblo*. Further internal problems surfaced at the end of 1976, resulting in the departure of another group of journalists. For four months the magazine was unable to publish, due to financial difficulties. Then there were pressures from those in the Colombian establishment who disapproved of the paper's political aspirations (its motto was: 'to dare to think is to begin to struggle'); there were violent attacks on the paper's offices, and attempts to disrupt distribution; and when, in 1979, the magazine was finally driven to seek advertising revenue, after a previous courageous refusal to do so, pressures from various sources ensured that no such financial support was forthcoming. The magazine was finally forced to close down in March 1980.

Over the past decade or so, García Márquez has been widely active in the field of human rights. In 1974, he served on the Russell Tribunal which investigated the abuse of human rights in Latin America, and in 1978 he founded a human rights organization called *Habeas* in Mexico City. Despite his close friendship with Fidel Castro, he has worked on behalf of political prisoners in Cuba, and he played a key role in the release, in 1982, of the poet Armando Valladares, who had been held in prison in Cuba since 1960. He also worked, with the novelist Graham Greene, to secure the release of two British bankers who were kidnapped by Salvadoran guerrillas in 1979, and he has continued to make use of his journalistic experience to support his political and human rights objectives. Since 1979, he has been a consistent defender of Nicaragua against the hostility of the United States, and he has generally been active in support of the countries of the Third World, in their efforts to resist the political, economic, or military intrusions of the western powers. One of the best of his recent journalistic pieces was a long article which appeared in 1983, on the strange circumstances surrounding the disappearance of Jaime Bateman Cayón, the leader of one of the main Colombian guerrilla groups. Curiously, just two years before, García Márquez had made a precipitate exit from Colombia, claiming he was about to be arrested on charges of involvement with the Colombian guerrillas. The Colombian government stated at the time that he was simply trying to gain advance publicity for his new book, *Chronicle of a Death Foretold*. At all events, García Márquez considered himself an exile from Colombia from March 1981 until, following a change of government, he felt able to return, in April 1983, to supervise the preparations for the launching of a new Colombian daily paper.

His international reputation as a writer was confirmed by the award of the Nobel Prize for literature in October 1982. García Márquez was the first Colombian and the fourth Latin American to win the prize, following Gabriela Mistral in 1945, Miguel Ángel Asturias in 1967, and Pablo Neruda in 1971, the first and third of whom were Chilean poets, the second a novelist from Guatemala. In his acceptance speech in Stockholm, at the end of 1982, García

Márquez looked back on the eleven years since Neruda came to
Stockholm, and the long list of terrors through which Latin America had lived in so short a time: the Chilean president, Salvador
Allende, dying alone in the burning presidential palace in Santiago,
the military tyranny in Argentina, the twenty million children who
failed to survive their first year of life because of malnutrition and
preventable disease, the 120,000 people who disappeared under
repressive regimes, the 100,000 dead in the Central American states
of El Salvador, Guatemala, and Nicaragua. He also called on
Europeans to reconsider their attitude towards Latin America, to
attempt to see through eyes other than those of a supposedly
rational culture at the end of a long process of development, to
remember that the tragedy of Latin America is not an exotic
aberration, but one that Europe, too, has known: 'It is understandable', he said, 'that the rational talents on this side of the world,
exalted in the contemplation of their own cultures, should have
found themselves without a valid means by which to interpret us. It
is only natural that they insist on measuring us with the same
yardstick that they use for themselves, forgetting that the ravages of
life are not the same for all, and that the quest for an identity is as
arduous and bloody for us as it was for them.'

In the context of the problems of Latin America and the Third
World generally, and in the face of the relentless pursuit, by the
more prosperous countries of the world, of the apocalyptic ideal of
mutually-assured destruction, what role remains for the writer?
Simply, it seems, the role which writers have always had: it remains
for them, as 'the inventors of tales, who will believe anything',
continually to assert, despite all provocation to despair, that human
beings are capable of creating a different kind of future, and a different kind of world, one in which 'no one will be able to decide for
others how they die, where love will prove true and happiness be possible, and where the races condemned to one hundred years of solitude will have, at last and forever, a second opportunity on earth'.

García Márquez's speech was followed by a party, for which Fidel
Castro provided a large consignment of Cuban rum. The head of
protocol at the Swedish Foreign Ministry protested that Swedish
alcohol regulations had been violated, while *The Times* (London),
equally alert, if more partisan, carried a story under the heading
'Castro's Rum Starts an Anti-American Orgy'.

III

Two stories of the *Violencia*

> In this country there isn't a single fortune
> that doesn't have a dead donkey behind it.
> (*In Evil Hour*)

(i) *No One Writes to the Colonel*

The central − almost the only − figure in Samuel Beckett's play *Happy Days* is a woman called Winnie. She is about fifty years old, and she spends the entire play buried in the earth, up to her waist in the first act, literally up to her neck in it in the second. From this unpromising and obviously declining position, anchored in the midst of an unbroken plain under a merciless light, she manages to sustain a dialogue with herself, constantly giving herself encouragement or reassurance, somehow getting through the day with the kind of routines that mark and condition a life, brushing her hair, going through the contents of her bag, and occasionally speculating on the way things are, though always in a manner designed to distance her from the possibility, or the threat, of change. Her world is apparently as self-contained as a world could be, drastically limited in space, essentially reduced to the dimensions of repetitious speech. Yet other worlds do intrude, memories of happier times and other places, above all the vague presence on stage of another character, Willie, a man in his sixties, someone with whom Winnie has had a long and progressively more limited relationship. Willie sits or crawls, mostly in silence, apparently more animal than human, yet still important to Winnie because, withdrawn and laconic as he is, he offers the last remaining hope that her voice will be heard by someone, that she may not, after all, be so totally alone.

The play contains much that is deeply moving, much, too, that is very funny − as a character in another of Beckett's plays remarks:

'Nothing is funnier than unhappiness.' However, the play also raises ethical questions that invite no easy response. What little remains of Winnie's life is being systematically destroyed; of that there is no doubt. Were the play to move to a third act, we should expect to find the central character fully absorbed into the earth and finally silenced. But how should the spectator respond to this process? In one way, Winnie's voluble adaptability to the increasing hopelessness of her situation, her determination to remain cheerful and to keep talking, her concern for order and appearances as a means of survival, all arouse in the audience not merely feelings of sympathy, but a sense of being witness to a struggle that is altogether heroic. If the encroaching mound of earth suggests the decline of old age and the inevitability of death, then Winnie's attitude, a warm and even passionate dramatization of old clichés ('One mustn't grumble', 'One should learn to make the most of things'), stands out as a message of a very positive kind, a refusal to surrender to the logic of despair. However, seen from another point of view, perhaps it is not so much the earth which is rising as Winnie who is falling? Perhaps she is falling, being sucked ever deeper into the morass, precisely because she is so relentlessly capable of making the most of things, of adapting with such apparent dexterity to a pattern of life that seems in the end to be a denial of life itself. At the end of the play, she watches as Willie tries to climb up the mound in which she is imprisoned. His errand is uncertain; perhaps he wants to kiss her, or perhaps to kill her and so end the misery of her private world or the torture of their shared existence. Winnie recognizes her complete helplessness, a passivity that has now become absolute: 'There was a time when I could have given you a hand', she says, 'and then a time before that again when I did give you a hand.' What has happened here? Does the problem lie in the nature of life itself, in the irresistible process of physical and mental decline? Or does it lie in Winnie's refusal or inability to counten-ance revolt, to take a stand, in her endless acceptance of life as it is given? Should we admire Winnie's resilience in the face of an unendurable pressure, or should we recoil in the face of her seemingly limitless capacity to reach an accommodation with the wretchedness of her condition? The play, clearly, will offer no resolution of this dilemma, recognizing that no resolution is possi-ble outside the limits of an individual consciousness, but it does allow the complexities and the poignancy of the situation to emerge in a particularly challenging way.

García Márquez's long short story *No One Writes to the Colonel*, written while he was in Europe in the 1950s, presents the reader with rather similar problems, and, in a sense, the problems are more complex still, because – whether intentionally or otherwise – the moral ambiguities raised within the story are not subject to the same rigorously neutral control as exists within Samuel Beckett's play. García Márquez's story seems at times to be searching for some form of resolution of the dilemmas it contains, while at other times it appears to take refuge in the inscrutable nature of those same dilemmas. Moreover, the story deals with issues of both a personal and a social kind, whereas Beckett's concerns in *Happy Days* are almost exclusively personal. Whatever their differences, however, both the story and the play are deeply involved with the problems of how to live in a world which is seen as ultimately unacceptable and unendurable, and both are far more productive of thought than their relatively simple narrative structures would suggest. *No One Writes to the Colonel* is set in the tropical lowlands of Colombia, in a place which resembles Sucre, the inland river port in the department of the same name where García Márquez's family lived in the 1940s. The central figure of the story, the colonel of the title, is a man seventy-five years of age, a veteran of the War of a Thousand Days, the Colombian civil war of 1899–1902. We learn that the colonel fought on the losing Liberal side and that he was present at the signing of the Treaty of Neerlandia on 24 October 1902. This treaty, as we have seen in an earlier chapter, marked the end of the military ambitions of the Liberal general Rafael Uribe Uribe, while in García Márquez's fictional world this same act of surrender brings to an end the military career of Colonel Aureliano Buendía, described in *No One Writes to the Colonel* as the 'quartermaster general of the revolutionary forces on the Atlantic coast'.

The events in *No One Writes to the Colonel* take place in the year 1956, when Colombia had already suffered through nearly a decade of the *violencia*; it is also the year, as the story twice reminds us, of the Suez crisis in Europe. For the central figure of the story, the half-century that has elapsed since the end of the War of a Thousand Days has been generally uneventful, but it has been dominated by a single, inescapable passion: the colonel's desire to obtain the war

veteran's pension that was promised by the government in the wake
of the surrender at Neerlandia. Every Friday, when the mail
arrives, brought by river launch from a town eight hours away, the
colonel goes to see if there is any news of his pension, and,
inevitably, there is none. As the postmaster succinctly puts it: 'El
coronel no tiene quien le escriba,' the flat and dismissive statement
that gives the story its title. Still the colonel refuses to give up hope
and patiently keeps on waiting for the next Friday to come around.
His desire for his war pension is doubly motivated. Most obviously,
he is in desperate need of the money: the colonel and his wife are
living in conditions of great material deprivation, and have long
suffered from the effects of chronic undernourishment. They live on
the outskirts of town in a house with a palm-thatched roof and
flaking whitewashed walls. The house is mortgaged and repayment
is due in two years' time. The couple's only son, Agustín, has been
shot nine months before by the local police for distributing clandestine literature, thus removing a vital source of economic, as well as
emotional, support. They have sold nearly everything they have
and now face the end of their lives with only the prospect of
wretched ill-health and slow starvation. However, the colonel is
also concerned with what he sees as the morality of the situation. He
has an unshakeable sense that the war pension should be his by
virtue of natural justice, that the cause he fought for in the civil war,
'to save the Republic', as he puts it in a conversation with his lawyer,
was a just cause, that defeat was not humiliation, and that, however
long the process may take, justice and truth must surely triumph in
the end.

   The colonel's optimism, which is not, in fact, quite as unwavering
or as unreflective as some critics have suggested, has produced very
different responses among readers. According to one editor of the
story: 'A state of innocence and truth protect the colonel's inner life
from the contaminating evils around him,' and the writer goes on to
suggest that there is a general lesson here: 'A capacity for love and
sacrifice are the safeguards of Man's happiness and, armed with
these qualities, he can spiritually survive' (Giovanni Pontiero).
According to another editor, however, the story 'shows a man who
is victimized by his pride, dignity, and quixotic hopes as much as by
the realities of history, government, and society' (Djelal Kadir).
Clearly, the discrepancies reflect very different basic attitudes and

values, and return us to the kind of dilemmas which face the audience in Beckett's *Happy Days*. Is the colonel's persistence in trusting to the future − a future in which we, as observers of his situation, can see little obvious reason for hope − a form of heroic madness in a world where values have become so distorted under the impact of endless violence, poverty, and repression that sanity appears a mockery? Or is the colonel's optimism a kind of suicide, a blank refusal to accept the reality of a world which is inevitably impinging upon him, an attempt to live according to values that are unsustainable except by an act of wilful blindness, a perverse effort to try to redeem the inadequacies of half a century by proving himself to have been right all along? These dilemmas are always near the surface of the tale, not least in the passages dealing with the relationship between the colonel and his wife. Where he is quixotic and optimistic, she is practical and, understandably, often near to despair, and, in one beautifully simple exchange between them, we see a confrontation between what are, in effect, two utterly distinct world views:

'You can't eat illusions,' said the woman.
'You can't eat them, but they feed you,' replied the colonel.

The general situation is complicated in a variety of ways by the fact that the couple have inherited from their dead son a fighting cock, an animal which, in the context of their society, represents potential wealth, either as an object to be sold immediately, or − more problematically − as an investment, which will pay off should the bird turn out to be a good fighter in the pit. Naturally enough, the colonel's wife is for selling the bird, putting their finances in order, and having something decent to eat; but the colonel, though hesitant at times, is driven by a desire to keep the bird. He knows that it costs more than they can afford to feed it, but, because it once belonged to their son, it represents an almost magical link with the past, it is wondrously and intensely alive, where so much else seems dead or dying, and it carries with it the possibility of hope, one that is more than simply financial, something strangely indefinable that appeals to the colonel more than the arid certainties of an immediate cash transaction. Inevitably, critics have argued that the fighting cock should be interpreted as a symbol of some kind, of revolt, of trust in the workings of fate or resignation to them, of the collective hopes of a people for whom chance alone appears to offer some possibility of release from their troubles, but this is a matter to which I shall return later.

The tale is told in an apparently simple and direct way, and, as we have seen, this directness was the result of a conscious decision which García Márquez took in the 1950s to move away from what he felt was the excessively literary style of his first novel, *Leaf Storm*, in order to try to deal more authentically with the rough realities of contemporary Colombia. The colonel of the story is never named. We are told that he grew up in the small town of Manaure, situated to the east of Riohacha, in the department of La Guajira in north-eastern Colombia. We learn nothing about how or why he came to fight on the Liberal side in the civil war; given that he is seventy-five years old in 1956, he would have been eighteen at the start of the War of a Thousand Days, and, according to his lawyer, he was a colonel by the time he was twenty. At some point he became associated with the town of Macondo, the legendary setting for *One Hundred Years of Solitude* which is generally identified with Aracataca, García Márquez's birthplace in the department of Magdalena. His distinctive, if problematical, honesty is reflected in his appointment at the time of the civil war as 'treasurer of the revolution in the district of Macondo'. He faithfully made the journey to the surrender at Neerlandia, travelling for six days with the funds of the rebel forces contained in two trunks tied to the back of a mule. He arrived just half an hour before the signing of the treaty, and obtained a receipt for the funds from Colonel Aureliano Buendía.

In an interesting passage from *One Hundred Years of Solitude*, this latter incident, which is only briefly described in *No One Writes to the Colonel*, is filled out in greater detail, and in a way that gives some insight into García Márquez's continuing thoughts about the character of his colonel some ten years after the writing of the story in which he first appears. In the later novel, the two trunks which the colonel brings to Neerlandia are revealed to contain solid gold; Aureliano Buendía is in the process of signing the final copy of the surrender document when:

> . . . a rebel colonel appeared in the doorway of the tent, leading by the halter a mule laden with two trunks. In spite of

his extreme youth, he had an arid appearance and a patient
expression. He was the treasurer of the revolution in the
district of Macondo . . . With a deliberation that was exasperating, he unloaded the trunks, opened them, and placed on the
table, one by one, seventy-two gold bricks. Everyone had
forgotten the existence of such a fortune . . .

The passage is interesting because it suggests that the colonel's
honesty, one of the most obvious aspects of his character, should
not be viewed in a wholly simple light. Certainly, in a time of civil
war, there is something remarkable about the way he has behaved;
he could so easily, amidst all the chaos of defeat, have taken the
Liberal gold for himself and lived for ever in comfort. But, at the
same time, there is something exasperating about his meticulous
concern for the details of his task. It has a hint almost of the
bureaucratic, suggesting a form of honesty that is hard, at times, to
distinguish from the simply obstinate. It might be said in reply,
perhaps, that it is only such forms of honesty that are likely to
survive under the pressure of war and the debasement of moral
values, a point which brings the reader back once again to the
difficult question of the appropriateness of the colonel's obstinate,
absurd, or heroic resistance in the short story of which he is the
subject. It is clear, at least, that the colonel is meant to be no simple
hero, no mere moral counterweight to the chaos that surrounds
him.

Following the Liberal defeat the colonel seems to have done very
little, except to wait for his illusory pension. After the signing of the
Treaty of Neerlandia he lives on in Macondo for a few years, but
then the banana fever, symbolized by that same 'innocent yellow
train' which appears in *One Hundred Years of Solitude*, comes to
change the way of life in the town for ever. The colonel is unable to
tolerate the invasion:

In the drowsiness of siesta time, he saw a dusty, yellow train
arrive, with men and women and animals suffocating in the
heat, crowded together even on the roofs of the carriages. It
was the banana fever. In twenty-four hours they transformed
the town. 'I'm going,' the colonel said then. 'The smell of
bananas is rotting my insides.'

So, we are told, he left Macondo in June 1906; fifty years later we find him settled in a remote and terrorized town further south, where he continues his life of endless expectation. Now, in 1906, he would have been only twenty-five years old, and the apparently uninterrupted period of passive waiting that has filled more than half a century of his existence seems scarcely credible. In reality, however, the story is told in a way that does not encourage the reader to reconstruct the past in any great detail. García Márquez is clearly not interested primarily in establishing a wholly plausible sequence of events to sustain the image of his central character. He is concerned above all with what the colonel is now, with what remains to him of life, with the psychology of waiting, and with his struggle to survive, spiritually and materially, in an increasingly enclosed world. Once, we learn, the colonel belonged to a veterans' association that included members of both political parties, but, as he says, 'all my comrades died waiting for the mail', and he is now left to face his problems alone.

Nothing very much happens in the course of *No One Writes to the Colonel*. Indeed, the story is constructed in such a way as to convince the reader that the chances of something ever happening in the town are extremely limited. What we are given is a sense of the unending pressures which weigh down upon the colonel's life: the forces of personal poverty, the tyranny of the climate, and the collective fear which is the mark of the years of the Colombian *violencia*; and it is only in the context of these seemingly invincible pressures that we can form any sense of the meaning — if there can be one — of the colonel's dogged resistance. The poverty in which he and his wife live is made explicit from the very opening lines of the story. He opens a tin of coffee and finds there is only a teaspoonful left; he uses a knife to scrape out the inside of the tin, in order that nothing should be wasted, and so another day begins. The dull precision of the gestures confirms the impression of an unending round of attempts to deal with a situation that has, imperceptibly over the years, become an impossible one. This search for a way out of the enclosed world of poverty colours the entire narrative.

The couple have nothing left to sell, except a clock and a picture, and no one wants to buy them, the clock because it is now old-fashioned, since clocks with luminous dials have begun to appear on the local market, and the picture because almost everyone in town has an identical one. The couple's poverty has become a powerful force of isolation, for they have struggled to maintain appearances, and this has led to desperate subterfuge: 'Several times I've put stones on to boil', his wife says, 'so the neighbours wouldn't know that we've gone for days without putting the pot on the stove.' Within their relationship, too, the long-term effects of poverty and the attempts to conceal it have been corrosive. When the colonel's wife goes to the local priest, Father Ángel, in an effort to raise some money on their wedding rings — and is rebuked by the priest with the cliché that 'it is a sin to trade with sacred things' — she cannot tell her husband at first, and offers a half-hearted explanation for her absence. The colonel, sensing her hesitation, sees the moral clearly: 'The worst thing about a bad situation', he says, 'is that it makes one tell lies.' It would be a mistake, however, to conclude that the description of the couple's poverty conveys only despair. On the contrary, *No One Writes to the Colonel* represents García Márquez's first important attempt to explore the humorous dimensions of a serious subject, revealing an approach that is characteristic of much of his best work and one that is very different from the heavy and sombre style of his earliest writings. At various points in the story, the colonel is able to contemplate his predicament with a wry sense of detachment, and, on one occasion, faced with the interminable problem of where to find something to eat, he argues with unanswerable false logic: 'If we were going to die of hunger, we'd have died already by now.'

To the troubles of poverty are added the trials of the climate. The story takes place between the months of October and December, and the weather during those months provides a kind of external image of the colonel's inner struggle. Throughout the Caribbean lowlands of Colombia, there are two distinct seasons, marked not by variety in temperature, as in the temperate zones of the world, but by the presence or absence of rain. The rainy season is called winter, and lasts from late April to November or early December, while the dry season, summer, runs from December to April. The heaviest rains come in May and October, and García Márquez set two of his early stories in those months: the *Monologue of Isabel Watching It Rain in Macondo*, which dates back to 1952, describes the sudden onset of winter with a rainstorm in May, while *No One*

Writes to the Colonel opens with a picture of the rains in October. In each case, there is a firm link between the coming of rain and a feeling of unease and disgust, allied to a sense of sadness, desolation, and disintegration. In the former piece, the approaching rainstorm produces an immediate physical reaction in the narrator: 'I felt shaken by the slimy sensation in my stomach,' she says, and then later, as the rains fall unceasingly, 'I felt changed into a desolate meadow, sown with algae and lichens, with soft and sticky toadstools, fertilized by the loathsome flora of dampness and shadow.' The colonel, too, experiences 'the feeling that toadstools and poisonous lilies were sprouting in his stomach', and his wife, thinking of a man who has recently died in the town, says 'it must be horrible to be buried in October', as if there is something truly terrifying about the rapacity of the earth under the tropical rain. As the rainy season gives way to summer towards the end of the story, the change, both physical and psychological, in the colonel's condition is immediately apparent. 'The whole year ought to be December,' he says, for with the onset of the dry season life seems possible once again.

However, throughout most of the story, the town is in the grip of the winter rains, suffocating and unhealthy. Such, too, is the quality of the political and social atmosphere. By 1956, the worst years of the *violencia* were over, and García Márquez was concerned, as we have seen before, not so much with detailing the horrors that had recently overtaken rural Colombia as with trying to understand the effects on those who had survived. There is nothing overtly dramatic, therefore, about this story of the *violencia*. On the contrary, the reader is quickly made aware of the dull and restricted nature of life in a community where repression has become institutionalized. Violence here has been so completely absorbed into the fabric of everyday life that most people seem hardly conscious of the forms it has taken. The colonel waits for curfew to be sounded in order to set his clock; we learn that it is years since elections have been held, and that it would be foolish to expect any change − as the local doctor puts it: 'We're too old now to be waiting for the Messiah.' The press is censored. It is possible to read about the Suez crisis, but not about what is happening in Colombia: 'Since there's been censorship', the colonel says, 'the newspapers don't talk about anything except Europe,' and he goes on to make a remark that, in its very naïvety, underlines something close to a simple truth: 'The best thing would be for the Europeans to come over here and for us to go to Europe. That way, everyone would know what's going on in their own country.' The colonel and the local doctor belong to a resistance group that is responsible for circulating clandestine information, and, later in the story, on a sweltering Sunday night, while the colonel is watching a game of roulette in the town's billiard hall, he is caught up in a police raid. He realizes he has a clandestine paper in his pocket. He comes face to face with the killer of his son, and in circumstances very like those in which his son was shot, but the moment of confrontation swiftly and safely passes, and García Márquez makes no attempt to heighten the sense of drama; for the clandestine paper, the police raid, even the son's violent and unnecessary death, have all become part of the regular and expected pattern of life in the town. It is perhaps this acceptance of violence as an inevitable condition of life, something like the weather which must be endured because it cannot be changed, that constitutes the saddest, and also the most dangerous, legacy of the Colombian *violencia*. It is, once again, only in the context of such an apparently closed and hopeless situation that we may try to understand the importance of the colonel's own affirmative view of life.

In many ways, *No One Writes to the Colonel* reveals a town that is not only isolated from the larger world, but also bitterly divided within. Cut off from the rest of Colombia, it yet reproduces all the most dismal features of contemporary Colombian life. The town is highly stratified, both socially and economically. We see the world of Don Sabas, 'with a two-storey house that isn't big enough to put his money in', and we learn that he is the only Liberal leader who has been able to survive the years of persecution, having come to an agreement with the local mayor (on terms that are fully clarified in *In Evil Hour*), and subsequently growing rich by buying up the property of his fellow partisans as they were systematically driven from the town or assassinated. By contrast, we get occasional glimpses of the poor parts of town, as when a funeral procession passes by and the women from the 'barrios bajos' watch it go, 'biting their nails in silence'. We see the world of the colonel's corrupt or ineffectual lawyer, with his endless complacent explanations of the intricacies of the Colombian bureaucracy, and a chair 'too narrow for his sagging buttocks'. There is also the local priest, Father

Ángel, a man concerned principally with the proper observance of the forms of religion, who uses the ringing of the church bells to propagate a system of ecclesiastical film censorship, and then sits at the door of his office to check on those who have disobeyed his instructions. For a year now the only films on offer have been condemned as 'bad for everyone', but the cinema still functions, showing films with mildly provocative titles like *Midnight Virgin*. We see the town's mayor, on the balcony of the police barracks, appropriately enough, dressed in his underwear, and with his swollen cheek unshaven, the latter detail also to be explained in the course of *In Evil Hour*.

Finally, on the margins of this society, there are the 'foreign' merchants, called variously Syrians or Turks. These names are widely applied in both Central and South America to a class of immigrants who came to the Caribbean in the late nineteenth century from Syria, Lebanon, and Palestine. They were mostly Christians fleeing from Turkish persecution, and they initially found work in the Caribbean region as itinerant salesmen. In recent times, their descendants have become fully integrated into the social and political life of a number of Latin American countries, but in García Márquez's writings they are invariably portrayed as alien, unassimilated, and exotic. In *One Hundred Years of Solitude*, the 'Street of the Turks' is described as the place 'where the Arabs languished who, in times past, used to exchange trinkets for macaws'; while in *No One Writes to the Colonel*, the extent to which the colonel's wife registers her decline in the society of the town is emphasized by her remark that, in the course of trying to sell off their unsellable picture, she has gone 'even to the Turks'.

This, then, is a town that seems altogether lost, a town described in a marvellous phrase as 'ravaged by ten years of history', dwelling in a kind of lethargy that appears to be beyond hope of reversal. This town, rendered mute by the excesses of its own familial savagery, stands, too, for so many others in the Colombia of the mid-1950s. The formal structures of social and political life offer no hope. If there is anything positive to be found, one must turn elsewhere. Some individuals, it seems clear, have managed to survive the horrors of the past without succumbing to the sterility of the present. There is the doctor who attends the colonel's wife, and who is also active in the local resistance; he shares much, incidentally, with the doctor of *In Evil Hour*, despite some superficial differences in the detail of their age and appearance. He refuses to accept payment from the colonel for his medical services, as he refuses to drink the coffee he knows the couple cannot afford to offer him, and, in both cases, his refusal is conveyed with an instinctive awareness of the importance of the couple's pride and dignity which allows the relationship between the three of them to remain as one between equals. The doctor has survived as a human being, events have not defeated him, and, if he declines to speculate on the coming of a Messiah, it is from a position of strength, not of despair.

Then, perhaps, there is the example of the colonel himself, though no final judgment is possible here because, as I have suggested, the colonel remains a controversial figure. Some would argue that his capacity to retain a faith in the future is all that matters in the context of the kind of world in which he is forced to live, and I think that might well be the best reading of his role in the story. According to such a reading, the problems surrounding the way the colonel thinks and acts are largely irrelevant. The fact that he is there, continuing to insist that his pension will arrive, that things will improve, that the fighting cock will bring an end to his financial problems, is enough in itself; and the question of whether he is right to have such faith, whether it makes any sense, whether or not it is even responsible in the circumstances, these are, arguably, all secondary issues. Such an approach is, I think, supported by the importance given to the colonel's sense of humour. It is difficult to account logically for the power of humour, but it is often far more influential in life than other things which ought logically to matter more. In the case of the colonel, his sense of humour allows him to express a detachment from the miserable conditions in which he is living, somehow making the misery less threatening, less all-encompassing. We are given a fine example of this process in the opening pages of the story. The colonel's wife is watching as he dresses to go to a funeral:

> 'You look as though you're ready for a special event,' she said.
> 'This burial is a special event,' the colonel said. 'It's the first death from natural causes that we've had in years.'

The positive value of such an attitude, in such adverse circumstances, is beyond analysis.

As soon as one tries to explore the detailed working out of the story, however, questions do arise, and they come to focus in the end on the colonel's concern for the fighting cock that he has inherited from his son. He longs to keep the bird, but comes very near to parting with it, under the general pressure of his financial situation and the constant pleading of his wife. He has reached the point when he has decided to sell the bird to Don Sabas; but then, while he is out of the house one day, the friends of his dead son, who have recently taken over the expense of feeding the bird, arrive to carry it off, saying that it belongs not simply to the colonel and his wife, but to the whole town. They take the bird to a trial fight in the cockpit, and there, almost by chance, the colonel comes to see it perform. This sequence of events implies that the author is seeking to turn the fighting cock into a symbol of some kind, a representative, perhaps, of the collective hopes of the people, an embodiment, as Vargas Llosa suggests, of the people's intense desire for change and renewal after the events of the past decade. It is clear, I think, that García Márquez is concerned in some way with developing the social dimensions of the colonel's private struggle, but a problem arises as soon as one looks at the description of the cock fight itself. The colonel perceives nothing but the sadness and absurdity of the event:

> He saw his fighting cock in the centre of the arena, alone, defenceless . . . with something like fear visible in the trembling of his feet. His adversary was a sad and ashen cock . . .

The birds go through the motions of fighting, and the crowd respond with wild enthusiasm; but the colonel cannot share in the excitement:

> The colonel noticed the disproportion between the enthusiasm of the ovation and the intensity of the fight. It seemed to him a farce to which − voluntarily and consciously − the fighting cocks had also lent themselves.

This last observation seems more appropriate as a comment on the years of the Colombian *violencia* than as an affirmation of the possibilities of escape. Nevertheless, the colonel goes home applauded by all the poor people of the town, and the narrator tells us that 'that afternoon . . . the people had awakened'. The colonel reaffirms his intention not to sell his fighting cock, and later, when his wife challenges him by saying 'you're dying of hunger, completely alone', he answers, with an evident reflection of the communal enthusiasm, 'I'm not alone'. So something has obviously happened, but just how and why the enthusiasm of the crowd has transformed the sad farce of the cockpit into something vital and sustaining is not really clear. The tumult of the crowd reminds the colonel of happier and freer days in the town, in the time when there were elections and functioning political parties, but much remains unexplained. Perhaps one of the problems here stems from the choice of the fighting cock as a potential symbol. García Márquez has said that he originally intended to end the story with the colonel wringing the cock's neck and serving the bird up as soup, and that he changed his mind on this only at the last minute. Clearly, the tone of the remark reveals his exasperation in the face of some of the more sublime efforts of critics to turn the fighting cock into appropriate symbolic terms. But there may also be a frustrated realization that perhaps the bird was not the best possible symbol for some of the things he wanted to suggest.

A final problem of interpretation arises in connexion with the closing lines of *No One Writes to the Colonel*. One might have expected to look there for some confirmation of the general direction that the story has been taking, but, in fact, the conclusion resolves nothing. For the climactic note on which the story ends is in itself ambiguous and opaque in its implications. We are given what is in many ways a typical short story ending, one that seeks to imply, through the device of its restricted space, that far more is involved than could adequately be explained to the reader. The colonel's wife has returned to her regular line of questioning. Now that the fighting cock is not to be sold, what are they going to eat, and what will happen if, at the cock fights the following month, the bird turns out to be a loser? As dawn breaks one Sunday morning, the couple exchange the following words:

'He's a cock that can't lose.'
'But suppose he does lose?'
'There are still forty-five days to begin to think about that,' the colonel said.
The woman grew desperate.

'And meanwhile, what do we eat?' she asked, and seized the colonel by the collar of his flannel night-shirt. She shook him hard.

'Tell me, what do we eat?'

The colonel had needed seventy-five years — the seventy-five years of his life, minute by minute — to reach this point. He felt pure, explicit, invincible at the moment of replying: 'Shit.'

Once again, it is clearly stated that this is a moment of conse-quence, but it is difficult to say precisely why. We are told that a lifetime's experience has gone into the final word, *mierda*, but what does that really imply? In an obvious way, we could say that this is an act of rebellion, symbolized by the colonel's use of a word that would never have normally entered his vocabulary — earlier in the story, indeed, he has reacted in a predictably offended way on hearing the word uttered by Alfonso, one of the former companions of his dead son, though the point of this parallel is lost in the English version by J.S. Bernstein, who translates Alfonso's 'Mierda, coronel' as 'Goddamn it, Colonel'. For all that, it seems a rather limited act of rebellion in the circumstances. Some critics, sensing this, have argued that the ending of the story changes nothing. So Giovanni Pontiero writes: 'The colonel gives vent to his frustrations without attempting to answer his wife's anguished questions or resolve anything. We leave the town and its inhabitants exactly as we found them — still waiting for the miracle that will transform their lives.' For other critics, however, the colonel's act of self-assertion, if that is what it is, presages a radical change in his attitude towards his situation. Vincenzo Bollettino, for example, argues that the final word of the story is critical for an understanding of the whole work. At this point, he believes, the colonel finally comes face to face with the absurdity of existence, and thus of his own existence; he at last understands that death is the necessary and inevitable end of all life's struggles, and this newly acquired realiz-ation conditions the violence of his final dramatic affirmation. Bollettino writes: 'His life has been nothing but a desperate attempt to evade reality, taking refuge now in his pride as a soldier, now in his veteran's pension, now in his fighting cock, but all in vain. Sooner or later, he had to come face to face with reality. At least now he does not have to conceal the fact that life is "shit".'

These differences in the response to the final lines take us back to some of the fundamental differences of approach that I have tried to explore with regard to the work as a whole. Such differences are not, I think, reconcilable, for the story allows many possibilities to emerge and never appears to decide between them. Much, naturally, depends on the values and expectations that the individual reader brings to the work, though these will always be, in themselves, complex and difficult to define. A number of terms that I have used in the course of this discussion, such as optimism and resistance, carry a wide range of implications, both positive and negative, and frequently serve only to conceal the thing one wants to talk about. If the colonel's irrational and often infuriating optimism is thought of as fundamentally self-deluding, then one will more naturally look for an ending to the story which will suggest a break with the habits of the past — and this is the approach which writers like Vincenzo Bollettino take. If, on the other hand, the colonel's optimism is felt to be the only valid mechanism by which he can deal with a world that would otherwise be perceived as intolerable, then one will tend to see the ending of the story as a reinforcement of his determination to continue his struggle as before. The former view is certainly easier to defend logically, but I suspect that the latter may be the more profitable reading. The more one thinks about the position of the colonel and his town, the more one is likely to be drawn by a logic of despair, and yet the book does not seem to be a tale of despair, or even simply one that encourages a realistic acceptance of things. If neither the colonel, nor the reader, nor the author can precisely articulate the nature of the alternatives, that may be because of the nature of hope itself, always dependent, to some degree, on faith rather than reason. Such a view, of course, invites charges of pure sentimentality, but the fact remains that many of the colonel's long-term problems cannot be met by any obvious solutions, and I think that is what gives his struggle an enduring interest and complexity. A comparison with *In Evil Hour* makes the point very well. That story is also about an intolerable world, but a potential solution is held out strongly at the end of the book, as people take to the hills to continue their struggle by force of arms. Such a solution may be more immediately satisfying and uplifting than the ambiguities of *No One Writes to the Colonel*, but it is one that can make sense only in a limited range of situations. The colonel's problems, of poverty, old age, and a life unfulfilled, remain to be faced, intractable and apparently beyond redress, and in the end, perhaps, it is only with a recognition of the true nature and extent of those problems that one might come to understand the significance of the colonel's quixotic resistance to them:

'You can't eat illusions,' said the woman.
'You can't eat them, but they feed you,' replied the colonel.

The English translation of *No One Writes to the Colonel* provides, on the whole, a good sense of the original, but there are one or two places where the meaning is obscured, usually because a Spanish idiom has been too literally translated, or, perhaps, misunderstood. I give two examples here. When the colonel's wife sees her husband off one morning, she reminds him to make sure that the doctor calls round to visit her, saying: 'Pregúntale al doctor si en esta casa le echamos agua caliente.' This literally means: 'Ask the doctor if we pour hot water over him in this house,' and is more or less rendered thus in the English version: 'Ask the doctor if we poured boiling water on him in this house,' whereas something like 'Ask the doctor what we've done to scare him away' might have been more appropriate. Then, later, when the colonel's wife is talking to her husband about changing their lawyer, she says, in effect, 'what use is money to us when we're dead?': literally, 'we get nothing out of it if they put [the money] in our coffin the way they do with the Indians', a reference to the Indian custom of burying the dead with their possessions. The English version, 'we're not getting anything out of their putting us away on a shelf as they do with the Indians', is simply wrong. Lastly, and incidentally, the presence of a significant trio of names − those of Álvaro, Germán, and Alfonso: see above, p. 42 − is obscured in the English version by the rendering throughout of the name Germán as Hernán.

(ii) *In Evil Hour*

In terms of its subject matter, *In Evil Hour* clearly belongs to the same period as *No One Writes to the Colonel*; and, in fact, it was while García Márquez was working on the former that the idea for the latter emerged, so that, having spent the first months of 1956 on the composition of *In Evil Hour*, he postponed work on it in order to concentrate on the writing of the short story. *In Evil Hour* was eventually submitted in 1961 for a competition sponsored by the Esso Company in Bogotá, where it won the first prize. It was sent to be printed in Spain, and there the text was emended, without consultation with the author, to make it conform to the conventions of peninsular Spanish; words and phrases that appeared obscure were altered or omitted, and, when the novel was published in 1962, García Márquez wrote to the Bogotá newspaper *El Espectador* publicly disowning the work. The second edition of the novel, published in Mexico City in 1966, is thus the only reliable text.

The affinities between *In Evil Hour* and *No One Writes to the Colonel* are, in many respects, very close. The town portrayed is clearly the same in each case, as is the importance, both physical and psychological, of the suffocating October climate. A number of the characters from *No One Writes to the Colonel* reappear in the later novel, and we come to learn a good deal more about two of them in particular, the unnamed mayor of the town and the local priest, Father Ángel. But if the two accounts have much in common in terms of their setting, the tone of *In Evil Hour* is generally darker, and the influence of the years of the Colombian *violencia* more immediately apparent. There is perhaps no clearer image of the tragic absurdity of the *violencia* than the picture of the mayor wandering desperately about the town with a toothache, unable to go to the local dentist because the mayor is a Conservative and the dentist a Liberal. It all seems so much like a routine family quarrel, something that could so easily be sorted out, if only people could agree to forget the errors of the past and bury their differences. But García Márquez is trying to show how vital it is that the past should not be forgotten; the worst years of the *violencia* may be over, but we come to see that the town is living through a peace that can only be temporary, that the *violencia* will return because its causes remain unresolved. So, as the mayor is forced to reveal the full extent of the savagery which underlies his control of the town, the reader is inevitably brought to reflect that the dentist's attitude towards his political opponent is not only correct, but courageous. Here lies, I think, one of the major strengths of a novel which has found less favour among readers and critics than most of García

Márquez's other works. It is all too natural, too emotionally enticing, to subscribe to a rhetoric of peace and reconciliation, particularly in times when people have suffered much from the effects of violence, but the novel enables us to see that there are some forms of peace that are simply the continuation of war by more convenient means, and that it is essential to understand the workings of this process if the desire for a genuine peace is not to be systematically exploited.

The novel also enables the reader to understand something of the mechanisms and the psychology of the *violencia*, and that is important, given that in Colombia the *violencia* remains both highly controversial and, in some ways, little understood — in this connexion, incidentally, it is interesting to note that a televised version of *In Evil Hour* was shown in Colombia in 1975. It is probable that about a quarter of a million people died in the course of the *violencia*, some 112,000 of them between 1948 and 1950, and such statistics are, in themselves, almost impossible to grasp. But, more than that, the form which the violence took, the fact that gratuitously brutal methods of torture and assassination became a commonplace in rural Colombia, and that, in the small towns and villages, the violence was frequently perpetrated by people who had known their victims for years, this, truly, seems beyond comprehension. What García Márquez does, however, in the course of *In Evil Hour*, is to take the abstract and terrifying concept of 'the *violencia*', and to explore its meaning in terms of the relationships between a few ordinary people in an ordinary Colombian town. The reader is left in no doubt that the savagery is real, but it is also made very clear that there is nothing mythological about it, nothing that belongs in the realm of primitive superstition and fear. The terror can, it seems, be brought down to the level of the purely human, the only level at which it can ultimately be understood and, possibly, confronted. It is interesting to note that, in his determination to understand what is happening in Colombia, García Márquez consistently avoids the use of political labels. As we have seen earlier, the *violencia* is traditionally thought of as the product of a political struggle between Liberals and Conservatives, but that is not how it appears in García Márquez's novel. We can always, if we wish, determine with reasonable confidence the political affiliation of the various characters in the book, but it is clear that such labelling

explains very little about the nature of a struggle the ideological
content of which was, in fact, remarkably thin.

   The entire action of *In Evil Hour* takes place over a period of less
than three weeks in the month of October; the year is not specified,
but it must be around 1954. A reference by one of the characters to
Colombia as 'this savage country where they assassinate students in
the street' almost certainly recalls the events of 9 June 1954, when
twelve students were massacred by the army in the centre of Bogotá
as they marched in protest against the killing of a student leader the
day before. In general, the novel seems to belong to that period late
in 1954, when the relative peace which had accompanied the *coup
d'état* of Rojas Pinilla in 1953 was giving way to the second, and
more confused, phase of the *violencia*. The novel begins in what its
shrewder or more honest characters recognize is a period of illusory
peace, and ends with the re-establishment of violence as the characteristic feature of life in the town. One night, as the community
waits on the threshold of the renewed violence, the doctor thinks
back to the earlier phase of the *violencia*:

> His wife was sleeping. In former times, they would both stay
> awake until dawn, trying to determine the place and the
> circumstances of the shooting. Several times, the sound of
> boots and weapons reached the door of their house, and they
> both waited, sitting in bed, for the hail of bullets that would
> break down the door. Many nights, when they had already
> learned to distinguish between the infinite nuances of the
> terror, they stayed awake with their heads resting on a pillow
> stuffed with clandestine leaflets for distribution.

So, as in *No One Writes to the Colonel*, the doctor is a member of the
local resistance. Also a member, it turns out, is the town's barber, a
point that wittily gives the lie to the lofty assertion, made by the
newly appointed judge, that 'in the whole history of humanity . . .
there hasn't been a single barber who was a conspirator'. The judge
has been in the town for less than a year, and, in a memorable
conversation with him towards the end of the book, the barber
speaks for all those who have lived through the terrors of the past:
' "You don't know what it's like", he said, "to get up every morning
with the certainty that they're going to kill you, and ten years pass
without them killing you".' When the judge admits that the barber

is right, that he doesn't know what it's been like and that he doesn't want to know, the barber says to him quite simply: 'Do all you can . . . so that you'll never know,' advice which the judge clearly takes to heart, for he abandons the town shortly afterwards.

If the *violencia* provides the central theme of *In Evil Hour*, the novel nevertheless opens with a series of incidents that seem, at first sight, to be unrelated to it. The priest, Father Ángel, awakens to what promises to be another ordinary day in a dull town, with familiar images of 'the desolate square, the almond trees sleeping under the rain', and the town 'motionless in the inconsolable October dawn'. Very soon, it is true, we learn about the presence of something new in the town: the *pasquines*, lampoons or satirical notices which, suddenly and mysteriously, have begun to appear in the night on people's doors; but even when one of these, suggesting sexual infidelity on the part of a man's wife, leads to the murder of the woman's supposed lover, the event still seems like an isolated act of revenge, local and containable – the mayor moves quickly to arrest the killer, and, with a cynical display of newly found bureaucratic zeal, he even gives orders for the doctor to perform an autopsy. Nevertheless, the lampoons do come to play an important role in the resurgence of generalized violence in the town, and it is interesting to note exactly how and why this happens. It is clear in the first place, I think, that the lampoons are not to be taken as the prime cause of the renewal of violence, for, as we have seen, the violence is perceived as something that will return in any case. The lampoons are, it is true, mysterious: as readers, we are never given a glimpse of them, nor will we ever find out who has been putting them up. But their mysteriousness has nothing intrinsically problematic about it; on the contrary, as the judge argues early on in the book when he responds to the challenge of trying to identify the source of the lampoons, the whole affair is only a kind of game, an enigma out of a detective story. Moreover, we are clearly told that the lampoons contain nothing new or particularly sensational, nothing that everyone does not know already. They only become a problem, the focal point for the expression of underlying tensions, when the élite families in the town recognize that the existence of the lampoons, and the apparent inability or unwillingness of the authorities to do anything about them, is undermining their own position of authority and control. In the houses of the poor, the lampoons have become a source of 'healthy amusement', and this requires correction. Events swiftly move towards a violent conclusion, a process in which, as we shall see, the local priest, Father Ángel, is deeply implicated.

Here it may be useful to make two points about the position of the Catholic Church in Colombia. In the first place, it is an organization that has long maintained considerable influence over daily life in the country. Robert Dix, in his book on Colombia published in 1967, refers to J. Lloyd Mecham's *Church and State in Latin America*, published in 1934, and he writes: 'What Mecham said thirty years ago . . . that "the Catholic Church has been more tenacious in its hold upon national and civil life in Colombia than in any other Latin-American country", is probably still the case'; and Dix goes on to note that 'Colombia has a ratio of one priest per 3,650 Catholics, a proportion of clergy exceeded in South America only by Chile, Ecuador, and the Guianas.' The second important point is that, since at least the middle of the nineteenth century, the Catholic Church in Colombia has been almost totally identified with the Conservative party. Given the great influence of the Church in secular matters, this was of obvious significance in the political context of the *violencia*, and there were widespread attempts by Church officials to identify Liberalism with a variety of undesirable forces, most notably that of 'atheistic Communism'. Paul Oquist quotes from a joint pastoral letter, issued by two Colombian bishops in the late 1940s, which makes the point clearly enough: 'All Catholics of our jurisdiction are obliged in conscience, and under mortal sin, to vote for candidates who they are certain, before God, will not be dangerous to the Church or favour communism.'

So we can see that Father Ángel's natural allies in his town are the influential, the powerful, and the Conservative, and this, I think, largely accounts for his behaviour in the matter of the lampoons. He is one of those intermediary figures in the book, neither irredeemably corrupt, nor conspicuously courageous. He is not without humanity, but he lacks imagination. Faced with a child who has been ill for two years, he is affected by 'a terrified pity', but all he can do is suggest that the child be brought to confession. He is, as he was in *No One Writes to the Colonel*, principally concerned with fulfilling the formal duties of the priesthood, and he is one of those who subscribe to the dangerous fiction that the town is an exemplary, devout, and law-abiding place, ruled by a mayor whose barbarity has recently given way to enlightenment. Father Ángel is sufficiently aware to be troubled by thoughts of the future – he ends a letter he has written with the words: 'I think that bitter days await us' – but in the end, whatever his natural inclinations, he allows himself to respond to pressure from 'the respectable families' of the town to do something about the lampoons. He goes to see the mayor, who has his own reasons for not wishing to intervene and, in a fatal phrase, he finds the point of contact between the mayor's world and his own: the lampoons represent, Father Ángel suggests, 'a case of terrorism in the moral order'. The threat of the word *terrorismo* is enough to persuade the mayor to give way, the curfew is reintroduced, and vigilante patrols are sent out on to the streets to defend 'the principle of authority'.

Father Ángel discovers that everything has now passed beyond his sphere of influence, and that the consequences of his intervention have been quite unpredictable. The vigilante patrols fail to catch or to intimidate the perpetrator of the lampoons, and the lampoons continue to appear; the town, the mayor observes, is 'dying with laughter'. The people, far from being cowed by the mayor's attempt to impose his authority, display, rather, 'a feeling of collective victory in the confirmation of what was in everyone's consciousness: things hadn't changed'. For just as the lampoons merely bring to the surface what everyone already knows, so the mayor's forced reversion to his normal violent methods of control brings the town back to a true sense of itself. There is no longer any need to pretend, the community is openly at war.

From this point, the situation deteriorates rapidly. A boy of about twenty, Pepe Amador, is brought into the police station, having been caught, like Agustín in *No One Writes to the Colonel*, in the act of distributing clandestine literature. The mayor gives orders for the boy to be tortured, in order to find out the names of those involved in the resistance network, and he replaces the vigilante patrols with three thugs, 'common criminals, taken out of prison and disguised as policemen', as he had earlier described them, and whom he had, until now, kept confined in the police barracks. Towards the end of the book, Pepe Amador is killed in police custody, leaving the mayor in a position where all he can do is to lie – he pretends uselessly that the boy has escaped – and to threaten to shoot the doctor and Father Ángel when they come to demand a sight of the boy's body. The mayor cynically recalls Father Ángel's involvement in what has taken place, saying: 'You ought to be pleased, Father: that boy was the one who was putting up the lampoons.' The priest turns away, overcome. It is left to the doctor to try, as he has done on several previous occasions, to bring Father Ángel closer to an understanding of the true nature of the situation: 'Don't be surprised, Father,' he says to him. 'All of this is life.' The way in which things have turned out may seem to be a personal tragedy for the priest, but there is an underlying process at work that also needs to be acknowledged. What has happened is not simply the result of a series of calamitous judgments; in another society, at another time, the same mistakes would have had a happier ending.

Father Ángel has played a part in an action the deepest significance of which will always escape him; and, in fact, his rigidity of mind, his ability to ignore what he cannot deal with, enable him to survive the horror of these events relatively unscathed. The character whom García Márquez wishes to portray as the paradoxical victim of the violence is, of course, the mayor. Here, as elsewhere in his writings, García Márquez tries to defuse the mythical fear which so often surrounds the exercise of absolute power by revealing the abject and very human solitude in which the powerful condemn themselves to live. We are given a clear picture of the day when the mayor first arrived in the town: at dawn, 'he disembarked furtively with an old cardboard suitcase tied up with string and the order to subdue the town at any price.' He has come to terrorize the town, and yet, on the morning of his arrival, 'it was he who had known terror'. With the help of 'three hired assassins' and an unnamed 'obscure government supporter' who was a member of the local community, he has accomplished his task of subjugation, but, however powerful he may have become, he remains 'bogged down in a town that continued to be impenetrable and alien, many years after he had taken charge of its destiny'.

What the mayor has done in the years he has been in the town is to use his power to make money, and in this he is typical of the many people who made fortunes out of the lawless conditions of the *violencia*. The judge puts it clearly: the mayor, he says, 'is sinking into the town. And every day he sinks deeper, because he has discovered a pleasure from which there is no return: little by little, without making a lot of fuss, he is becoming rich.' That is why the mayor wants a peaceful town. Having achieved a position of power by violent means, he now seeks to consolidate that position by extending his control into new, more directly productive, areas. He wants land, and cattle, as the rewards for a difficult job well done. In observing how he goes about his project, we can learn a good deal about the way local power structures functioned at the time of the *violencia*. Early on, as we know from *No One Writes to the Colonel*, the mayor made a deal with Don Sabas, one of the Liberal leaders in the town, and, in the course of *In Evil Hour*, we learn the terms of the deal: Don Sabas handed over a list containing the names of those who were in contact with the local guerrilla movement, and that is how he was able to survive, and, in his turn, to prosper. It is through the continued application of such policies of collusion and extortion that the mayor is now systematically working his way towards the attainment of an economic position that will more accurately reflect the apparently absolute nature of his political control.

'This is a happy town', the mayor says, and we shall find the identical sentence spoken about Macondo in *One Hundred Years of Solitude*, at precisely the moment when the death squads are out on the streets at night, rounding up those who have been involved in the strike on the banana plantations. The fostering of an illusion of peace and contentment can be a highly sinister and very effective element of policy, as García Márquez clearly recognizes. That is why, every time the mayor is forced to resort to violence, compelled to reveal the true nature of his position in the town, it is felt to be a defeat for him and a victory for those whom he oppresses. We see this early on in the book, when the mayor is tormented by tooth-ache, a condition which, incidentally, explains his appearance, with swollen cheek unshaven, in *No One Writes to the Colonel*. He would love to be able to deal reasonably with the dentist, but the dentist has struggled to survive through the years of persecution and refuses to co-operate. So, finally, the mayor is forced to send his men to break down the door of the dentist's office, and he then has his aching tooth extracted under the cover of a gun, a curiously resonant version of the self-inflicted wound. The events which follow in the book continually work to expose the fictions which the mayor seeks to sustain, confirming publicly and unambiguously that his power depends on violence alone, and that only through violence can it be resisted. The lampoons which have been the catalyst in this process of revelation are, by the end of the book, nothing but 'a picturesque anecdote from the past', but they have served their purpose. Men leave for the hills to join the guerrilla struggle, the treacherous peace is over. Only with a realization of the precise nature of their condition, the novel implies, can people fully respond to the challenges of that condition. Only then can the possibility of change seem anything more than a pious or sentimental dream.

García Márquez's two stories of the Colombian *violencia, No One Writes to the Colonel* and *In Evil Hour*, are remarkable both for their restraint in dealing with the details of the terror and for their refusal to countenance attitudes of incomprehension or despair in the face of what was happening. There was certainly much in the Colombia of the 1950s to support a view that terror was being visited on the people in some blind spirit of cosmic revenge; that the world had gone mad. There seemed no end to the futility of it all, no sense to be gathered from the grotesque accounts of what people were prepared to do to each other in the name of partisan politics. When Gerardo and Alicia Reichel-Dolmatoff made their important study of the village they called Aritama in northern Colombia, they found that even in such a relatively remote place, in the foothills of the Sierra Nevada de Santa Marta, the political polarization of contemporary Colombian society was so completely accepted as an inevitable condition of life that the very saints had been integrated into the process: 'The Virgin, San Rafael, and San Antonio', they reported, 'are said to be Conservatives, associated with the colour blue, while the Sacred Heart of Jesus and San Martín de Loba are Liberals and therefore "reds".' For García Márquez, on the other hand, the important thing was to try to understand the nature of the terror in purely human terms, to identify the ordinary, the everyday, problems behind apparently motiveless and incalculable cruelty. In *No One Writes to the Colonel*, he goes beyond the immediate context of the *violencia*, to look at more general problems of death, and poverty, and disease, but always the aim is the same: to resist, in the face of the misery of existence, the seemingly inescapable logic of despair, to insist on the everlasting possibility of alternative ways of seeing and thinking, and to reach towards an optimism that is more than sentimental posturing, an optimism that seeks, responsibly, to free the future from the limitations of our ability to deal coherently with it in the present.

IV

After success: *The Autumn of the Patriarch*; *Chronicle of a Death Foretold*; and *El amor en los tiempos del cólera*

When it is all over you will be glad
of my savings.   (Napoleon's mother)

The success of *One Hundred Years of Solitude*, following its publication in 1967, was on a scale that most writers would have found daunting enough. For García Márquez, perhaps, the problem of where to go next was heightened by the fact that his novel of Macondo was one that he had been working towards all his life. Once completed, and with Macondo obliterated from memory in the closing lines of the book, a successor was needed that would constitute a clear break with the past. Since 1967, García Márquez has published only three novels: *The Autumn of the Patriarch*, in 1975, *Chronicle of a Death Foretold*, in 1981, and *El amor en los tiempos del cólera*, in 1985, a novel which, at the time of writing, has yet to appear in English translation. All three works are certainly very different stylistically from *One Hundred Years of Solitude*, as they are also very different from each other. *The Autumn of the Patriarch* is García Márquez's most self-consciously literary work to date, a highly complex, poetical meditation on the world of dictatorship and the solitude of absolute power, his first novel to be without a specifically Colombian setting. *Chronicle of a Death Foretold* is, by contrast, a deceptively straightforward account of an episode from García Márquez's own past, and concerns the murder of a friend in Sucre in 1951; while *El amor en los tiempos del cólera*, a long novel about romantic love, is a kind of 'populist' reply to the powerful literary claims of *The Autumn of the Patriarch*. The three books taken together, then, represent García Márquez's intriguing, and varied, response to the challenges of his own success.

(i) *The Autumn of the Patriarch*[1]

This novel was, on its own evidence, some seven years in the making, between 1968 and 1975, and the fascination with the psychology of power which it reveals goes back very much further than that in García Márquez's experience. In chapter II of the present book, we have seen a number of the influential events that contributed to the development of his interest: the presence, in the Aracataca of his childhood, of refugees from the dictatorial regime of Juan Vicente Gómez, his visit to Moscow in 1957, where he saw the body of Stalin in the Lenin Mausoleum in Red Square, the overthrow of the Pérez Jiménez dictatorship in Venezuela in 1958, and the trial of Sosa Blanco in Havana in 1959. His fascination seems always to have been with the *solitude* of power, and this suggests natural psychological links between *The Autumn of the Patriarch* and his earlier works. But his increasing success as a writer has also introduced a new element: 'There is nothing which more closely resembles the solitude of power', he has said, 'than the solitude of fame.' This implies that *The Autumn of the Patriarch* cannot be judged as a simply objective attempt to enter into the mind of a savage and alienated Latin American dictator; rather, the novel depends fundamentally on an underlying relationship between writer and subject that is complex and difficult, and which was clearly the source of many problems during the writing of the book, problems both technical and moral.

In an interview with *Playboy* magazine in February 1983, García Márquez gave a detailed account of the various stages through which his novel passed. At first, he said, he tried to work from the memory of the trial of Sosa Blanco. That trial took place in a large baseball stadium, and, as he watched the prisoner, García Márquez found that he was fascinated by 'the literary possibilities' of the situation. He thought of trying to turn the figure of Sosa Blanco into that of a supreme dictator, finally brought to justice after a long

---

[1]In writing about *The Autumn of the Patriarch*, I have made particular use of the book by Michael Palencia-Roth, *Gabriel García Márquez: la línea, el círculo y las metamorfosis del mito* (Madrid, 1983).

career of crimes against the people. 'However, as I began writing', he says, 'the idea quickly fell apart. It wasn't real. Latin American dictators, the great ones, all either died in bed or escaped with huge fortunes.' Indeed, García Márquez's patriarch, in the final form of the novel, dies from nothing but natural causes. The second version of the novel was to take the form of a 'fake biography', but this turned out to be stylistically too close to *One Hundred Years of Solitude*, and was therefore abandoned on those grounds. His third, and final, attempt was to create 'a structure based on multiple monologues – which is very much the way life is under a dictatorship. There are different voices who tell the same thing in different ways.' Then, he goes on, 'after some time, I reached another block. I personally had never lived under one of the old dictatorships. To make the novel work, I wanted to know what daily life was like in a very old dictatorship. While I was writing, there were two of interest: in Spain [where Franco had been in power since 1936] and in Portugal [under Salazar since 1932].' So he moved to Barcelona. He returned to the Caribbean, however, at a critical point in the writing of the novel, in order to recover his sense of the atmosphere of the region, and this return visit finds an intensely lyrical and nostalgic expression at many points in the book.

García Márquez has said that 'the dictator is the only mythological figure that Latin America has produced'. Certainly the mythical possibilities of the dictator figure have been much explored in contemporary Latin American fiction, and, in an interesting article published in 1980 in the Soviet journal *América Latina*, following on the theme of an earlier interview in 1976, García Márquez spoke about the place of his novel within this literary context. He says that around 1968 the Mexican novelist Carlos Fuentes had the idea of promoting a kind of collective fictional study of Latin American dictators to be called *Los padres de las patrias*; to this project a number of contemporary novelists were to contribute, each writing about a dictator from their own country. So, Miguel Otero Silva was to write on Juan Vicente Gómez, Carlos Fuentes on Santa Anna, Alejo Carpentier on Gerardo Machado, Juan Bosch on Trujillo, Augusto Roa Bastos on José Rodríguez de Francia, and Julio Cortázar on Evita Perón. The list is interesting in its diversity, both geographical and chronological, and clearly shows the extent to which an experience of dictatorship was felt to be part of a broad

Latin American inheritance, and, as such, a suitable area for collective literary exploration. Gómez was president of Venezuela from 1908 to 1935, Santa Anna the dominant force in Mexican politics from the late 1820s to the mid-1850s, Machado president of Cuba from 1925 to 1933, Trujillo dictator of the Dominican Republic from 1930 to 1961, Rodríguez de Francia Supreme Dictator of Paraguay from 1814 to 1840, while Evita Perón was one of the most powerful political figures in Argentina in the late 1940s and has, of course, achieved legendary status world-wide.

I am not sure whether this collective project was ever as clearly defined as I have implied, but one thing is certain: García Márquez's idea for a novel of dictatorship could never have fitted very easily into the scheme. He is a Colombian, and Colombia has never had a dictator on the lines of Gómez or Trujillo. The dictatorship of Rojas Pinilla, for example, lasted only four years, from 1953 to 1957, and left no enduring mark on the country. So the patriarch of García Márquez's novel is not a Colombian; he is a composite figure, and, although García Márquez has said on several occasions that his subject owes more to Gómez of Venezuela than to any other single model, he is not to be closely identified with any of the historical dictators. Now, of course, it would be wrong to suppose that the long list of dictators above has anything uniquely Latin American about it, in terms either of the sort of men they were or of the problems they created for themselves and those around them. The account which Cicero gives, for example, in the *Tusculan Disputations* (V 20), of Dionysius, tyrant of Syracuse, belongs quite clearly to the same tradition. Dionysius seized control of Syracuse, which had been a democracy, in 405 BC, and he remained in power until his death nearly forty years later. He brought a certain prosperity to his city, and enjoyed considerable popular support. He also brought violence and repression on a massive scale, and he lived, as tyrants will, in constant fear of assassination. Cicero reports that he was unable to trust anyone, and, as he was afraid of barbers, he had his own daughters instructed in the art of shaving instead. Then, as they grew up, he felt he could no longer trust them with a razor either, so they were compelled to singe off his hair with red-hot nutshells. The pursuit of absolute power tends to lead everywhere to the same kinds of excesses and to the same kinds of absurdities.

But if the figure of the dictator is not uniquely a Latin American one, the phenomenon of dictatorship has been of particularly pressing importance in Latin America in the twentieth century. To talk of dictators in this way is not, however, to talk of a single, unified model. In the same interview with the Moscow journal *América Latina*, for instance, García Márquez himself insists on a clear distinction between the older 'feudal' dictators and the more recent technocrats, the 'prefabricated' or 'computer' dictators, as he calls them. As a writer, he has no real interest in the sort of bureaucratic authoritarianism that has characterized recent military interventions in Brazil (1964), Argentina (1966 and 1976), Uruguay (1973), and Chile (1973), where the military has taken power as an institution, rather than, in the traditional way, as the motor force behind some individually charismatic officer. Nor, for very different reasons, is García Márquez interested in the purely literary possibilities of genuinely populist dictatorships, such as those of Juan Perón in Argentina or Getúlio Vargas in Brazil. It is the older generation of dictators that fascinates him, men who were as corrupt and as brutal as their modern successors, but who were often able to mobilize a considerable degree of popular support, who took advantage of the widespread ignorance of their people and the generally undeveloped state of their country to set themselves up as gods, awesome, terrifying symbols of absolute power. García Márquez talks of the broad popular appeal of Gómez, once reputed to be the richest man in all of South America, and it is clear that it is the magical possibilities of such a life that interest him as a writer, the ability of such a man, an illegitimate cattle driver with almost no formal education, to establish himself for twenty-seven years as the centre of national power and the embodiment of popular fantasy.

What García Márquez is seeking to do in *The Autumn of the Patriarch* is to explore how lives are turned into myth, in order to encourage an understanding of the process and of the illusions which always lie behind it. Inevitably, such a project runs the risk of doing more to sustain the fascination of illusions than to undermine them, and García Márquez was well aware of the dangers. The book tries to overcome the problem by offering itself as a kind of maze from which the reader instinctively wants to escape; we are brought to experience a sense of the hopeless circularity of life in a dictatorship, a circularity which can only be finally broken with the end of dictatorship itself. The further you read in *The Autumn of the Patriarch*, the less you feel sure about what is going on; all is rumour, lies, supposition, distortion. Even in the presence of the dead body of the patriarch, one of the anonymous narrators of the book can say: 'we knew that no evidence of his death was conclusive, for there was always another truth behind the truth.' There seems no end to this process of unravelling that leads always into uncertainty; and the answer seems to lie, not in seeking to establish the real truth, for within the closed world of dictatorship the truth is irrecoverable, but in trying to reaffirm the validity of a kind of collective common sense, a trust that, in the most adverse of circumstances, there is a life to be led which cannot be contaminated, and which will ensure survival until better days arrive.

In Latin America generally, the tendency towards the establishment of authoritarian forms of government is closely linked to the confused and unstable political situation of the post-independence period. Spanish control of South America had rested on a powerful and highly centralized bureaucracy; by the end of the colonial period, however, the power of the state had been seriously weakened, due in large measure to the decline of Spain's international standing in the face of British expansion. Consequently, when the Spanish colonies took their independence from Spain in the early years of the nineteenth century, they inherited all the structural weaknesses of a decayed absolutist system with no compensating experience of democratic traditions. Out of this confusion and instability, and in the absence of any clear structures of authority, there emerged the *caudillo*, the classic nineteenth-century figure of the strong man, the man on horseback, a leader who grouped his followers around him on the basis of his own strength and ability, and for whom ideologies or political parties counted for very little. The tradition of *caudillismo* survived for a long time in Latin America, and, in some countries, played a very powerful role in inhibiting the development of democratic institutions. Some of the modern 'strong men', such as Somoza in Nicaragua or Trujillo in the Dominican Republic, have even been able to appropriate entire national economies for their own private use. García Márquez's patriarch has many of the attributes of the traditional *caudillo*. He is, according to at least some accounts within the novel, a leader who emerged out of the conflictive post-independence period, a time of short-lived governments ('illusory presidents of a single night') and civil war between Liberal and Conservative factions. He has, it seems, brought a measure of stability to his country, but, with the passing of the years, this has come to resemble the stability of the dead, rather than of the living.

People living in democratic states tend, on the whole, to be suspicious of dictatorship, though there is sometimes a more marked willingness to concede that dictatorship might be a useful or, indeed, a necessary form of government for others. Latin America has found people enough, both externally and internally, to justify the long succession of authoritarian regimes it has experienced, and there are times when the whole continent seems reduced to a passing show of endless figures in military uniform and dark glasses, endlessly replaced and replaceable − a stereotype that is wittily parodied in the long succession of United States ambassadors, indistinguishable except for their names, who pass through the pages of *The Autumn of the Patriarch*. Arguments in support of dictatorship in Latin America range from crude assumptions about the inherent instability of the Latin race to more sophisticated approaches such as those of Jeane Kirkpatrick, US ambassador to the United Nations under the first Reagan administration, who maintains that, at least, right-wing dictators do not survive as long as left-wing 'totalitarian' regimes and may, moreover, serve western interests in helping to prevent the spread of such regimes. There is often a recognition that the 'excesses' of dictatorial governments are regrettable, but those excesses, it is argued, are something one has to live with, for, without them, the situation might be yet worse.

A powerful argument often heard in defence of dictatorship is that, in certain countries at certain times, such a system of government is genuinely in the long-term interests of the people concerned. Some dictators, it is held, are able to turn the stable conditions they have instituted to creative use. These are the 'modernizers', the magicians of progress; they provide an attractive environment for much-needed foreign investment; in the terms of the inevitable cliché, they make the trains run on time, not necessarily, it must be said, a negligible achievement. Gómez managed to pay off the entire Venezuelan foreign and domestic debt by skilful handling of the oil industry; Trujillo in the Dominican Republic was able to embark on a thorough modernization of the financial infrastructure of his country; Estrada Cabrera, the Guatemalan dictator who was the subject of an important novel (*The President*) by Miguel Ángel Asturias, made attempts to improve public health, he built roads and railways and schools, and he also indulged in some mildly eccentric cultural projects, such as the Festivals of Minerva that were celebrated in mock Greek temples. These dictators had their defenders, and still do, and there is no doubt that as leaders they were able, at times, to mobilize the support of large numbers of their people. Their detractors would argue that the schemes for modernization and public works were as nothing compared with the massive injustice and corruption that lay behind them, that such schemes only ever benefited a small section of the population, that they were, in the end, mere cosmetic devices to win the support of a gullible people.

This cosmetic aspect of authoritarian beneficence is satirized at a number of points in *The Autumn of the Patriarch*, most extravagantly, perhaps, towards the end of the first section of the novel where, we learn, the patriarch has decided to abandon for a time his pursuit of security through torture and assassination, and is looking instead to rather different methods: 'he ordered a free school to be set up in each province to teach sweeping and the girls who attended, fired by the presidential stimulus, went on sweeping the streets after they'd swept their houses and then they swept the highways and the byways, so that the piles of rubbish were carried backwards and forwards from one province to the other without anyone knowing what to do with them . . .' This variation on the more traditional exercise of digging holes and filling them in reflects a sceptical view of the kind of job-creation schemes that attract various governments from time to time. Doubtless, the motivation behind such schemes is not dissimilar in most cases. The patriarch's view is that people in his country have too much time on their hands, too much time to think, and the free sweeping-schools have much the same function as his other ideas for keeping the people occupied: he restores the tradition of the annual beauty contest, he brings back the March poetry festival (reminiscent of Estrada Cabrera's Festivals of Minerva), and he orders the construction of the largest baseball stadium in the Caribbean.

There is, however, another aspect of dictatorship that García

Márquez clearly sees as of considerably greater importance, one that is the focus for much of the course of the novel. The real danger of dictatorship, he suggests, lies in its long-term psychological effects, and the presence of the word 'patriarch' in the title points directly to the nature of the problem. The ability of some authoritarian leaders to establish themselves plausibly as the guardians, saviours, and father confessors of their people, to identify themselves so completely with the destiny of their country that they and the country are felt to be one and inseparable, this inherently duplicitous talent is the source of enormous potential power. For, once accepted, it reduces the status of everyone else to that of children in the face of a stern (though, of course, always loving) father, or to that of supplicants at the feet of an absolute monarch or undying god. De Gaulle sought to offer himself in this kind of way to the French people, and, at times, he was considerably successful at so doing. He projected himself as the guardian of an unchanging image of France, as the incarnation of a France that was glorious and powerful, quite unrelated to the reality of the disaster of 1940 or the political instability of the post-war Fourth Republic. The ambiguous nature of this sort of relationship is clearly identified by Alexander Werth, one of his biographers: De Gaulle, he wrote, 'had much contempt for his fellow-humans and especially for his fellow-Frenchmen . . . If he loved France with a kind of mystical love, he did not love the French, or at least not very many among them.' Indeed, the problem of the attitude that is for ever associated with Louis XIV ('L'État c'est moi', 'I am the State') is, of course, that it renders the leader essential and the people superfluous.

There are a number of important passages in *The Autumn of the Patriarch* which point to the terrible consequences of this kind of dependent relationship for a people who submit to it. One of these passages occurs early in the sixth section of the novel. With the passing of the years, people have given up all hope that the patriarch's rule will one day come to an end. Now, suddenly, he is dead, and we discover that, although this should obviously have been a moment for national celebration, the hated leader has become so intimate a part of people's lives that he seems irreplaceable. They have waited for years in the hopeless expectation 'that one day the repeated and always denied rumour that he had at last succumbed to one of his many royal illnesses would be true, and yet we didn't believe it now that it was certain, and not because we really didn't believe it but because we no longer wanted it to be certain, we had ended up not understanding what would become of us without him, what would become of our lives after he was gone'; and, similarly, from a time when the patriarch is still alive, some lines from a brilliant passage in the third section of the book: 'the only thing that gave us security on earth was the certainty that he was there, invulnerable to plague or cyclone . . . invulnerable to time, dedicated to the messianic happiness of thinking for us'; and, from the early part of the fifth section: 'there was no other country but the one made by him in his image and likeness where space was changed and time corrected by the designs of his absolute will.' The nostalgia for the passing of such a leader is rooted in a dangerous submissiveness to an illusion of eternal order and power. The people come to believe that there is, after all, an order and a life eternal, for they think they see eternity incarnate before them in the monstrousness of unending dictatorship, and they yearn for the illusion and cannot bear the thought of its destruction. It is this mentality, above all, that the novel seeks to undermine from within, to force an awareness that there is only one life and that it is ephemeral, and that it is only with an awareness of the fact, and the courage to face it, that happiness or authenticity can be possible.

There is another aspect of the psychological appeal of dictatorship that is, in its way, almost as problematical. The exercise of absolute power can create a focus for a very wide range of fantasies connected with the purely everyday conduct of life. These may seem comparatively trivial in nature, but may yet have a deeper underlying significance. In this respect, there are links between the fantasies attendant on the arbitrary exercise of absolute power and those surrounding the casual display of wealth that is one of the distinctive features of constitutional monarchy, or, indeed, of the very rich in general. The dictator and the millionaire are, according to an illusion which must never be undermined if their attractiveness is to be maintained, able to do entirely as they please, to act without consultation or even reflection; it is enough for a desire to be formed for it to be satisfied. This apparent freedom from the constraints of ordinary existence is clearly a source of attraction, particularly, perhaps, for those who have very little; for if there is never any hope of gaining what you need or most wish for, then here, at least, is a chance to live vicariously through the medium of someone who has everything. In a different sense, this attractiveness is problematical for the novelist as well, for the magical absurdity of power or money can offer many creative possibilities to the literary imagination. In his Nobel Prize acceptance speech in Stockholm, García Márquez recalled some of the strange stories attached to the history of dictators in Latin America: Santa Anna, the Mexican soldier, who held a state funeral for the right leg that he lost in battle, Hernández Martínez, the Salvadoran dictator who had the streetlights draped in red paper to ward off an epidemic of scarlet fever. There are endless similar stories, and they seem to retain an unfailing power to charm, fascinate, or amuse. They apparently offer proof that the wildest constructions of the imagination can, after all, be validated in the world of experience, and they are, for that reason, perhaps, particularly seductive for both novelist and reader alike. It may be true, as Seymour Menton suggests in an interesting article on *The Autumn of the Patriarch*, that the proliferation of dictator novels in Latin America in the 1970s revealed a growing awareness that the age of the classical dictator was drawing to a close; and perhaps the comic tone which characterized many of these novels reflected a concerted effort finally to exorcise a dangerously dynamic myth that would not easily die.

In the light of these remarks, we can see that *The Autumn of the Patriarch* is a novel that is working in several directions at once. On the one hand, it seeks to re-create an experience of the mythical world of dictatorship, to impose on the reader a sense of the hopeless circularity of apparently unending power, while, on the other, it seeks constantly to force an awareness of the illusory quality of this mythical world. So, for example, many of the voices in the novel do speak in support of the idea that the world of the patriarch is eternal, and that he is a god. Indeed, he is more than that, in a sense, because, as 'corrector of earthquakes, eclipses, leap years and other errors of God', he is worshipped as one who has the power to put right the things that God had got wrong. He is entire, complete, self-defining: 'al fin y al cabo yo soy el que soy yo' ('after all I am what I am'), and he has a son called Immanuel. He has imposed upon his city a 'lethargy of centuries', for time, too, has been at his disposal: 'once he asked what time is it and they had answered him whatever time you command general sir.' None the less, we are also conscious that this is a world that does change, however much the rhetoric of the regime may attempt to disguise the fact. The patriarch is now in the autumn of his power, no longer that other legend who used to go about the country years before, informing himself about crop yields, the condition of livestock, talking to the people, and bringing home runaway husbands. Now he has withdrawn into the solitude of the presidential palace, and his control over events has progressively weakened as 'life kept going on behind the back of his power'.

It is this power that is everywhere the object of scrutiny. Surely the patriarch is all-powerful? Anyone who can have prisoners thrown to the crocodiles must at least be that. Yet, where exactly does his power lie? It seems in practice to be constantly displaced. There is the patriarch's mother, Bendición Alvarado, who has considerable influence over him; he visits her every day, and her death is the great and lasting sorrow of his life. He decides to have her declared a saint after her death, and, when the Catholic Church refuses to go along with the plan, he orders the expulsion of all Church officials from the country. Then there is his wife, Leticia Nazareno, who subtly engineers the return of the expelled officials. She teaches the patriarch to read, persuades him to marry her, and, in the end, manages to acquire 'more power than the supreme command, more than the government, more than he . . .' She thereby arouses the hostility of the armed forces, and is torn to pieces by wild dogs in an assassination that the patriarch knows he is powerless to prevent and in which he is compelled to acquiesce. Then there is the grim sadist, José Ignacio Sáenz de la Barra, who is brought in ostensibly to avenge the murder of the patriarch's wife, but instead unleashes a reign of terror so horrific that even the limited sensibilities of the patriarch cannot bear the reality of it.

So the portrait of supreme power is constantly undermined. Sometimes this is done by use of the comic weapon, as when we find the patriarch reduced to writing in his own honour, on the toilet walls of the presidential palace, 'long live the general', conscious, as he is, that, in these most private of quarters, he will be the only one to do it. This comic absurdity is also revealed in one of the book's most serious and significant episodes, when the patriarch, for all his apparent power, is shown to be powerless in the face of external aggression, and loses the one thing he really cares about: the Caribbean sea.

From the opening pages of the novel, we have heard that the sea has mysteriously departed from the shores of the country, and, gradually, this mystery is clarified. The patriarch has been besieged by a long line of United States ambassadors who claim the Caribbean as surety for the enormous interest payments due on the country's foreign debt; finally, under the threat of an invasion by the marines, the patriarch caves in. With characteristic efficiency, the United States government removes the sea, which is then dispatched, in numbered lots, to Arizona. The patriarch's sense of loss is clearly coloured by García Márquez's own nostalgia for the beauty of his Caribbean homeland; here is part of a passage in which the patriarch seeks to dissuade one of the faceless ambassadors from pursuing his course of economic piracy:

> . . . imagine, what would I do alone in this huge house if I couldn't see it [the sea] now as always at this time like a marsh in flames, what would I do without the December winds that come barking through the broken window-panes . . .

Later, one of the anonymous voices of the novel puts the United States policy in the context of the endless exploitation of Latin America by a succession of foreign countries:

> . . . we had exhausted our last resources, bled white by the age-old necessity of accepting loans in order to service the foreign debt ever since the wars of independence and then other loans in order to pay the interest on the overdue interest, always in exchange for something general sir, first the monopoly of quinine and tobacco for the English, then the monopoly of rubber and cocoa for the Dutch, then the concession on the highland railway and the navigation of the river for the Germans . . .

The importance of such a passage does not lie simply in its value as protest, but in its clear understanding of where power truly lies, in its implicit recognition that the economic system places severe limitations on the megalomania of even the most awesome tyrant.

So far I have said little about the plot of *The Autumn of the*

Patriarch. This is mainly because it does not really have one, in any conventional sense. As I have suggested, part of the novel's strength lies in its ability to replicate the psychological conditions of life under a dictatorship, a life in which things rarely seem to develop in any rational or understandable way. The book can seem difficult of access, and was much criticized in Latin America on its first appearance, with the result that García Márquez has been more openly defensive about it than about any of his other books. The novel is difficult partly because of its allusiveness; García Márquez makes use of the diary of Christopher Columbus, for example, or the poetry of Rubén Darío, or the accounts in Plutarch and Suetonius of the death of Julius Caesar, to say nothing of allusions to specifically Colombian figures such as 'Negro Adán' ('the perpetual delirium of the mythical paradise of Black Adán'), a Barranquilla restaurant-keeper − and something rather more than that − whose local fame is explained by Jacques Gilard (*Obra periodística*, vol. 4, 18). These references, particularly in the case of Columbus and Darío, can often be structurally significant, rather than simply illustrative. The novel is also difficult in terms of its form. It is divided into six sections, and the number of sentences within each section progressively diminishes as the length of individual sentences increases, so that, for example, the first section contains thirty-one sentences and the final section only one. This is not, of itself, a major problem for the reader, since the discrete sense-units within the massively expanded sentences are very carefully punctuated. What is disconcerting, though, is the range and number of the anonymous voices who carry the narrative; sometimes these voices are difficult to identify, and there are frequently abrupt changes of voice within a single line of text. Who are the people who lie behind the omnipresent first-person pronouns? Which of them, if any, can be trusted? This uncertainty is, of course, part of the novel's psychological project, and, once accepted as such, many of the apparent problems recede.

If the book plays continuously on our uncertainties, we do, nevertheless, learn a good deal about the patriarch's world as the narrative progresses. The incomprehensible reference in the opening lines to 'the hearse from progress in order', for example, will be clarified when we find out that 'progress in order' is the official slogan underpinning José Ignacio Sáenz de la Barra's reign of terror; the 'year of the comet', which is also mentioned in the opening lines, will similarly be linked with the patriarch's absurd platonic passion for the beauty queen Manuela Sánchez. Like Gómez of Venezuela, the patriarch is a highlander, and various references, such as an early one to 'the glacial and deserted villages of his native highlands', serve to reinforce a picture of him as an unredeemable intruder into García Márquez's Caribbean world of heat and light. When we are offered such conflicting stories as those surrounding the details of the patriarch's conception, we have no difficulty in distinguishing between the school text-book account that his conception was immaculate, and his mother's version that she conceived him standing up in the back room of a bar, with her hat on to keep the flies away. The uncertainties about his age (between 107 and 232), and about his historical origins, are also easily reconcilable with the myth-making machine: in some accounts, he seems to have been already in power when Columbus arrived in the Americas, at other times he is thought to have come to prominence during the nineteenth-century civil wars between Liberals and Conservatives (the latter referred to as 'Goths' in the text, 'godos' being a common term in Colombia for Conservatives). In general, we are able to form a clear picture of the machinery which keeps the patriarch in power: a combination of animal cunning, immense brutality, financial corruption, and, above all, an ability to secure the continuing allegiance of the armed forces, the key to the success of Gómez, Trujillo, and so many others.

In other ways, however, we seem to understand less and less as we discover more and more, and this process of progressive disenlightenment is well illustrated by a comparison of the openings of the six sections of the novel. Each section begins with a version of the same event: the discovery of the patriarch's body and the immediate aftermath of his death. The opening of the first section is magnificently clear:

> During the weekend, the vultures went in over the balconies of the presidential palace, pecked through the wire netting over the windows and with their wings stirred up the stagnant time inside, and at dawn on Monday the city awoke from its lethargy of centuries with the soft warm breeze of a great man dead and of rotten grandeur.

Only when the vultures have gone in first do the people dare to follow. They search the presidential palace and they find the dead tyrant, dressed in his uniform, with the golden spur on his left heel as the symbol of his power, lying on the floor face down, with his right arm folded under his head. By the time we reach the sixth section of the novel, however, this apparently straightforward account has been so undermined that all is confused and confusing; here are the opening words:

> There he was, then, as if it might have been he even though it were not . . .

The Spanish text ('Ahí estaba, pues, como si hubiera sido él aunque no lo fuera') mingles indicative and subjunctive moods, so that fact ('There he was') and supposition (all that follows) are opposed within the grammatical structure of the phrase itself. Whose is this corpse that has now turned so problematic? Is it that of a real man, decrepit in his immense age, or is it that of the legendary dictator, father of the nation and symbol of its destiny? Or, perhaps, it is something, or someone, else entirely? The answers to such questions cannot ultimately be found, but it is in asking them, and continuing to ask them, that we come to share a sense of the maze-like quality of the world that the novel seeks to re-create. Already in the first section of the book, we learn that those who come across the body fail to identify it; it is so long since the patriarch has appeared in public that no one who is alive has ever seen him, and, certainly, the man they find bears no resemblance at all to the heroic images which adorn the country's coins and stamps. What, indeed, could be the reality of a man whom no one knows except in terms of a myth that has long ago acquired its own identity?

The people who discover the patriarch's body in the first section of the novel are afraid to believe that the tyrant is really dead; they do not recognize him, and they cannot be sure that they are not going to be the victims of a trick. That they have some reason to be afraid is supported by the story of Patricio Aragonés, the patriarch's double. He was a man who, long ago, was found wandering about the country making a living by impersonating the patriarch. He was subsequently brought into the dictator's service, where he played a useful myth-supporting role, allowing his master to appear magically in two places at once. When Patricio Aragonés is assassinated, the patriarch is able to observe in secret the jubilation of the many and the sadness of the few, all, quite naturally, believing that it is the leader of the nation who is dead. He is then in a position to take revenge on all those who have too precipitately shown their hand, and so, this time, now that he seems once again to have died, the people have grown more cautious.

But there is a further element of confusion for those who seek to unravel the mystery of the body and its identity. This concerns the position in which the body is allegedly found. As we have seen, in the first section of the novel the patriarch is discovered face down on the floor in his uniform, and this account is supported by the opening of sections two and three. At the beginning of the fourth section, however, we have no mention of the position in which the body was discovered, but, rather, a reference to 'the procedure for arranging and embalming the body', and, in the opening of the fifth section, we are given an insight into the further progress of these arrangements: 'Shortly before nightfall, when . . . we had put a little order into that fabulous disarray, we had still not succeeded in making the corpse look like its legendary image . . .' (As Michael Palencia-Roth points out, the English translation by Gregory Rabassa seems to be in error at this point.) So, we have one group of people who discover the patriarch's body lying on the floor, and another group – or, possibly, the same one – who then take it upon themselves, for whatever reason, to prepare the body for display. The members of this latter group, if, indeed they are distinct from the former, are clearly interested in perpetuating a patriarchal myth beyond the grave, by ensuring that the body is transformed in accordance with its legendary status. Now, by the sixth and final section of the novel, this process of transformation seems to have been completed. The body is decked out with flowers, and displays all 'the feminine splendour of a dead pope'. Those who have achieved this effect have recast the patriarch in terms of their own, they have established their own version of his legend, so that now they can reasonably say that 'for the first time it was possible to believe without any doubt whatsoever in his real existence, although truly no one looked less like him.' They can fully believe in the new image, because it is they who have created it. Yet the indecision we noted in the opening words of the sixth section reflects the fact that the patriarch himself would never have identified the garlanded corpse as his: 'truly no one looked less like him'; and we know this, because, once before, he had seen the body of his double, Patricio Aragonés, similarly decked out with flowers, 'more dead and more adorned than all the dead popes in Christendom', and he had been appalled at this effeminate transformation of his own macho self-image: 'Hell, that can't be me, he said to himself in a fury, it's not right.'

So, through the actions and attitudes in the last three sections of the book, we gain access to a moment of myth-making. Henceforth, the image of the patriarch which will be presented to the world will be one that he himself would never have recognized. However, the complications do not end there. For, by the end of the novel, it is clear that the description of the body in the first three sections has also been subject to a mythologizing process. We are alerted to the fact that something might be wrong when we find out that the conditions in which the patriarch was apparently discovered are precisely those that had, long ago, been foretold by an old fortune-teller whom he had gone to consult. She had shown him all the details of his death, how he would be found lying face down, with the golden spur and the military uniform, and, indeed, when Patricio Aragonés was killed, this was exactly how the patriarch had arranged the body of his double, before, as we have seen, other mythologizers came to garland it with flowers. From the testimony in the first three sections, it looks as if the fortune-teller's prophecy has indeed come true, but any doubts we may have about this coincidence are confirmed in the closing lines of the book. There the patriarch is visited by the figure of death who tells him that, after all, he will not die in his sleep, or in his military uniform, but in the full horror of consciousness, 'barefoot and in the clothes of the poor . . .' Those who say they found him, then, have lied in order to sustain a myth, as those who prepare the body for display will lie in order to sustain a different myth. Neither of the versions that will emerge of the patriarch's death will be true; both are mythologized versions of a truth that has been so tortuously deformed that it can never be recovered.

García Márquez has said that *The Autumn of the Patriarch* is 'a poem on the solitude of power', but it is also, and inevitably, a book concerned with the general relationship between writing and power, between literature, myth, and truth. In the act of writing, the writer seems condemned simply to perpetuate the myth-making process, to be just another voice offering just another illusory point of view. As one set of myths is undermined, a new set is created, for there is 'always another truth behind the truth'. The patriarch can declare by decree that the tatty cathedral in his city is 'the most beautiful in the world', but, for all that, the cathedral remains what it always was; and so with writing. Literature can make claims to power, or to magic, seductiveness, or even subversion, but its ability to alter the substance of the world it reflects, or creates, is extremely limited. García Márquez's attitude seems to be that by insisting on the inevitably fictitious nature of the literary process, by exploring and re-creating the methods by which fictions are developed and sustained, the boundaries of the real may be more clearly delineated. His story of the patriarch contributes to that end.

There is a fascinating passage early in the fifth section of the novel that brings together a range of reflections on writing, myth, and reality. The patriarch is thinking about what looks like a simple event in the long history of his power: the building of a railway up into the highlands. Why he decided to have such a railway built, we never learn, because the explanation he gives is altogether fantastical. He imagines it was a response to an incident that belongs, it seems, to the world of his childhood. He thinks he remembers a long train of mules climbing into the highlands, with thirty grand pianos on their backs, destined for the masked balls on the coffee plantations, and, 'by chance', he happened to look out of the window at the precise moment when the last mule in the line lost its footing, dragging the whole train down into the abyss. He was the only one who heard the terrified shrieks of the animals, the sound of the pianos playing all on their own as they fell through the air, he alone can bear witness to the truth. It was to prevent such a thing ever happening again that he built the railway. Then, there is a moment of self-doubt: did he really see the incident, or did he simply hear someone talk about it years ago, or did he, perhaps, see a picture of such a scene in a travel book? The patriarch tries for a moment to separate fact from fiction, and then goes on: 'but none of that mattered, what the hell, they'll see that with time it will be true.' Under his rule, the truth is what he declares it to be, his power is its guarantor.

The same applies to the writer: if a story is well told, we cease to care whether it is true or not, or to wonder in what sense any story could ever be said to be true. The power of the writer carries all such concerns before it, as the story takes on its own magical, independent, and illusory, existence. This independent power of language is reflected in the passage which immediately follows the story of the mule-train. The patriarch turns to thinking about another childhood, one that alone now seems real to him, that delayed childhood when his wife, Leticia Nazareno, would sit him down every afternoon between two and four in order to teach him how to read and write. As his wife chanted the reading lesson to the rhythm of a metronome, 'there was in his vast kingdom of sorrow no other truth but the exemplary truths of the school-book', truths locked into the succession of childish jingles with which he manages to confuse a Dutch treasury minister who comes to talk to him about the real things of the world, of money and foreign debt.

Central to these issues of literature and power is the presence in the novel of the Nicaraguan poet, Rubén Darío (1867–1916). García Márquez has said that *The Autumn of the Patriarch* is a tribute to Darío, to the extent, even, that it 'was written in the style of Rubén Darío'. An analysis of the claims to such an affiliation is outside the scope of this book. Nevertheless, the presence of Darío in the novel can be explored in broad terms, and it reveals itself to be interestingly and significantly ambiguous. Darío was the founder of the modernist movement in Latin American poetry, a movement that began in the 1880s, and reached its high point at the turn of the century. The enormous significance of the modernist movement is underlined by Antoni Kapcia: '*Modernismo* can . . . be considered as the first real attempt by Latin American literature to define a Latin American literary identity.' Gordon Brotherston, while retaining reservations about the long-term value of the movement for Latin American people themselves, makes a similar point in his anthology entitled *Spanish American Modernista Poets*: modernist writers, he suggests, might even be said to have produced 'the first body of literature which can be meaningfully called Spanish American.' Jean Franco, in the same vein, writes that Darío 'can be regarded as the first truly professional writer of Latin America', while José Coronel Urtecho, himself a Nicaraguan poet and novelist, offers a different, but equally positive, perspective: he recalls how, in the early years of the twentieth century, Darío was looked at with disfavour by some of the more traditionalist elements in Nicaraguan society, and how to believe in the aesthetics of Darío at that time 'was like believing politically in Sandino [the Nicaraguan guerrilla leader], a little later on'.

So the main reason for Darío's inclusion in *The Autumn of the Patriarch* is clear. Here is one Latin American writer paying tribute to another, to one of the great literary myths of the continent, to the 'poet of America' who had given the literature of Latin America an international prestige and a sense of its own continental identity. But we might also expect a novel like *The Autumn of the Patriarch* to question Darío's mythical status in some way, and this, implicitly, is what it does. Darío was certainly a very popular figure among the people of Central America, and yet there are some strange aspects to this popularity. He was a man with distinctly aristocratic leanings; more than that, he wrote within a poetic tradition that looked for inspiration to some of the most austere and complex tendencies in the literature of nineteenth-century France. Gordon Brotherston summarizes the forces at work here: 'Under the decisive influence of the French Parnassians and the Symbolists, and as a reaction to the unfriendly illiteracy of the societies out of which they [the *modernistas*] emerged, they emancipated art from civic and municipal obligations and cultivated it determinedly for its own sake.' This self-conscious aestheticism is gently mocked in some lines from Pablo Neruda's *Canto General* (IV, 33), where Darío, 'the young Minotaur enveloped in river mist', is pictured in the house of the aristocratic Chilean president, José Manuel Balmaceda. So a different image of Darío begins to emerge, as the novel encourages us to wonder what relevance the poetry of writers like Darío could have for the Latin American world that *The Autumn of the Patriarch* seeks to re-create. Could Latin American literature really only come into its own to the extent that it turned away from the problems of its homeland?

Darío is mentioned only four times by name in the course of the novel, though there are also a number of concealed allusions as well as references to certain of his poems. By far the most important passage in which he appears is to be found almost exactly half way through the fifth section of the book, where we hear of an imaginary visit which Darío, as a young man, makes to the patriarch's city. He comes to give a poetry reading at the National Theatre, and, prompted by the social and cultural aspirations of Leticia Nazareno, the patriarch consents to go and listen. Here the full scale of the irony of Darío's presence in the novel is revealed. What will the poetry of the man whom García Márquez also calls the 'minotaur' have to say to a brutalized and semi-literate tyrant? As it turns out, the patriarch is overcome by what he hears; he feels 'diminished and alone', suddenly conscious of his true state, and forced to accept that there are worlds that are different from his, larger, wider, and more glorious. García Márquez intersperses the narrative with clear references to one of Darío's own poems ('Marcha triunfal'), and, deeply affected by this 'revelation of written beauty', the patriarch is driven to wonder 'how is it possible for this Indian to write something so beautiful with the same hand he wipes his arse with.' The patriarch goes home, and, 'in the tepid cowshit olympus of the milking stables', he struggles to memorize the poem he has just heard. So great art does have power; it can move even the most degraded of people. But the irony here is deeper. For to be moved by art is not necessarily to be changed by it. There seems to be no way in which the patriarch can ultimately connect what he hears with what he does. Shortly after the poetry reading, there is an attempt on the life of Leticia Nazareno, and the patriarch senses at once that he must come down to earth: he has been so wrapped up in poetry that 'his exquisite instinct of a man-eating tiger had not recognized in time the old and sweet smell of danger.' The random savagery of his regime will continue. Darío has come and gone; the patriarch's world remains as before.

The imaginary visit by Darío to the patriarch's city recalls the real visit which Darío made, at the end of his life, to Estrada Cabrera, the Guatemalan dictator. Whatever the precise nature of the visit, it seems clear that Darío, dispirited and in poor health, allowed his prestige as an artist to be used by a man whose conduct no one should have excused. Estrada Cabrera had been in power since 1898, and had enjoyed an early reputation as a good 'public works' kind of dictator, but, by the time of Darío's visit in April 1915, that phase had long gone. Darío was humiliated by his host, who kept him waiting long hours for an audience before finally refusing to receive him, and yet Darío publicly proclaimed his admiration for the dictator's achievements: he praised the railways and the schools and all the rest. He even subscribed to the cult of the dictator's dead mother, and wrote a poem for the anniversary of her birth. It was a sad end to a life, one latently acknowledged, perhaps, in the passing reference, early in *The Autumn of the Patriarch*, to the 'forgotten poet Rubén Darío'.

A final example of García Márquez's interest in the ambiguous power of myth concerns his treatment of Christopher Columbus. Columbus is mentioned half a dozen times in the course of the narrative, though never by name. He is usually identified by the phrase 'admiral of the ocean sea', the title given to him by Fernando and Isabel of Spain in recognition of his voyages of discovery. The negative possibilities of the Columbus myth are deeply felt by García Márquez, and it is easy to see why. Columbus is now everywhere famous for having discovered America in 1492, for having introduced the Age of the New World. Of course, the American continent had been occupied for thousands of years before Columbus found it, and it could only have been new in the restricted sense that it was new to Europeans. However, because the European conquest effectively destroyed the pre-existing cultures of both North and South America, the version of history which the Europeans imposed is the only one to have flourished. That is not all. It is well known that Columbus originally sailed west in the hope of opening up a lucrative trade route to the east. He wanted gold and spices, and, partly to safeguard his own financial position, he refused to accept he had found anything other than the place he had set out to find, even making his men swear that they were on the mainland of Asia when they were, in fact, on the island of Cuba. So, to set beside the glorious and romantic visions of a New World, we can see the possibility of an alternative myth of America: an America that was almost accidental, the marginalized product of a journey to somewhere else. To think of Columbus in these terms is to recall the whole tangle of error, chance, and exploitation that lies at the heart of the European conquest. As Michael Palencia-Roth suggests: 'If the colonial mentality had been other than it was, the whole history of America would have been different.'

There is a fascinating irony in the fact that the heroic myth of Columbus took a relatively long time to establish itself in the European imagination. J.H. Elliott, in his account entitled *The Old World and the New, 1492–1650*, writes as follows:

The treatment of Columbus by sixteenth-century writers indi-
cates something of the difficulty which they encountered in
seeing his achievement in any sort of historical perspective.
With one or two exceptions they showed little interest in his
personality and career . . . It seemed as though Columbus
might be doomed to oblivion, partly perhaps because he failed
to conform to the sixteenth-century canon of the hero-figure,
and partly because the true significance of his achievement was
itself so hard to grasp.

So the myth of Columbus emerged as a late creation, almost
independent of the historical figure to whom it related. What
García Márquez tries to do, in an early and important passage in
The Autumn of the Patriarch, is to undermine the myth by taking a
satirical look at the traditional 'great moment in 1492', the day when
Columbus finally came to reveal the New World to the inhabitants
of the Old. In this key passage, which occurs at the very end of the
first section, García Márquez draws on what is usually called the
Diary of Columbus, an extremely interesting document that is, in
fact, a digest made by Bartolomé de las Casas of Columbus's lost
log-book from the time of his first voyage to the Americas. Working
from this account, which English readers will find admirably translated in J.M. Cohen's *The Four Voyages of Christopher Columbus*,
García Márquez transforms the perspective, and reveals the
accidental, almost commonplace quality of the great event by
describing the arrival of Columbus through the eyes of those who
were already there, the indigenous people who, through another of
those absurd errors that conquest alone has the power to invest with
the semblance of truth, have continued to this day to be called
'Indians'.

Columbus arrived in his new world on Friday 12 October 1492,
landing at a place that is probably to be identified with the Island of
San Salvador (or Watling Island) in the Bahamas. He brought three
ships: his flagship, the *Santa María*, the *Pinta*, and the *Niña*. These
are the 'three caravels' that appear at several points in *The Autumn
of the Patriarch*. When the 'historic Friday in October' comes
round, it seems that the patriarch is already well established in his
power. At dawn, he suddenly discovers that everyone in the presidential palace is wearing red hats, and it is this colourful, but

insignificant, detail that alerts the reader to the fact that Columbus has arrived. For Columbus notes in his *Diary* that he offered presents to the people he met, in order to win their friendship: 'I gave some of them red hats and glass beads which they hung around their necks, and many other things of little value, with which they were much pleased,' and, in return, he says, the people gave him parrots and balls of cotton thread and spears. This moment of unequal exchange clearly has great symbolic potential, and the way García Márquez treats it is interesting. The people in his novel say: 'they traded everything we had for these red hats and these strings of little glass marbles that we hung round our necks to amuse them.' García Márquez recognizes the exploitation involved; he cannot alter the fact that it took place, but he seeks to change our way of seeing it. He refuses to allow the indigenous people to appear as the gullible innocents of traditional travellers' tales; he makes it clear that his people are well aware that what they are given by Columbus is almost entirely worthless, and, if they hang the glass beads around their necks, it is not out of some childlike sense of pleasure, but out of a sophisticated realization that it is the kind of gesture the visiting strangers will find amusing. This difference in emphasis is marked throughout the whole passage. Where Columbus gives us a primarily physical account of the people he meets, commenting on their nakedness and their use of body paint, the people in *The Autumn of the Patriarch* look in civilized wonder at the Europeans all dressed up in the heat, and reveal that their body paint is not so much a heathen exoticism as a practical means of protection against the sun's rays. Incidentally, a comparison between García Márquez's text and that of Columbus's *Diary* confirms that the phrase 'ellos son de la color de los canarios', which Columbus applies to the indigenous people, means 'they are the colour of the Canary Islanders', not, as Gregory Rabassa rather fancifully renders it, 'they are the hue of canary birds'.

So Columbus stands primarily as a symbol of all the greed and exploitation that was to follow upon the European discovery of the Americas. This negative view of the great explorer is further stressed when we learn, in the fifth section of the novel, that the golden spur which the patriarch wears on his left heel was given to him by 'the admiral of the ocean sea so that he might wear it until death as a sign of the highest authority'. In the closing pages of the novel, García Márquez allows himself a passing moment of consolation, of the illusory kind that literature works so seductively to permit, when he takes his revenge on the discoverer of the Americas. In a brilliant manipulation of the ahistorical framework of the book, we catch a final glimpse of Columbus through the windows of the patriarch's limousine, but this time it is a Columbus who seems fully conscious of the terrors he has brought upon the New World, a Columbus concealed in 'a brown habit with the cord of Saint Francis around his waist shaking a penitent's rattle among the Sunday crowds in the market-place'. The patriarch's aides try to catch hold of him, but he vanishes, the insubstantial embodiment of a myth, colourful but devoid of reality, memorable, certainly, but, in the end, a vision no more true, no more false, than any of the other representations of Columbus that literature and history have handed down.

Though the presence of Columbus in *The Autumn of the Patriarch* is clearly to be understood negatively, we would not expect it to be altogether unambiguous. In fact, García Márquez has long been fascinated by the figure of Columbus and the myths attaching to it; he has said that the *Diary* of the explorer is the first work of magical literature to have been produced in the Caribbean, and, indeed, the whole literary context of Columbus's travels is one that cannot fail to engage the reader's interest. There is so much absurdity surrounding the events, an absurdity cloaked in the disarming certitude and high seriousness of a distinctly European rationalism. On Columbus's first voyage, for example, he took with him a converted Jew who spoke Arabic, on the confident assumption that Arabic would be the natural language of the Indians, Chinese, and Japanese he was sure to find on his journey west. Then, on his third voyage, we find him theorizing about apparent deviations in the course of the Pole Star, which led him to conclude that, although the earth may seem round from a European perspective, it is, in fact, pear-shaped, and that, moreover, in travelling west, he had also been going up hill, which helped to explain how mild the weather was. There are also numerous conflicting accounts of his birth and death. Though he was Genoese, some said he was a Majorcan Jew, and, as late as the 1930s, the issue was joined by a patriotic Greek, Spyros Cateras, who, from his exile in the United States, published a book with the proud title *Christopher Columbus Was a Greek*

(Manchester, New Hampshire, 1937). The death of Columbus was no less a matter of mystery, and a passage in *The Autumn of the Patriarch* reflects the fact that his body has been claimed by the cities of Santo Domingo, Havana, and Seville: 'he had been buried in three different tombs in three different cities in the world although he really wasn't in any of them.' That particular controversy is still alive, and is summarized in an interesting review of *The Autumn of the Patriarch* by Graciela Palau de Nemes, published in *Hispamérica* in 1975. These brief indications are enough, at least, to suggest that the figure of Columbus, for all its negative implications, is one that is also rich in elements of irony, ambiguity, and magic.

The Autumn of the Patriarch is a vast tangle of myth, deception, and untruth. Its central figure is a nameless dictator, a composite creation formed from the writer's wide reading in the history of Latin America, as well as from personal contacts and experience. Its setting is also a composite one, made up of memories of Barranquilla, Cartagena, Panama, Havana, and many other locations in the Caribbean. Out of this tangle, one truth alone can emerge: that the world of the patriarch is violent and brutal beyond all hope of change. At the same time the book reveals how difficult it is to hold on to this simple truth, how, through fear or fascination, hopelessness or an anguished refusal to know, the mind can so easily take refuge in what is not real, in myth and legend, in that illusory timelessless of a life in which one is always spectator of the deeds of another. The book plunges us into a world that constantly encourages a surrender to the unreal, and seeks to hold us there until, of our own will, we struggle to find a reference point outside, from where alone the reality of the patriarch's power can be exposed as the common experience of thousands upon thousands of people throughout all time:

Oh, to be able to sleep in your own bed tonight
Without the fear of being woken up and taken from your
house,
The fear of the knock at the door and the bell in the night!
(Ernesto Cardenal, 'Zero Hour')

Pedro Joaquín Chamorro, the Nicaraguan newspaper editor who was assassinated in January 1978, the year before the overthrow of the Somoza dynasty, has left an account of the time in 1956 when he was tortured by agents of the Office of National Security, some of whom, incidentally, had been trained by police officers from Britain and the United States. The details he gives of his sufferings are those that characterize human rights reports from around the world. But then he mentions something else, something he used to see from the cell in which he was held: the Somoza brothers, with their wives and relations and children strolling past the cages of the family zoo, where prisoners were kept, along with lions and panthers, in the garden of the presidential palace.

That is the way of dictatorships. Within the closed circles of apparently absolute power, it seems there is nothing so fantastical or depraved that it cannot be made true. In such a world, human bestiality appears limited only by the limits of the individual imagination, and, once again, the mind turns aside from the horror, unable any longer to trust its grasp over what is real and what is not. It is because literature has this same power of distortion, the power to mask the differences between truth and fiction, that *The Autumn of the Patriarch* can stand as a kind of model of the thing which it most abhors. The reader is given something of the sense of what living under a dictatorship might be like, with all the fears, uncertainties, and attractions of the absolute. At the same time, however, the novel also conveys a sense of the enormous importance of refusing to submit to the power of this fallaciously eternal world. García Márquez's dictator dies in utter solitude. He, at least, is fully conscious of the contradictions that his reign has sought to conceal; he knows he is not immortal, or destined to endure in the memory of the people:

> he had arrived without surprise at the ignominious fiction of commanding without power, of being exalted without glory and of being obeyed without authority . . .

Out of this sickening morass, there comes the final, anonymous voice of a tyrannized people, affirming that there is a world that is different from the patriarch's, one governed by different values, a fleeting world of hardship and suffering that is worth more than all the lying eternities of all the patriarchs in history. It is for them to assert their identity in the face of a patriarchal myth that is now dissolving, a myth whose insidious power has long since eroded the identity of the patriarch himself. It is for them to reaffirm a faith in:

> this life which we loved with an insatiable passion that you never dared even to imagine for fear of knowing what we knew only too well that it was arduous and ephemeral but that there wasn't any other, general, because we knew who we were while he remained without knowing it for ever . . .

With the death of the patriarch, the time of eternity, the time of myth and legend, is over. Now all is possible once again.

(ii) *Chronicle of a Death Foretold*

If *The Autumn of the Patriarch* is García Márquez's most complex work to date, *Chronicle of a Death Foretold* is perhaps the least so. It was published in 1981, and tells the story, or a story, about the murder of Cayetano Gentile (called Santiago Nasar in the novel), a friend of the author from the time when he lived with his family in Sucre in the 1940s. The man was murdered for having been allegedly the clandestine lover of Margarita Chica (Ángela Vicario in the novel), a woman who, on her wedding night, had been unable to satisfy the harsh conditions of virginity, and had, therefore, been returned to her family by an outraged and disconsolate husband. Within the cultural setting of a small Colombian town, the affair was immediately perceived as one that affected male honour, and the woman's brothers, having found a name on which to hang the deflowering of their sister, cut down her supposed lover with butcher's knives in the doorway of his own home. In García Márquez's telling of the story, the utter pointlessness of the act, along with its apparent inevitability, are clearly marked. It becomes obvious that the woman's brothers had no desire to kill their victim, and that they did all they could to encourage someone to stop them; but although the people in the town had no desire for the killing either, they felt restrained by an archaic culture of honour and the concept of a just revenge for the transgression of a sexual taboo, and this, together with a chain of unhappy accidents, led to a murder that was not only senseless and unjustifiable in absolute moral terms, but also in the relative sense that the man who was named by the woman as her lover seemed to most of those who knew them both to have been a highly improbable choice. The novel seeks to understand how an event that was so little desired by all concerned came to take place, and it also raises obliquely the more difficult question of just how much one can ever hope to know about the past, a question fundamental, once again, to the relationship between literature and reality.

After the publication of *The Autumn of the Patriarch* in 1975, García Márquez entered into a much-publicized literary silence, saying that he would publish no more works of fiction as long as the Pinochet regime retained its power in Chile. What happened in Chile in 1973, when the armed forces overthrew the democratically elected government of Salvador Allende in one of the most savage coups of recent times, caused an enormous shock, and not only in Latin America. So García Márquez's wish to take a public stand on the issue was reasonable enough, and, in a way, admirable. But dictators, as he might have known, have a tendency to survive; by the end of the 1970s, Pinochet was still there, and showed every sign of staying. So García Márquez broke his literary silence with the publication of *Chronicle of a Death Foretold*. There has subsequently been some rather arid discussion among critics as to whether the book is indeed a work of literature, rather than of investigative journalism, but the point here seems to be a relatively simple one: creative writers need the challenge of writing and of publication; and, moreover, it is difficult to see that there was much to be gained in political terms from a continued literary silence. Beyond this, however, is the possibility that the silence of the late 1970s may have been necessary from a very different point of view. In an interview with Ernesto González Bermejo in 1970, García Márquez was already announcing that he would write no more novels after *The Autumn of the Patriarch*; that novel, he added, 'closes the cycle of solitude . . . you can't ask for any more solitude now'. It seems clear that the successful completion of the project which found its fullest expression in *One Hundred Years of Solitude* has left the writer with considerable problems in terms of defining a new direction in which to go.

Superficially, *Chronicle of a Death Foretold* looks as if it might be a fairly straightforward narrative, but the book very quickly turns out to be full of self-conscious inconsistencies, alerting the reader to the fact that this can only be a version of the story, with no claim to the superior status of objective truth. The narrator, who, García Márquez has suggested, is to be taken as the voice of the author himself, implicitly acknowledges that his own view of the affair is a partial one, limited by state of mind and by circumstance. For, on the one hand, he claims that he had just got engaged at the time, and, on the other, that he spent the decisive period leading up to the murder fast asleep in the local brothel. Indeed, the whole town seems distanced from the event in various ways, unable to recognize its potential significance until it is too late to act. Most people are caught up in what they imagine will be the main event of the day, a pastoral visit from their bishop. This event, ironically, turns out to have no significance at all, for the bishop never gets off the boat that brings him into town; he simply makes a few pious gestures in the general direction of the crowd, and then goes away again. So the novel constantly reminds us of the difficulties involved in trying to understand the meaning of events as they are experienced, and, at the same time, it reflects on the illusory, almost random, quality of all retrospective attempts to organize those same events to form a pattern in the mind.

This confusion is reflected in almost all areas of the book. There are the different registers of names, for example; some of the characters are disguised under a pseudonym, as we have seen, while others, such as Luisa Santiaga, García Márquez's mother, are given their own names, and the border between the real and the literary is further blurred by the inclusion of one of García Márquez's own fictional characters, Colonel Aureliano Buendía, as a distant participant in the story. Then there is a manifest confusion over the dating of the events. The murder in Sucre occurred in the early hours of Monday, 22 January 1951. The murder in *Chronicle of a Death Foretold* cannot be dated. It does take place on a Monday, but in February, on a day that was bright and clear, according to the memory of some, or suitably funereal, according to the memory of others. The year floats about to suit the demands of the narrative. At one point, for example, the narrator mentions his engagement to his future wife Mercedes, and refers to their marriage fourteen years later. Since García Márquez and Mercedes Barcha were married in 1958, this would place the action of *Chronicle of a Death*

Foretold in 1944. None the less it is clear from other points in the story that the setting must be later — a reference to a time in the past when German knives were unavailable because of the war suggests this, along with a number of other inferences about the age and situation of various characters. There is no point in seeking to resolve these contradictions, for they are deliberately contrived to undermine any sense that the narrator's version of events is somehow more reliable than anyone else's might have been.

This abdication of responsibility in the face of a truth held to be beyond recall works to the great advantage of the story-teller. Once you admit that all accounts of the past are alike in their untrustworthiness, then the narrator's prime responsibility is to tell the story as well as he can. *Chronicle of a Death Foretold* is a good story in this sense. There is the constant stringing together of chance events that is characteristic of all good stories. The fact that the local doctor leaves town because he does not want to be around when the bishop arrives means that the local priest, who had once been a medical student, has to perform an amateur autopsy after the murder, an act which results in the second butchery of the body of Santiago Nasar. Then there is the witty parody of the painstaking investigator, in the figure of the narrator paddling about in the tide-washed offices of the Ministry of Justice in Riohacha, pursuing the truth relentlessly for five years, only to discover that the official report on the murder now contains 322 pages, instead of the more than 500 he assumes (but how could he know?) that it must once have had.

The danger, or delight, in this method of story-telling is that it recognizes no limits. Two accounts which García Márquez has given of *Chronicle of a Death Foretold* show just how easily the confusions generated within the book can be replicated outside it. These accounts both appeared in 1981, one of them in the November issue of the French *Magazine Littéraire*, the other in the September/October issue of *Cuadernos de Marcha*. The French text, entitled 'Le Récit du récit', is entirely literary and inventive in its approach. First of all, García Márquez writes about the extraordinary reconciliation which concludes the story of *Chronicle of a Death Foretold*. From the book, we know that Ángela Vicario becomes passionately attached to her husband of a single night, Bayardo San Román, and that, after he repudiates her, she writes to him for seventeen years without ever receiving a reply. In the end, he comes back to live with her, bringing the great bundle of letters, carefully preserved but all unopened. In the article for the *Magazine Littéraire*, García Márquez says that the account of the reconciliation of the couple was told to him by his friend Álvaro Cepeda Samudio, shortly before the latter's death in 1972, and that it provided him with a conclusion to a story that he had long been hoping to write. Having always felt that the emotional focus of the story would be located in the violence surrounding the death of a friend, he now came to see that it lay instead in the secrets of 'un terrible amour'.

In search of this love-story, he says that he went to visit the couple in Manaure, to the north-east of Riohacha, a visit which provides for an interesting chance encounter, on the way to a village called Manaure that turns out to be the wrong Manaure, with a man who claims that his grandfather had been killed by García Márquez's grandfather; this encounter then leads to a week of wanderings around the Guajira peninsula. Eventually, García Márquez comes to the right village, finds the couple, and gives a description of the event more or less after the manner of the novel. His account then moves on to talk about other aspects of the story, including a second chance encounter: this time it is with the priest who performed the massacre of the autopsy, whom he comes across in Spain, in Calafell, near Barcelona. Finally, he tells us of his vision, at the airport in Algiers in 1979, of an Arab prince, who reminded him so forcefully of Santiago Nasar (one of the Christian Arabs who appear frequently in García Márquez's novels) that the story could no longer remain unwritten.

If some of this seems too magical, too consciously literary to be true, it probably is. In a much more prosaic mood, in the interview which appeared in *Cuadernos de Marcha*, García Márquez rejects the whole romantic story of the reconciliation of Ángela Vicario and Bayardo San Román, saying that it is entirely fictitious; the couple did re-establish contact after a while, and did discuss the possibility of a reconciliation, but, for reasons of social propriety, they remained apart. The novelistic version is certainly more entertaining to read than the other, but there are potential dangers here. The assured facility of the practised story-teller can lead to a disregard for everything except the glories of the narrative. *Chronicle of a Death Foretold* is a good story, but, of all García Márquez's novels, it is perhaps the one that leaves the reader with least to think about. That is not necessarily a bad thing, of course: it all depends on what the reader expects from a novel. However, if one compares the work of García Márquez in the decade following the publication of *The Autumn of the Patriarch* with the work in the decade preceding it, it is hard to escape the sense of an impoverishment, in terms of both quantity and quality. There may have been many reasons for this, not least García Márquez's deliberate policy of self-censorship in the wake of what happened in Chile in 1973. At all events, with the publication, in December 1985, of his long new novel, *El amor en los tiempos del cólera*, a period of relative inactivity was formally, and conclusively, brought to an end.

(iii) *El amor en los tiempos del cólera*
(Love in a Time of Cholera)

For a long time before the publication of *El amor en los tiempos del cólera*, García Márquez had been talking about the romantic novel he was writing. He would say that the project was something he had always wanted to do, something that would be his private consolation after so much writing about solitude, violence, and repression. In the end, the novel *is* about love, and, intermittently, about cholera, too, but it is also concerned with problems that take us back to the world of *No One Writes to the Colonel*, problems of old age and death, about the significance of a life spent in apparently futile suspension waiting for the great event which will finally give that life its meaning.

El amor en los tiempos del cólera is a daring novel, particularly so for a writer so recently canonized by the Nobel Prize for literature, because it is firmly based on a model of 'bad' romantic fiction, the sort of fiction that is read the world over and that critics the world over so frequently reject as unworthy of discussion or even of recognition. It is a novel that deals confidently in cliché and improbable exaggeration, searching for the truths about emotional life which, the book implies, are as solidly embedded in the language of the popular imagination as in the most subtle language of psychological analysis. So the novel is, on one level, about a refusal to be made respectable as a writer, a refusal to be constrained by the challenge of the conventionally literary; while, on another level, it is also clearly about the author's own private war against the problems and fears of old age, a defiant statement of faith in the validity of the years still to come.

The world of *El amor en los tiempos del cólera* is immediately accessible, in keeping with the kind of fictional model which it imitates. There is a wealth of detail and incident, but only three principal characters: a woman, Fermina Daza, and the two men who share her life, Juvenal Urbino, her husband for half a century, and Florentino Ariza, her much devoted aspirant, and, in the end, her lover. The plot is a simple one, so implausible as to invite the reader's outright rejection of it as a medium for psychological insight, but one which finally offers a curiously subtle validation of the clichés which have dominated it. Florentino Ariza sees Fermina Daza once, when she is thirteen and he is eighteen; a single glance, and he falls hopelessly in love. After much feverish, but totally innocent, activity, Fermina agrees to marry him. Then Fermina's wicked father, a disreputable mule-dealer, finds out about the relationship. He has hopes of higher things for his daughter, and threatens the young hero, who refuses to be dissuaded. Fermina is then sent on a long journey so that she might forget all about Florentino, but he keeps track of her with the help of a confraternity of telegraph operators. Fermina returns, now eighteen years old, and, on an impulse, breaks off the relationship. She then marries Dr Juvenal Urbino, immensely respectable, wealthy, and patrician, and they live together in what looks, from certain angles, very much like happiness; Florentino, on his side, remains faithful to the memory of Fermina through over fifty years and more than six hundred sexual encounters. Finally, Juvenal Urbino dies, at the age of eighty-one, when he falls off a ladder as he climbs a mango tree in search of a beloved parrot which has escaped from its cage. Florentino, now seventy-six years old, immediately renews his pursuit, even though he and Fermina have never once in over fifty years seen each other alone. After a great deal of prevarication, the couple make love at last, in the Presidential suite of a boat on the Magdalena river, destined, in a mad sort of way, to live happily ever after.

This summary is not, I think, a misleading account of a plot which is, itself, a conscious exaggeration. The strange thing is that the reader comes to the end of the story with a sense of wonder at what has happened; it is a novel which constantly challenges the reader to adopt a knowing, cynical, or sophisticated response to the events described, and then works hard to ensure victory for a certain kind of innocence. The discovery of a great physical passion at the age of seventy-six might seem to be the prelude to a cruel joke at the expense of the traditional romantic notion of happiness 'ever after', but that is not what the book allows. Even if the reader is only momentarily convinced, we do finish the novel with a feeling that the significance of a life is not to be measured in terms of knowledge gained or time well spent, but by some other irrational standard that is beyond the reach of any language, whether subtle or clichéd, and which is rooted in an obscure, apparently all-redeeming, capacity for complete commitment. Florentino's life has been, by all logical criteria, an absurdity, locked into the monomania of adolescent fantasy, naïvely dedicated to proving the reality of romantic love by artificially perpetuating its tyrannical hold. But the truth is that Florentino does make his love last a lifetime, and, in the end, the account of his strange self-sacrifice and his belated triumph does not allow him to be ridiculed.

The novel is set between the late 1870s and the early 1930s. The country is certainly Colombia, for the capital city is named as Santa Fe (for Santa Fe de Bogotá), while the city in which much of the action unfolds is very closely modelled on Cartagena. Cartagena, sometimes called Cartagena de Indias to distinguish it from the Cartagena in Spain, lies on the Caribbean coast of Colombia, some sixty miles to the south-west of the mouth of the Magdalena river. It is a place that García Márquez knows well; it was there that he began his career as a journalist in 1948, and it was his parents' home from the early 1950s. References to the city in the novel are often precise and unmistakable: to the then newly-established residential quarter of La Manga, for example, or to the old artisan quarter of Getsemaní (Gethsemane), or to the dancing at carnival time on the Plaza de la Aduana. But more significant than the detail is the general physical presence of Cartagena, which is strongly felt from the earliest pages of the book.

The entry for Cartagena in the eleventh edition of the *Encyclopaedia Britannica*, published in 1910, notes that 'the mean annual temperature in the city is 82°', and it goes on to say that 'the port is

classed as very unhealthful, especially for unacclimatized for-
eigners'. It also notes that Cartagena has the best harbour on all the
north coast of South America, a geographical chance that has given
the city what the guidebooks would call a long and glorious history.
It was founded in 1533, and quickly became rich and famous as one
of the key centres of communication and trade within the Spanish
empire. It was once the headquarters of the Inquisition in South
America, and the Palace of the Inquisition remains one of today's
tourist sights ('a fine example of colonial baroque', in the words of
the *South American Handbook*). The city was also an important
centre for the slave trade, as García Márquez reminds the reader
very early on.

Cartagena's wealth and position always attracted the envious. It
was plundered by pirates in 1544, captured by Francis Drake in
1585, and by the French in 1697. It was unsuccessfully attacked by
Admiral Vernon in 1741. In 1811, it was the centre of the first
rebellion against Spanish colonial power in Colombia, and later
suffered a terrible siege of almost four months, surrendering to the
Spanish only after the death of a large part of its population. For its
dedication to the cause of independence, Simón Bolívar gave it the
title 'Ciudad Heroica' (Heroic City). Characteristically, however,
García Márquez is not concerned with Cartagena's formidable past,
but with the period of decline which set in during the years after the
War of Independence.

A problem for Cartagena has always been one of inadequate
connexions with the interior of Colombia; during the colonial
period, a canal (the Canal del Dique, or, in the words of the novel,
the 'old Spanish passage') was cut through the marshes and lagoons
to the east of the city, giving access to the Magdalena river at
Calamar. In the early post-colonial period, with the decline in
Cartagena's population and commercial activity, the canal fell into
disuse. In the early 1880s, the canal was reopened for steam
navigation, but this renewal of Cartagena's fortunes is seen in the
novel as precarious, and when Florentino and Fermina pass through
the canal in the 1930s on their way up the Magdalena, Calamar has
changed in just a few years from a place of perpetual carnival to 'a
port in ruins with desolate streets'. The only person they see there is
a woman dressed in white who waves at them with a handkerchief,
and who turns out to be a half-remembered ghost from the past.

So García Márquez's novel is set in a city with a spectacular history and a dull present. The gorgeous background remains: the huge encircling walls, the narrow streets, the great fortresses, described by the *Area Handbook for Colombia* as 'some of the finest examples of Spanish Renaissance architecture in the New World', the famous Cathedral, and water everywhere; the Caribbean sea to the west, the Bay of Cartagena to the south, the lakes and lagoons to the north and east. But the real city of the novel is narrowly provincial, uncertain of itself, still 'dreaming of the return of the viceroys', a city where the poor live miserably and where the great families struggle to maintain the illusion of their power in the face of palpable evidence of decline. There are still some former slaves to be seen, distinguished by the mark of the branding iron, but the wealth which such slaves once represented has gone, and the world in which Juvenal Urbino is born and brought up exists in a 'state of honourable decadence', an arid city, lying 'at the margin of time', suffocating in the heat, and steadily growing old 'amidst faded laurels and rotting marshes'. It is in the context of this underlying sense of collective failure that García Márquez sets the apparent worldly success of Juvenal Urbino and the apparent emptiness of the life of Florentino Ariza, to challenge the reader to reflect on the ways in which we give significance to the lives around us.

The world of the novel is extraordinarily intimate, like Joyce's Dublin. The estimated population of Cartagena in 1905 was only 14,000. Everyone knows everyone and everything, though social distinctions are rigidly maintained, in keeping with the insecurity of a society which finds itself under threat. The novel is composed of six sections. The first describes the events of Juvenal Urbino's final hours of life, and takes place around the year 1930; this date is suggested by two references: firstly, to the recent success of Remarque's book *All Quiet on the Western Front*, and, secondly, to the fact that a Liberal president has just been elected after forty-five years of Conservative rule. The remaining sections of the novel then retrace the story of the lives of the three main characters, beginning from a point nearly sixty years before, finally rejoining the moment of Juvenal Urbino's death in the fifth section, and passing beyond it in the sixth.

The book opens, however, with what might seem to be a false

start. We are given an account of the death by suicide of Jeremiah de Saint-Amour, Juvenal Urbino's chess partner, a refugee from the West Indies who once was supposed to have beaten the Cuban chess prodigy Capablanca. Urbino attends to the delicate matter of the funeral arrangements for his dead friend, and then, in a scene which owes something to Conrad's *Heart of Darkness*, he has a meeting in the old slave-quarter of the city with the woman from Port-au-Prince who had long been Jeremiah de Saint-Amour's secret lover. Given the drama of this opening scene, its prominent place in the novel, the reader might expect the story to be developed somewhere later on, but this never happens. Jeremiah de Saint-Amour is briefly recalled a couple of times towards the end of the book, but only in passing. His status as an 'atheistic saint' – which, in turn, must owe something to the aspirations of Jean Tarrou in Camus's *The Plague* – is never clarified. He simply vanishes from the novel after the initial pages.

In those early pages, we do, however, learn why he has taken his own life: Juvenal Urbino sums it up, with a certain self-satisfaction, in the word 'gerontophobia'. Jeremiah de Saint-Amour turns out to have been a man who has loved life with a deep passion that cannot survive the prospect of old age and decay; long ago, he decided he would never grow old, and vowed, with the passive acceptance of the woman who loved him, to end his life at the age of sixty. It is clear, then, that his absence from the rest of the book is only a formality: the whole of *El amor en los tiempos del cólera* stands as a kind of answer to Jeremiah de Saint-Amour's decision, offering a wildly affirmative and irrational refutation of a seemingly unbreachable logic of despair. In a way that reminds us a little of *No One Writes to the Colonel*, the triumph of the novel seems to lie in its act of defiance, its refusal to accept a logic of decline, and its attempt to recover old age as a vital area of human experience, one unconstrained by what may have preceded it or by what must necessarily come after, the sense of a moment of life, pure and autonomous.

The three major characters in the book are, I have suggested, figures whose primary function is to sustain the outline of a traditional romantic fiction, though they are all seemingly capable of escaping from the stereotypes which the form of the novel imposes on them; or, more precisely, they are all capable of revealing the complex truths which all stereotypes more or less successfully conceal. Of the three characters, perhaps the most formally interesting is Juvenal Urbino. He is an immediately recognizable type, a parody not simply of the middle-class professional in general, or of the Colombian oligarch in particular, but of the educated Latin American who, at a critical moment in the nineteenth century, goes to Europe and comes under the influence of the dominant political philosophy of contemporary liberalism. This doctrine, with its faith in the ability of unfettered economic competition to create a pattern of endless growth and progress, held an enormous fascination for many educated people outside Europe, and was particularly influential among those Latin Americans who saw their mission as one of bringing Latin America into the nineteenth century, rescuing it from the dark ages of superstition, savagery, and neglect. The transparent failure of the liberal dream to solve the acknowledged problems of Latin America is implicit throughout García Márquez's novel, and is linked, often satirically, with the generalized failure of the rational approach to life which Urbino struggles so conspicuously to personify; while, in the political context of the book, the failure of the dream is all the more significant, given that there are many neo-liberals today whose preferred solution to the economic problems of Latin America has a deep affinity with the free-market triumphalism of mid-nineteenth-century Europe.

So Juvenal Urbino is, first of all, a caricature of a certain kind of Latin American, 'a perfect oligarch of the kind you don't see any more', as García Márquez once wrote of Gabriel Turbay, one of the two unsuccessful Liberal party candidates in the presidential elections of 1946. Urbino is a doctor, like his father before and his son after, the career being the fate, or the privilege, of the first-born son of each generation, as the narrator points out. He is, inevitably, a Liberal, like his parrot which has learnt to cry 'Long live the Liberal party', but he is fundamentally a man who thinks of himself as above politics, a Liberal 'more by tradition than from conviction'. He defines himself as 'a natural pacifist', one who believes in the importance of a civilized reconciliation between the two sides in the civil war, for the good of the country.

In the context of that reconciliation, we are given an interesting insight into the relationship between the Colombian political élites and the realities of the War of a Thousand Days. Just before his death, Urbino attends a gala banquet, given in honour of one of his colleagues. There he talks to the archbishop who points out that the banquet is the first occasion, since the ending of the civil war nearly thirty years before, at which both sides have sat down together, and that it is, therefore, something of an historic event. But Urbino reflects to himself that the truth is rather different. Nobody who is there has been invited because of what they think, only because of the distinction of their ancestry; and a distinguished ancestry has always been above 'the accidents of politics and the horrors of war'. The banquet simply represents an example of the élites at play, divorced by wealth and position from the realities of political conflict, self-satisfied, and self-perpetuating.

Regardless of such displays of self-satisfaction, however, the values of the élite are being progressively undermined. Urbino himself is acutely conscious that he is, in a way, the last of a line. His son is a doctor of no consequence, his daughter has married a bank employee from New Orleans, and his wife, Fermina Daza, has broken into his class from a social position that is far beneath him. As the novel draws to an end, the ruling élite discovers that it is powerless to prevent the rise of a new newspaper called *La Justicia* (Justice), a paper dedicated to spreading scandal about the most respected people in the city; while a portrait painted of Urbino shortly after his death, which is on display for many years in the School of Fine Art, will one day be taken out by art students and burned, as a symbol of a hated aesthetic and a hated past.

As the last incident suggests, the cultural values of the élite are also under attack, and this is reflected in a deeply-felt cultural insecurity. One of the most amusing incidents in the novel recalls the public outcry which follows after an utterly obscure Chinese immigrant wins 'the most coveted prize in national poetry' at the annual literary festival. Men like Urbino, who have travelled widely, are highly aware of what they take to be the inferiority of their own country in the face of the artistic productivity of western Europe. Urbino's house is full of original English furniture and French porcelain. His parrot speaks French and Latin, and almost the last words that Urbino himself ever speaks are in French. His library is a retreat from the noise and smells of the port, plunged into a sort of timeless ecclesiastical anonymity, with three thousand volumes, all identically bound in calfskin and with his initials on the spine. His books, of course, come from Europe, and he inevitably pays more attention to the literary fashions of France than to those of Spain. He reads all the authors that a fashionable man of his time should be acquainted with: Anatole France, Pierre Loti, Rémy de Gourmont, Paul Bourget, none of whom, interestingly, has fully survived the test of time, unlike Zola, whom he resolutely refuses to read.

Juvenal Urbino, as one fully conscious of the social responsibilities of his class, does not keep his cultural discoveries to himself. He is an endless proselytizer. He sees to the restoration of the old Teatro de la Comedia, which since colonial times has been turned into a venue for cock-fighting. A regular season is established there on the lines of the great European centres, and, in deference to European tradition, the wives of the distinguished go to first nights in their fur coats, defying the furious heat of the Caribbean. The direction of this cultural parody is obvious. It was precisely because men like Urbino felt that their own country could contribute nothing to a process of cultural resurgence that there was no possibility of dialogue between Europe and Latin America. For so long, Latin American culture saw itself as merely imitative, and it is in that context that we can understand the importance of a writer like Rubén Darío, whom Urbino would never have read. The question also has a more topical dimension, for a tendency towards a supine acquiescence in the unquestioned superiority of North American cultural values has been characteristic of large sections of the Latin American middle class in the twentieth century; and in *that* context, we can judge something of the importance of a writer like García Márquez, someone who has never failed to acknowledge the problems of his own country, but who has never doubted for a second that those problems were worth writing about.

If Juvenal Urbino is an obvious figure of parody, this does not mean, however, that García Márquez has an uncomplicated relationship with him. García Márquez is himself a man who has increasingly lived within the circles of an international culture. He may continue to say that he has never forgotten that he is just 'one of the sixteen children of the Aracataca telegraph operator', but he knows that the truth is not so simple. He is a child of the Caribbean who has chosen to write about the Caribbean from more cosmopolitan centres, like Paris or Mexico City, where, he says, he always keeps his studio at an artificially stifling temperature, in order to remind him of the world he has left behind. So there is a finely ironical relationship between Juvenal Urbino sweating his way through the heat of Cartagena, dreaming of Europe, and García Márquez in his overheated studio in foreign lands, dreaming of Cartagena. Urbino is in many ways ridiculous, but he is also clearly a threat which the novel works hard to demolish.

Urbino is consistently undermined in the book largely because of his misplaced faith in the absolute power of reason. As a man, and as a doctor, his sense of his ability to establish the connexions which unify objects, states, or events is vital. As he grows older, he is forced to recognize the decline of this rational capacity, and is deeply distressed. Indeed, the narrator suggests that, had Urbino not been an entirely orthodox member of the Catholic church, he might have been won over by the logic of Jeremiah de Saint-Amour's despair, by the latter's sense that 'old age was an indecent state that ought to be prevented in good time'. As it is, the only consolation Urbino can find in old age is the coming of 'sexual peace', the gradual fading away of all instinctual desire and of all the chaotic problems that go with it. It is precisely this acquiescence in the apparently inevitable process of physical decline that will be challenged by Florentino and Fermina, in their triumph of sexual passion at the end of the book. Urbino, though, seems more and more to cling to life simply out of a fear of death; only the social conditioning implied by his religious orthodoxy, only those defences that are least personal to him, can save him from a purely reasoned terror in the face of old age. In the end, the diagnostic method upon which his whole life has been based inevitably fails to see him through.

So one of the sets of stereotypes which the novel creates is an opposition between reason and instinct, and we can gain some idea of the context in which the debate is taking place from an apparently trivial passage in the first section of the book. The narrator is talking about the way Urbino and his wife set about coping with the intense heat of the city. Instead of maintaining 'the Caribbean superstition of opening doors and windows to summon up a breath of air that in reality did not exist', they opt for the Roman tradition, which consists of keeping the house firmly shut during the heat of the day and opening it for the breezes at night. The narrator says that, as natives of the Caribbean, they find it hard at first to get used to the feeling of being shut in, 'but they ended up convincing themselves of the advantages of the Roman method . . .' This turns out to be less simple than it looks. On one level, of course, it is a simple parody of the returning traveller, for whom everything abroad is better than at home, and we are firmly told that the couple have to suffer at first in pursuit of their affectation. But the narrator goes on to note that their house is, in fact, the coolest in the whole district, a wonderful place to be during siesta time. So the European way *is* better; it works, and reason triumphs over superstition. There is a cost, though: for the Urbinos' house is closed all day not simply to the heat, but to the entire world around them. The symbolism of the passage is now clear, and reinforces our sense that one of the things the novel is most keen to do is to look critically at the invariable priority we attach to being *right*, and to restore to the reader the forgotten truth that being right almost always carries a hidden cost.

This theme is picked up at many points in the book. An obviously satirical example concerns Juvenal Urbino's brush with the local firemen just before his death. One of Urbino's civic achievements has been to secure the setting up of a professional fire service, a great advance on the previous self-help schemes which, as the narrator points out, sometimes caused more damage than the fires they were trying to deal with. Urbino knows from experience, moreover, that in Europe firemen do not only put out fires: he has seen them rescuing a child from a basement in Hamburg, and lowering a coffin from a balcony in Naples. So it is only natural that he should send for his new fire brigade when his parrot escapes from its cage. The gap, however, between conception and execution is vast. The firemen arrive with their high-pressure hoses and use them to try to scare the parrot into submission; this they fail to do, but they flood the house, and then set about the garden with their machetes. The fire service is an excellent institution in principle, but in practice its bungled efforts lead indirectly to the death of Urbino: in his own attempt to rescue the parrot shortly afterwards, he falls off a ladder and dies. This parody of the rational approach to practical matters is complemented, moreover, by a simple remark which the narrator makes about the emotional experiences of Urbino and his wife: 'If they had learnt anything together', he says, 'it was that wisdom only comes to us when it can no longer be used for anything.'

It is around the question of cholera and the city's responses to it that these ideas and ambiguities are most closely focused. Asiatic cholera is an acute bacterial infection, transmitted chiefly through contaminated drinking water. Endemic in India, it first began to spread on a world-wide scale in the period after 1817, probably because of India's growing links with the world economy at that time. After this first pandemic of 1817–23, there were further ones in 1829–51, 1852–9, 1863–75, 1881–96, and 1889–1923, while a seventh is currently affecting large areas of Asia and Africa. Where living conditions are poor and medical treatment inadequate, it is a disease with a potentially high mortality rate, and, in some epidemics, up to seventy per cent of all cases have ended in death. In Europe, there were four great cholera epidemics in the nineteenth century, and the third of these, in 1866, saw the rise to prominence in France of Dr Adrien Proust, father of the novelist Marcel. Adrien Proust did important relief work, and did much to promote the idea of the *cordon sanitaire* with such slogans as 'Egypt is Europe's barrier against cholera'. In the fictional world of García Márquez's novel, Juvenal Urbino goes to Paris to complete his medical training. While he is there, he learns of the death of his father in a cholera epidemic at home, and, as a result, he decides to find out all he can about the disease. He studies epidemiology under Adrien Proust, and so, when he returns to the Caribbean, he brings with him all that is best and most advanced in the contemporary European medical tradition, a tradition increasingly dominated, in the years after 1865, by the bacteriological successes of men like Louis Pasteur and Robert Koch.

Once home, Juvenal Urbino sets about transforming local medical conditions with the same modernizing zeal that he applies to everything else. The hospital where he works is still lost in superstitious darkness; it is a place where the legs of patients' beds are anchored in jars of water, in the hope of preventing the spread of disease. Urbino struggles successfully against the ridicule and scepticism of those around him. He has the city's first aqueduct built, in order to improve the water supply; he has the old open sewers replaced, and he secures the construction of a covered market, on the lines of one he has seen in Barcelona. When new cases of cholera appear, he takes the appropriate measures, and an epidemic is averted. He saves his city, acquires fame and distinction, and is admitted to the order of the Legion of Honour by the French government – like Adrien Proust in 1870, or for that matter, García Márquez in 1981.

In this respect, at least, Juvenal Urbino's life seems utterly beyond reproach, a perfect combination of applied scientific knowledge and high moral sense. When Urbino reflects on the way his father coped with the previous cholera outbreak, the importance of what has been achieved since then seems ever greater. His father had to face an epidemic in which a quarter of the urban population died in less than three months; he himself fell victim to the disease, and died alone, in voluntary isolation, leaving a farewell letter for his wife and children. Juvenal Urbino, years later, concludes that his father, with the limited knowledge available, probably did more to help spread the disease than to control it: his father's method 'had been more charitable than scientific', and, in many ways, 'contrary to reason'. Yet, in spite of all this, the novel somehow encourages us to think of Urbino's father as the truer hero, while Urbino's absurd death seems to represent the author's final refusal to grant him the undiluted credit which his reformist achievements apparently deserve.

Obviously, much of what Urbino achieves *is* admirable, but García Márquez clearly sees the dangers of mythologizing such a character, of legitimizing the whole set of attitudes and beliefs that underlie Urbino's position. Urbino's desire to be so thoroughly modern, to sustain the dream of that new priesthood of European professionals, whose mental horizons were constrained only by a sense of the limitless perfectability of a world made in their own image, could not fail to encounter an irreconcilable reality when transferred to a different context and a different continent. We are given a fine example of this discordant process in the account of Urbino's return home, after his long period of training abroad. When he was away in Europe, he had felt nostalgia for his native city; on one occasion, when he was most alive to the romance and glory of Paris, he had said to himself that he would sacrifice it all for 'a single moment of his Caribbean in April'. But then he returns, and his city looks mean and degraded. It is so intolerably poor and backward, with its streets full of rats, and, in a calculated phrase, the narrator tells us that Urbino 'found nothing that seemed to him worthy of his nostalgia'. In the coach bringing him home from the port, he dissolves into unseen tears.

Those tears, moreover, are not shed for the victims of the city's poverty, but out of private frustration at the sudden collapse of an ideal. Urbino does care for his city, but it is not clear that he cares for many of the people in it. One of the few things he ever does that seems out of keeping with his public image, according to the narrator, is to move from the house where his family have lived for over a hundred years into the developing rich suburb of La Manga. In making such a move, he is, of course, following a middle-class pattern that has become well-established in the twentieth century, as the centres of many cities in the world have been progressively abandoned, leaving them to survive as symbols of hopeless decay, fear, and endemic violence. There is, however, no escape for Urbino; he has to live on to acknowledge the failure of his modernizing dreams. At the turn of the century, as he is about to make an historic flight in a hot-air balloon, he is asked by a local journalist what his last words will be if the mission ends in disaster, and he replies: 'In my opinion . . . the nineteenth century is changing for all the world, but not for us.' Cholera may have been intelligently averted, but, as the balloon passes eastwards over the country, Urbino can see that people are still dying unnecessarily, not of preventable disease this time, but in the old-fashioned way, from civil war. At the very end of his life, some thirty years later, he is once again forced to recognize the squalor of the city, as he returns from his meeting in the old slave-quarter with the former lover of Jeremiah de Saint-Amour.

The two other main characters in the novel exist very much in relation to the power of Urbino and in reaction to it. In the vast spaces created by a half-century of life in a dull city, much that they do seems inevitably to lack form or solidity. Florentino Ariza spends a lifetime making love to innumerable women, besides working his way towards the Presidency of the Compañía Fluvial del Caribe (River Company of the Caribbean), but nothing can truly happen to him until the final liberation of Urbino's death. Fermina Daza, for her part, lives a strangely unformed life with Urbino, a mixture of accommodation and revolt. The early years of her marriage are the worst of her life, spent within the terrifying confines of a polite society in decline, a time of endless boredom in huge windowless rooms. Later on, the narrator suggests that she and her husband almost find love together, or, in García Márquez's more active language, that they are 'on the point of inventing it', but social constraints never seem to allow their relationship to break out of a certain inherited conception of the traditional marriage. Their relationship looks ideal from without, but they are uneasy about questioning its status from within. In later years, Fermina identifies the ambiguity of the life she has spent with Urbino: she sees herself as the 'absolute sovereign of a vast empire of happiness built by him and only for him'. She has been immured in a world of happiness from which there is no escape, in which she has largely ceased to exist except as the source of happiness and security for another, her husband's shield against the terrors of life and death. It is a relationship that has found its best moments in a carefully contrived harmony of apparently mutual support, but it has never quite passed beyond that.

There is much about Juvenal Urbino that is not entirely negative, but because he has so little sense of the extent to which he is defined by his class, so little awareness of the stereotype he embodies, he remains the centre of authority against which the book so joyously rebels. *El amor en los tiempos del cólera* is a vast celebration of all that Urbino is not: it is about spontaneity, disorder, vitality, and, above all, love. That is why the apparently implausible story of Fermina's final passion for Florentino Ariza can be sustained, even at the point when Florentino is old, and bald, and lame. For Florentino has nothing in common with Urbino, except Fermina; he is illegitimate, and has always lived at the margins of conventional society. In many ways he is hardly noticeable. The same reason which led Fermina to reject him in the early days — his shadowy unreality, his apparent nothingness — now allows her, at the end of her life, to begin again with him. Florentino's seventy-six years may seem to have been almost entirely wasted, but it is he who, after Urbino's death, can write to Fermina in a language which is not of the past, a language which gives her the courage to reject the prejudices of the class she has adopted, and to think of love, finally, 'as a state of grace that was not the means to anything, but an origin and an end in itself'.

The culminating moment of fulfilled sexual passion is reached in the course of a journey which Florentino and Fermina take on one of the wooden paddle steamers that used to carry passengers up and down the Magdalena river. The theme of travel has been an important one in the book. Urbino, characteristically, never travels in his own country, but Fermina and Florentino have, separately, made a number of journeys into the interior of Colombia before their final voyage of love. There is the early journey which Fermina is forced to undergo by her father, so that she should forget about Florentino; this takes her eastwards across the Sierra Nevada de Santa Marta as far as the town of Valledupar, and then on to Riohacha, a journey which allows García Márquez to express all his nostalgia for a world that is not Urbino's, a world of light and happy chaos, where every day is a fiesta and every house is open. Then there is the companion journey on which Florentino is sent by his mother, so that he should forget about Fermina. She arranges for him to go to work as a telegraph operator in the old colonial town of Villa de Leiva, more than twenty days distant in the mountains, but he simply takes the boat as far as its terminus, unintentionally losing his virginity on the way, and then returns, because he cannot bear to be parted from the city of Fermina. Much later, there is Fermina's absence of nearly two years, when, as a result of Urbino's one adulterous relationship, with the daughter of a Protestant minister, she goes to live with her cousin. She passes through her home town of San Juan de la Ciénaga, and there, in an echo of the story of *One Hundred Years of Solitude*, she experiences all the desolation of memory in the face of a town transformed by the invasion of the banana company.

The final journey in the book takes Florentino and Fermina up the Magdalena on a boat called the *New Fidelity*; the symbolism of the name is, on one level, obvious, but the narrator also tells us that this is the first of the river company's boats to have been built locally, rather than abroad, a detail which suggests another sort of fidelity. They go through the Canal del Dique, then on past Calamar and Zambrano. The river and the surrounding forests have been devastated by recent developments: the new steam ships which have revived Cartagena's fortunes have consumed vast quantities of wood, and the river is silting up through the effects of soil erosion. The parrots and the monkeys have gone; the manatees have been hunted to extinction, and the tanneries in New Orleans have killed off all the alligators. As a result of the shortage of wood, however, their boat is stranded for nearly a week in the sweltering heat of the river, and it is there, 'in an unreal lethargy in which it was easier to love one another without asking questions', that all the clichés of the novel are finally validated.

The boat goes on as far south as La Dorada, the terminus for navigation on the Lower Magdalena. Here they turn around, and Florentino, recognizing their need to be alone together, orders the captain to fly the cholera warning-flag from his ship, so that no one will come on board for the return journey. The old symbol of terror is defused and transformed into a symbol of love, and, in this unreal, but utterly committed, state, they prepare for a lifetime in each other's company, and for the wild gesture of affirmation with which the book comes to an end.

El amor en los tiempos del cólera is an imaginative re-creation of a forgotten period in Colombia's history. It is a book which is full of memories transposed from García Márquez's own past and from that of his parents. It reveals an almost tactile fascination with the objects of history, particularly with details of dress, so that, as one of the early Colombian reviewers suggested, reading the novel is like leafing through an album of faded family portraits. Above all, however, the novel is an attempt to reclaim the values of popular tradition. It takes its energy from a range of competing stereotypes, and its aim is not to transcend those stereotypes, but to squeeze them to the limit, in order to extract the truths which they contain. In the end, through a parody that is more than simply witty, the forces of enlightenment in the book are defeated by the dark forces of instinct, and we are left smiling, not at the absurd clichés of romantic love but at the rational follies of Juvenal Urbino, a man who has to take out a subscription to the Paris newspaper *Le Figaro* 'so as not to lose the thread of reality'.

This is not a naïve book, moreover. It is one which recognizes that the triumph of instinct is not obtained without a price: the purely rational suicide of Jeremiah de Saint-Amour at the beginning of the novel is carefully paralleled at the end of the book by the suicide of Florentino's former lover, the schoolgirl América Vicuña, who dies entirely for love and the bitter cliché of a broken heart. In spite of this, the novel is full of a sense of joy at the recovery of an attitude to life that is constantly felt to be threatened by authority in all its forms – the authority of class, of reason, of money, of religion, and, of course, of literary tradition. Juvenal Urbino, the symbol of correctness in literature as in everything, is condemned by his position to read only what is best in the field of contemporary writing, whereas Florentino reads simply for the love of reading, without caring about distinctions between good and bad. He has been brought up on the volumes of the Biblioteca Popular, a series which can be found everywhere and which contains everything, from Homer to the most derisory of local poets.

It is this kind of freedom that García Márquez is seeking in the novel, in opposition to the authoritarianism symbolized by a nineteenth-century European tradition and its twentieth-century adherents. In making its attack, the novel rejoins another tradition, one that Europe, too, has known, one capable of recognizing that there may be more to life than the simple glory of being right. That tradition finds its expression in the gnomic elegance of Pascal's famous remark, 'le cœur a ses raisons que la raison ne connaît point' ('the heart has its reasons which reason knows nothing of'), and it returns in the popular, harsher, but no less perceptive, language of the Caribbean: 'El corazón tiene más cuartos que un hotel de putas' ('the heart has more rooms than a whore-house'), Florentino's anguished words of self-discovery, as he stands alone among the crowds on the quayside, waving goodbye to one of the many women who have, unaccountably, and just for a time, filled out a little of that vast space reserved for ever in his heart for the incomparable Fermina Daza.

V

Macondo – i

An isle under Ionian skies,
Beautiful as a wreck of Paradise.
(Shelley, *Epipsychidion*)

Macondo is, in reality, the name of an old banana plantation, situated between the villages of Guacamayal and Sevilla, near García Márquez's birthplace of Aracataca. In an article published in 1971, Germán de Granda suggested that the name is probably of Bantu origin, and that it was brought to Colombia by Bantu-speaking slaves who worked the plantations of the Atlantic coast in colonial times. There is nothing improbable about this suggestion. Germán de Granda notes that a form 'makondo' has been recorded in Cuba, and John Kelly, of the Language Department of the University of York, tells me that the word 'kondo', plural 'makondo', turns up in a number of Bantu languages, mostly from the western part of the Bantu area, a point which would accord with what is known of the geographical origins of the Caribbean slave population. The word 'kondo', 'makondo', means 'banana', and Germán de Granda notes that, within the cultural world of the Bantu, the fruit carries a range of magical and religious associations: it has the power to cure serious illnesses; it is, at the same time, the favourite food of the devil. The potential symbolic irony here is obvious, in the context of García Márquez's literary Macondo, a world which is brought into prominence and then obliterated from memory in accordance with its rise and fall as a banana-company town.

But of course, the relationship between the real and the imaginary is of only passing interest here. García Márquez's Macondo is a primarily literary creation, the resolution of a long-meditated project, and the focus for a wide range of personal memories and experiences from childhood days in Aracataca. A comparison between the Macondo of García Márquez's first novel, *Leaf Storm*, and the later Macondo of *One Hundred Years of Solitude* shows just how vital is the force of imaginative transposition. For, where the latter is a world of light, energy, magic, and illusion, the former is dark, cold, and essentially cerebral. Yet, at the same time, the basic project of Macondo is already clearly sketched out in *Leaf Storm*, a novel García Márquez began around June 1950, seventeen years before the publication of *One Hundred Years of Solitude*. Already, *Leaf Storm* reveals a concern for the major theme of solitude, one that is both individual and collective; it describes a town that was founded with great hope and promise by refugees fleeing from the civil wars of the late nineteenth century, but which has gradually taken on all the fatal, and fatalistic, rigidity of a world that feels itself inescapably doomed to vanish without trace. The manner of its disappearance is already determined in *Leaf Storm*, where 'that final wind which will sweep away Macondo' looks forward to 'the wrath of the biblical hurricane' that will bring about the end of Macondo in *One Hundred Years of Solitude*.

Leaf Storm describes a period from the founding of Macondo down to 1928, the year of the author's birth and of the massacre of the banana-plantation workers which precedes the final destruction of Macondo in *One Hundred Years of Solitude*. The significance of the title *Leaf Storm*, or, in the original, *La hojarasca*, has already been mentioned (see page 37). It is the term which the patrician founders of Macondo apply to the surge of immigrants who arrive in the town in the wake of the development of the banana industry. The novel begins with this process clearly in mind: 'Suddenly, as if a whirlwind had taken root in the centre of the town, the banana company arrived, pursued by the leaf storm.' The prologue, from which these words are taken, is dated 'Macondo, 1909', and reflects the atmosphere of the early years of the banana boom, when Macondo was transformed into a typical frontier town, wild and tough, with 'the madness of its people who burned banknotes at parties'. From about 1918 decline sets in, and the decade which follows sees the town's slow death. With the departure of the banana company, all is desolation:

A ruined village was left here, with four poor, dark shops;

occupied by unemployed and resentful people, who were tormented by the memory of a prosperous past and the bitterness of an oppressive and static present.

The founding members of the town, represented by the nameless colonel who is one of the three voices who carry the narrative of the novel, feel they have lost everything. This is partly a reflection of the way in which the intrusion of outsiders has disrupted the traditional social hierarchy, but there is also a shrewd realization of the long-term damage that has been done by the creation of an illusory prosperity, which is dependent in the end not on people's ability to handle their own affairs successfully, but on the working of economic forces that lie beyond their control or understanding. There is no possibility now of returning to the ways of Macondo before the banana company came, for the mentality of the people has been altered beyond recall:

> It would have been enough to go out into the fields laid waste by the banana company; to clear them of weeds and start again from the beginning. But they had taught the leaf storm to be impatient; not to believe in the past or in the future. They had taught it to believe in the present moment and to satisfy its voracious appetites there. It did not take long for us to realize that the leaf storm had gone and that without it reconstruction was impossible. The leaf storm had brought everything and it had taken everything away.

This will be true also of the Macondo of *One Hundred Years of Solitude*.

The moral dilemma which lies at the heart of *Leaf Storm* is suggested by the lines from the *Antigone* of Sophocles that are placed at the beginning of the novel. In Sophocles's play we have a conflict between the claims of an individual conscience and the demands of social conformity. Antigone insists on giving her rebellious brother Polynices a proper burial, in defiance of the orders of Creon the king, and this clash of loyalties creates a situation which will end in her suicide. In *Leaf Storm*, too, there is a conflict over a burial: the colonel, who is closely modelled on García Márquez's grandfather, has agreed to ensure the funeral rites for a local doctor who, in obscure circumstances, has saved his life. The doctor is a cold and elusive figure; García Márquez has suggested that he is to be associated with the historical general Uribe Uribe, the Liberal leader who, as we have seen, also provides a model for Colonel Aureliano Buendía. The doctor in *Leaf Storm* arrives in Macondo in the early years of the twentieth century, and he lives with the colonel and his family for eight years, without their ever discovering much about him. His professional qualifications are in some doubt, and, with the arrival of the banana company, he is driven out of business. Gradually, he withdraws into total solitude, and then, one night in 1918, when there is an outbreak of violence at a political meeting, he refuses to come out of seclusion to help treat the wounded. He is thus hated by the people of the town. So now, with the news of the doctor's death by suicide, the colonel's private loyalties are in conflict with the vengeful anger all around him. The novel takes the form of a series of monologues by the colonel, his daughter, and his grandson, around the doctor's coffin, and the book ends with continuing uncertainty as to whether or not the people of Macondo will allow the burial to take place. This is only resolved in a passing reference towards the end of *One Hundred Years of Solitude*.

There is much that is uncertain in *Leaf Storm*. García Márquez's aim seems to have been to create an atmosphere of brooding menace, one which the principal voices in the novel register in terms of a burden of fate which must be endured because it can never be defeated. The very form of the interior monologue suggests a world in which people are continually turned in upon themselves, and the Macondo which emerges from the book is one that is totally closed, rigid and conformist, both in social and in emotional terms. Vargas Llosa, who gives what is probably the best account of the novel, in his book *García Márquez: historia de un deicidio*, sums up the condition of life in the Macondo of *Leaf Storm* as the 'glacial coexistence of solitary essences', and he goes on to suggest that the people's hatred of the doctor may be due not so much to his refusal to treat the wounded victims of the political violence as to the withdrawn and miserable quality of his life, an example which offers too harsh, because too truthful, a reflection of what life is like in general in this early Macondo.

With *One Hundred Years of Solitude* the project of Macondo is finally realized. Published in 1967, the novel was an immediate success and remains, for most readers, García Márquez's most important achievement to date. It reveals a world of diverse and engaging complexities, in which the strange and the magical are the common currency of life. Apparently free to operate according to its own laws and conventions, it is a world which, we come to see, is fated from the outset to suffer from external forces over which it has no control. The novel is about the solitude of a family, a town, a nation, and, ultimately, a whole continent; about history, about the history of Colombia, about a process of change and development the significance of which largely escapes the characters involved but which the reader is privileged to observe with some degree of understanding and recognition. Exceedingly funny, the novel offers a marked contrast between the exuberant manner of its telling and the frequent wretchedness of the reality and events which it describes. In the end, it draws attention to its own status as a work of fiction, and seeks, as does *The Autumn of the Patriarch*, to force the reader out of the imaginative world of the novel into a confrontation with the real world of experience and of suffering.

Leaf Storm gave us a picture of a Macondo founded initially as a refuge from the horrors of the long period of civil unrest in Colombia that culminated in the War of a Thousand Days (1899–1902); as the colonel's daughter puts it: 'Macondo was my parents' promised land . . .' But the circumstances surrounding the founding of Macondo in *One Hundred Years of Solitude* lie further in the past, are darker, more complex. For José Arcadio Buendía and his wife Úrsula, pre-eminent among the founders of Macondo, come there in flight from the horror of a violence for which they are themselves responsible.

They are cousins, from families with a long history of interbreeding, and over their heads is the constant threat that they will produce children who are genetically malformed. This history of interbreeding, along with the fear of the consequences of incestuous relationships, dominates the whole book, and is symbolic of the solitude which characterizes successive generations of the Buendías, a family whose members struggle in vain to engage successfully in relationships outside the tightly-controlled familial world; by extension, it symbolizes the inward-looking nature of their town, their culture, their continent, all locked into a permanent state of underdevelopment, unable to relate to the world outside on terms other than those of a deeply felt and crippling inferiority. Because of the fear of incest and its consequences, Úrsula refuses to have sexual relations with her husband. This provokes gossip in the village where they live, and, in the end, results in the murder of Prudencio Aguilar by José Arcadio Buendía, in a traditional gesture of offended sexual honour. It is this murder, and the subsequent inability of the ghost of Prudencio Aguilar to overcome his nostalgia for the world of the living, that leads the Buendías to abandon their village, and, eventually, to found Macondo, a Macondo which is described, not in the simple manner of *Leaf Storm*, but, on the contrary, as a refuge in a land 'which no one had promised them'.

And this distinction is significant. The Macondo of *One Hundred Years of Solitude* is not the promised land, nor could ever be. It is true that the novel opens with a marvellous sense of freshness, of a world made new, with an image of twenty houses on a river bank, in a distant past when 'the world was so recent that many things lacked names, and, in order to refer to them, it was necessary to point'. However, this freshness will be exposed as not merely subject to inevitable change and degradation, but as inherently illusory in itself. It corresponds to a deeply rooted fantasy, evoking the kind of joy we might feel if we could truly begin everything again from the beginning, if we could remake the world in our own image, rather than having to accept the reality of a world into which we are carelessly born, and which, through its gross imperfections, injustices, and disappointments, seems only to confirm its total independence of us. *One Hundred Years of Solitude*, however, is a book which recognizes the impossibility of ever beginning again; a book in which there are no second chances.

Macondo does not trace a simple process of decline from paradise into history, as is sometimes said. Rather, it recalls, with great nostalgia, the perception that paradise is a myth, and that behind every apparent new start there is always something else. Just as the 'New World' could only flourish as a concept through the obliteration of the original inhabitants for whom it was old, so the newness of Macondo conceals a tale of murder, and, behind that, a history of incestuous generations of Buendías about whom we know next to nothing, but whose existence is essential to the working out of the story we are reading. Only to the extent that Macondo is isolated from the rest of the world and from history can it briefly sustain the illusion of a new beginning; and this isolation is not the comforting security of an earthly paradise, but the vulnerable solitude of a people who will never survive to give their own account of what happens to them. Their history will always be constructed by others.

A spirit of predeterminism dominates the whole course of the novel, rather in the manner of a classical tragedy. Just as we can see that Oedipus behaves wrongly, but that his behaviour is simply the particular form in which the inevitability of a fate long since decided is being played out, so we can see that the Buendías are moving inexorably towards their own destruction, and that the inadequacies which they display in dealing with the world are, once again, simply the manner in which their fate is made manifest. We can observe here, too, how the theme of fatalism has developed since the time of *Leaf Storm*. In *One Hundred Years of Solitude*, we are no longer dealing with a vague sense of brooding menace; instead, we are made clearly aware that the fate of the Buendías is one which has been decided by an imperious external force, that of an omniscient narrator who wills the destruction of Macondo, and against whose decisions there can, of course, be no appeal. The narrator's representative within the novel is the elusive gypsy sage Melquíades. It is he who writes down, in advance, the story of the hundred years of solitude, encoded on parchment, for one of the last of the Buendías to decipher. From the outset, everything is known, willed, and controlled, but this knowledge is withheld from the Buendías themselves until the final moment of apocalypse. As the last sentence of the book makes clear, the Buendías have been 'condemned' to their solitude; they might have behaved differently, they might have behaved more generously, but the result would still have been the same in the end.

In the early days, Macondo is a village in which everyone is young, happy, and hard-working, and where death is unknown. The only contact the inhabitants have with the outside world at this time is through the gypsies, and foremost among these is the mysterious Melquíades. I have suggested that he is an authorial representative, but he is far more than that. His name means 'son of a king', from the Semitic root 'Melq-' and a Greek suffix. He has sometimes been associated by critics with Melchizedek, the ancient Canaanite priest-king of Jerusalem, whose name appears in both the Old and the New Testament. In a passage from 'The

Letter to the Hebrews', Melchizedek is described thus:

> He is without father or mother or genealogy, and has neither beginning of days nor end of life, but resembling the Son of God he continues a priest for ever.

Melquíades, too, is a kind of eternal priest-king. He has many of the attributes of a shaman, the traditional priest-doctor among the American Indians: shamans are pre-eminent in their knowledge of myths and of the meaning of myths; they are able to maintain close contact with the world of spirits, to travel to the spirit world, and to return with their knowledge enhanced; they have the power of bilocation, enabling them to be seen simultaneously in different places; they have skill in divination, in poetry, and in magical medicine, and, in general, they serve as the repository of a wisdom beyond ordinary people's power to attain. In the novel, Melquíades is an ambiguous figure. It is he who brings to Macondo both knowledge – itself a traditionally ambiguous gift – and death. He enchants José Arcadio Buendía with a series of seemingly miraculous inventions from the outside world, like the magnet and the magnifying glass; and José Arcadio Buendía develops such a passion for knowledge that he grows more and more detached from the social reality of Macondo, and eventually ends in a kind of righteous madness. More destructive yet, Melquíades is the first person ever to die in Macondo, 'for Macondo was a town that was unknown to the dead until Melquíades arrived and marked it with a small black dot on the many-coloured maps of death'.

On the other hand there is also something heroic about Melquíades, rather like the heroism of Shakespeare's Prospero in *The Tempest*. Both men are visionaries who, in very different circumstances, are brought to abandon their supernatural powers in order to retain their basic grasp on humanity. Melquíades, we are told, has already died once before, but he comes back to the living 'because he could not bear the solitude' of the dead; and then, 'repudiated by his tribe, bereft of all his supernatural faculties as a punishment for his fidelity to life, he decided to take refuge in that corner of the world that was still undiscovered by death'. So he returns to live in Macondo. Now reduced to the outward trappings of mere mortality, he very swiftly ages and becomes almost invisible, spending most of his time writing down, in anticipation and with full insight, the whole history of Macondo that is to follow. Appropriately, the language in which he writes will later be revealed to be Sanskrit, the distant parent tongue of Romany, the gypsy language.

Melquíades's second death takes place in Macondo, and it is one of the early indicators in the book that change and mortality are to be as integral a part of life here as anywhere else. As critics have often pointed out, however, one of the distinctive features of the novel is that, for most of the time, virtually all the characters are shown to be unaware of the existence or direction of change; they perceive their lives, on the contrary, as either rooted in stasis or subject to simple circularity. They reveal an almost total inability to situate their experiences in any sort of historical framework, and so, in a very real sense, they persistently fail to understand what is happening to them and to their village, losing themselves instead in an illusory timeless world in which all things seem to remain the same. Occasionally, they may have insights into the fact that the nature of life is different, but such insights are never helpful, never profound. So, for example, Úrsula at one point has the confused sense of what the narrator calls 'a progressive breakdown of time': ' "The years these days don't come round the way the old ones used to," she would say, feeling that everyday reality was slipping out of her hands'; but this response is a completely subjective one, a reaction of instinct, not of practical understanding. The reader, on the other hand, is privileged to recognize just how inevitably things do change in Macondo, and how there can be no safe refuge from this process:

A people without history
Is not redeemed from time, for history is a pattern
Of timeless moments . . .

(T.S. Eliot, *Four Quartets*)

Not only is the reader aware that things change, but also that, in this vulnerable community, all change will be for the worse. As Anna Marie Taylor puts it, in a short and lucid article entitled '*Cien años de soledad*: History and the Novel': 'The characters' perspective on the world is ahistorical and cyclical while the narration of Macondo's story, as seen from the perspective shared by author and reader, describes unrelenting decline.'

An early example of how this dual perspective works can be seen in relation to the plague of insomnia which strikes Macondo. This disease, one of the results of Macondo's increasing contact with the outside world, is brought to the town by two Indians who arrive one day 'in flight from a plague of insomnia that had been scourging their tribe for several years'. The two Indians, Visitación and Cataure, belonged to the aristocracy in their own society, but in Macondo they become servants of the Buendías. The plague of insomnia which they bring does not worry anyone in Macondo at first; after all, the town is such a lively place and there is so much to do that having to stay continually awake seems no great hardship. However, it becomes clear that one of the potentially disastrous effects of the plague is that it causes people to lose their memory. Visitación explains how

> . . . when the sick person became used to their state of wakeful-ness, the recollections of childhood began to be erased from their memory, then the name and the notion of things, and finally the identity of people and even the consciousness of their own being, until they sank into a kind of idiocy that had no past.

It is, of course, significant that it is the Indians who understand the nature and meaning of the plague of insomnia and loss of memory, and that the first person to catch the plague in Macondo is Rebeca, the child who arrives mysteriously in the village at the age of eleven, and who has apparently been brought up in a bilingual Spanish and Indian environment. Behind the new world of Macondo lie the thousands of years of Indian culture that have been effectively erased from memory by the European conquest. The continuity of the cultural tradition has been shattered, and its history is now largely irrecoverable, because it is the history of the vanquished. Likewise with the history of Macondo. It, too, is a history of the vanquished; it, too, is irrecoverable, along with the broken fragments of a childhood in Aracataca, for it belongs to a world that has ceased to have an identity. Only the magic of language and the apparent authority of a god-like narrator can create the illusion of a world brought back to life. That illusion is exposed in the end by the novel itself, with the clear recognition that, in the real world, there are no second chances, and that, for the defeated, no magic wand is ever waved.

In protohistoric and historic times, there were two important cultural units within the Indian population of Colombia. They are discussed by Gerardo Reichel-Dolmatoff, in his book *Colombia* (1965), and in his earlier, jointly-written, book called *The People of*

Aritama: The Cultural Personality of a Colombian Mestizo Village
(1961). The two groupings were the Chibcha, who occupied the
highland areas around Bogotá, and the Tairona of the Sierra Nevada
de Santa Marta, among whose descendants are the Cogui Indians of
modern Colombia. When the Spaniards reached Colombia in the
sixteenth century, they were amazed at the cultural level of the
Tairona, at their architecture, cultivated gardens, irrigated fields,
and paved roads; the chronicler Oviedo wrote that it all reminded
him of the way things were done in Europe, in Lombardy and among
the Etruscans.

Initially, contact between the Tairona and the Spanish was friendly
enough, but, under increasing provocation and exploitation, the
Indian population rebelled, and virtually the entire sixteenth century
was passed in savage warfare. Reichel-Dolmatoff cites an early
seventeenth-century decree by the governor of the region, Juan
Guiral Velón, which marked the effective end of the Indian resistance. By then, the Tairona had ceased to exist as a cultural unit, their
villages had been sacked, their fields laid waste, and their chieftains
taken prisoner. The leader of the final rebellion was ordered 'to be
dragged by the tails of two wild colts and torn into quarters and these
put on the trails, and the head put in a cage . . .' The governor's
decree continues with a long list of Tairona chieftains, concluding:
'All these Indians . . . I condemn and order to be hanged by their
necks . . .', that each 'be strangled in the usual form and that his body
be burned in live flames till it be turned to ashes, so that no memory be
left of him.'

This policy, not simply of conquest, but of annihilation, continues
to the present day in countries such as Guatemala, where the Indian
population remains proportionately large. The story of one Guatemalan Indian woman in her early twenties, published in English in
1984 under the title *I . . . Rigoberta Menchú*, shows clearly the
continuity of attitude and of method. The account which Rigoberta
Menchú gives of her early life, highly informative, and sad and brave
beyond measure, has found an audience only because, at a critical
moment, she made a conscious decision to break out of the linguistic
isolation of her people; at the age of twenty, she learned Spanish, the
language of the conqueror, and this alone enabled her to carry the
story of the suffering of the Guatemalan Indians to a wider world that
almost totally ignored their existence. She recalls the time in 1979

when her sixteen-year-old brother was tortured by members of the
Guatemalan armed forces:

> My brother was tortured for more than sixteen days. They cut off
> his fingernails, they cut off his fingers, they cut off his skin . . .
> He stayed alive . . . My brother suffered tortures on every part
> of his body, but they took care not to damage the arteries or veins
> so that he would survive the tortures and not die.

Later, her brother was one of a group of Indians who were burned to
death in front of the members of their family and community; not
long after that, her mother and father were also killed. So the
persecution of the American Indians is not something which can be
consigned, in civilized relief, to the memory of a barbarous past. It
continues, with varying degrees of subtlety or ferocity, and they, the
original inhabitants of the Americas, have survived to become, both
in popular speech and in official reports, the 'Indian problem'.

So the reader of *One Hundred Years of Solitude* is fully in a position
to understand the significance of the plague of insomnia and
forgetfulness which the two Indians bring to Macondo, and to
understand how it is that two Indians of royal blood come to be
servants in the Buendía household. The reader also gradually
becomes aware that the fate of the Indians will be mirrored in the fate
of their new masters, and that everyone in the book will be finally
condemned to the same horror of oblivion. The Buendías themselves
are only dimly, and intermittently, aware of the hopelessness of their
situation. They lack the tragic perspective. They are given nothing
comparable to those moments of genuine insight into the nature of
life which Homer gives to Hector in the *Iliad*. Hector has a passionate
sense of the inescapability of his fate, and, in his determination to
pursue his course to its appointed end, fully conscious of what awaits
him, he reaches towards a standard of heroic behaviour. The
Buendías are never given that kind of chance, never allowed to face
the world with a knowledge of their destiny: that is a privilege and a
challenge reserved for the reader alone.

This dual perspective, which firmly distinguishes between the
reader's perception of events and that of the characters within the
novel, is further illustrated by the way in which the Buendías respond
to the insomnia plague. As it becomes clear that loss of memory
might have serious consequences, and that even the names of

everyday objects are in danger of being lost, Aureliano discovers the importance of writing. He starts to put labels on the objects around him, as a way of trying to hang on to their identity. This practice is then extended throughout the village; tables and chairs, and clocks and doors, are all carefully labelled, while José Arcadio Buendía puts a sign around the neck of a cow:

> This is the cow, she must be milked every morning so that she will produce milk and the milk must be boiled so that it can be mixed with coffee to make coffee with milk.

The narrator comments: 'Thus they went on living in a reality that was slipping away, momentarily captured by words . . .' It all seems ridiculous, and, from a certain point of view, it is ridiculous. Nevertheless, the reader can also reflect that the reduction of objects and experience to writing is a significant step in the development of the human race; that writing is indeed a legitimate way in which people seek to hold on to an awareness of the past, as a means of giving some sense to their existence in the present, and that the novel we are reading is but one further attempt in this same direction, however forcefully it may, in the end, advertise its own inevitable failure to carry out its task successfully.

It is at this critical point in the development of Macondo that Melquíades returns to the village to escape from the loneliness of death. He produces a magical drink that immediately restores people's memory, and so the crisis of forgetfulness is temporarily resolved. However, for ever afterwards in the book, reality is felt to be dangerously precarious; and Melquíades, in the months he spends in Macondo before dying for a second time, devotes himself almost exclusively to the task of trying to define and preserve this threatened reality. He buries himself in the composition of his encoded manuscripts, and, with the new technology of his daguerreotype laboratory, he records 'everything that was recordable in Macondo'.

The response of José Arcadio Buendía to this recording process is interesting, for it tells us much about the kind of problems that successive members of the Buendía family will experience in their attempts to come to terms with the world in which they live. José Arcadio Buendía is fearful of the daguerreotype: he senses, quite rightly, that the photographic miracle which allows us to freeze a moment of experience also presses upon us the realization that reality is constantly in flux. However, as a member of a line he believes to be eternal, José Arcadio Buendía is unwilling to reconcile himself to the existence of change; for change, logically, might lead – as, inexorably, it will lead – to a world in which there are no more Buendías, and no more Macondo. So, for the rest of his life, he is trapped in a dilemma he cannot resolve. Faced with the terrifying and unacceptable truth, he looks at the world about him for the irrefutable confirmation that things do change, but he fails to find it, or refuses to see it. He finds only that things apparently remain always the same; the way the air feels, the buzzing of the sun, everything seems merely to replicate the way things were the day before, or the day before that. He loses his grip on sanity, and he smashes the daguerreotype laboratory; he is then forcibly restrained, and tied to the chestnut tree in the patio of his house, from which he will be released only at the point of death.

The inability to accept the fundamental conditions of life, to accept those things which, like change and mortality, cannot be altered, is a fatal disadvantage. The mad, magical world of the Buendías that is often so amusing, so enchanting, is also the solitary world of a people who have taken refuge in madness or magic as the only alternatives to a world whose preconditions they cannot endure. This inability to deal with the world on even terms, characteristic of so many of the Buendías, is treated by the author in ways both sympathetic and critical. The sympathy, on the one hand, is profound because, after all, the Buendías are seen as supremely vulnerable; every contact with the outside world is a challenge for which they appear hopelessly unsuited. The first gypsies who come to Macondo with Melquíades dazzle with the excitement of the new inventions which they bring; but these inventions are of no obvious relevance in the context of an isolated agrarian society. Later, another wave of gypsies arrives; they are no longer the ambiguous 'heralds of progress' from the days of Melquíades, but mere 'pedlars of amusements', and they succeed in turning the village upside down with their activities, so that 'the inhabitants of Macondo suddenly found themselves lost in their own streets', a clear foreshadowing of the depredations that follow in the wake of the banana fever later in the story. As we see Macondo transformed from an agrarian society towards one that is more commercially orientated, and as the various institutions of the state – the police, the Church, and the judiciary – begin to impinge upon the people, the impression we gain is one of a relentless decline in the quality of life. The response of the people of Macondo to these various intrusions is typified by José Arcadio Buendía's outraged innocence in the face of the newly-arrived magistrate, don Apolinar Moscote. The magistrate comes with an order that all the houses in Macondo should be painted blue, the colour of Conservatism. He bears a title that reeks of the Spanish colonial past, that of 'corregidor' (literally, 'corrector' of abuses), a title given to judicial and administrative officers of the Spanish crown. José Arcadio Buendía, who wants to paint his house white, says bluntly to the magistrate: 'We don't need any corregidor because here there is nothing to correct' ('no necesitamos ningún corregidor porque aquí no hay nada que corregir'), oblivious of the true significance of the arrival of the corregidor in the context of an ever-encroaching centralist state.

If it is clear that the Buendías are brought into contact with the world on fundamentally unequal terms, it is also clear that they are not to be thought of as wholly blameless in their plight. Anna Marie Taylor, in the article mentioned earlier, talks of 'the nihilism with which, to one degree or another, all members of the [Buendía] clan relate to the past', and of how 'the characters see the past in general as part of a circular pattern of recurring events and, in particular, as filled with negative personal experiences which they do everything possible to repress.' These familial traits, the corrosive inability to make anything of life in the present, and the distorted, repressed, or obsessional attitudes towards the past, are implicit in descriptions of the Buendías from the earliest pages of the novel. Aureliano, 'the first human being to be born in Macondo', is silent and withdrawn from childhood, while his brother, José Arcadio, in his first sexual experience, finds a path that leads only to loneliness and despair.

An incapacity for genuine affection is a burden carried by many of the principal characters. The rivalry between Amaranta and Rebeca over the Italian Pietro Crespi, for example, has little to do with love; it is a struggle for rights of ownership, the kind of passion that recognizes simply the imperious necessity of an object upon which to focus its obsessions, and its effects are entirely negative, leading to the suicide of Crespi and the self-willed martyrdom of Amaranta. In a perceptive article published in 1983, Arnold Penuel writes of Amaranta in the following terms:

Amaranta's fundamental problem is her virtually solipsistic narcissism which resembles that of the infant that has not yet learned that it must accommodate its impulses to the realities of the external world. When Amaranta's pathological narcissism comes into conflict with the uncontrollable realities of the external world, we witness the birth of her pride, which is inordinate precisely because of its defensive nature.

Úrsula Buendía, Amaranta's mother, reflects on the same problems in a different light. She comes to believe that behind Amaranta's apparently casual and callous behaviour there lies an emotional failure that is the product of her daughter's essentially passionate nature. Úrsula sees Amaranta as caught in 'a mortal struggle between a boundless love and an invincible cowardice', and concludes that 'the irrational fear that Amaranta had always had of her own tormented heart had triumphed in the end.'

Both Amaranta and Rebeca survive into old age to endure, or to savour, the solitude of a living death. Amaranta's long-preserved virginity is triumphant over a lifetime, feverishly sustained all through the dangerous excitement of an affair with her nephew, Aureliano José; she spends the last years of her life symbolically sewing her own shroud. Rebeca, on the other hand, seems mysteriously implicated in the death of her husband, José Arcadio, after which she withdraws from the world: 'As soon as they took the body out, Rebeca locked the doors of her house and buried herself alive', hardly ever to be seen again, and forgotten by almost everyone in Macondo, except, predictably, by her old rival, Amaranta, who continues to give some sort of shape to her own existence by feeding intensely on the absurd hatreds of the past. This rigid dependence on a falsified and simplistic model of the past is reflected, too, in the character of Fernanda del Carpio, the woman who comes to Macondo from Bogotá, or somewhere close by, and who is clearly the representative of García Márquez's hated world of highland Colombia. By seeking to impose the standards of a reactionary colonial culture and the observances of the most repressive form of Catholicism, she succeeds in making the house in Macondo as mournful as the colonial mansion in which she was brought up. She is one of the characters in the novel upon whom the most overt authorial criticism is directed; and, in a loathsome act that symbolizes everything that is wrong with Fernanda and her beliefs, she condemns her daughter, Meme, to a silent hell in the same convent in the highlands where she herself was educated as a girl, as a punishment for her daughter's affair with the apprentice mechanic, Mauricio Babilonia.

This life-denying attachment to images of a falsified past is widely shared by the characters in the novel. It is an implicit feature, for example, of the apparently endless reduplication of names throughout the book, all Arcadios and Aurelianos in a deliberately confusing cascade of generation upon generation of Buendías. Yet of all the characters, the one through whom the process of self-conscious and wilful alienation from life is most fully explored is Colonel Aureliano Buendía. We saw in chapter I above how Aureliano is loosely modelled on the Colombian Liberal general Rafael Uribe Uribe, and how, through the progress of his military career, we are given an insight into the utter futility of the twenty years of civil war that occupy so large a space in the development of Macondo, and which are the direct reflection of the long period of civil unrest in Colombia that ended with the War of a Thousand Days. At first, Macondo is a town 'without political passions', and Aureliano himself has only the vaguest ideas about the meaning of the terms Liberal and Conservative. However, with the increasing influence of the outside world, elections arrive in Macondo. Aureliano witnesses a crude example of electoral fraud, perpetrated by the Conservatives, and so he decides to become a Liberal. There follows his rise to power as a Liberal war leader, the miserable drama of his thirty-two lost military campaigns, the progressive degradation of his sensibility and humanity, and, finally, in the face of a reality that he cannot endure, the retreat into the solitude of his workshop where, determined to erase all painful memories, he lives out a mockery of a life, endlessly engaged in the production of tiny golden fishes.

One evening, at the end of the war, Aureliano comes to a clear recognition of what has happened to him when, 'for the first time in many years', he dares to look his mother in the face:

> . . . In an instant he discovered the scratches, the welts, the sores, the ulcers and scars that more than half a century of daily life had left on her, and he realized that these ravages did not even arouse a feeling of pity in him. Then he made one last effort to search in his heart for the place where his affections had rotted away, and he could not find it . . .

Later, his mother, Úrsula Buendía, reflects that the truth about her son is even bleaker than she had imagined; for she comes to feel that the civil war has been only an incidental, peripheral event in the process of Aureliano's disintegration as a human being:

> She realized that Colonel Aureliano Buendía had not lost his affection for the family because of the brutalizing effect of the war, as she used to think before, but that he had never loved anyone . . . She sensed that he had not fought so many wars out of idealism, as everyone thought, nor given up out of fatigue on the brink of victory, as everyone thought, but that he had won and lost for the same motive, pure and sinful pride. She came to the conclusion that the son for whom she would have given her life was simply a man incapable of love . . .

It is this truth that Aureliano flees, deliberately excluding the past by seeking to create the illusion of a timeless circularity in the solitude of his workshop, voluntarily reducing himself to the status of 'an artisan without memories, whose only dream was to die of weariness in the oblivion and wretchedness of his little gold fishes'.

It is only through the conscious repression of the past, and the invention of an artificial world that recognizes no past, present, or future, that Aureliano can stay alive. Significantly, therefore, his death is preceded by a momentary return to the world of memory: one afternoon, he hears the distant sounds of an approaching circus, and 'for the first time since his youth he consciously fell into a trap of nostalgia'. He allows himself to re-live that magical afternoon, heralded in the opening sentence of the novel, when his father had taken him to see the great block of ice which the gypsies had brought to Macondo. This fragment of a remembered past will prove too much for him to bear. In one of the novel's most moving passages, Aureliano stands to watch the circus parade pass by:

> He saw a woman dressed in gold on the neck of an elephant. He saw a sad dromedary. He saw a bear dressed like a Dutchwoman keeping time to the music with a ladle and a saucepan. He saw the clowns doing acrobatics at the rear of the parade, and he saw once more the face of his miserable solitude when everything had passed by, and there was nothing but the bright expanse of the street, and the air full of flying ants, and a few onlookers peering into the precipice of uncertainty.

A few moments later, Aureliano is dead, overcome by the terrifying nothingness that he has made of life, or that life has made of him. He dies unnoticed and alone, discovered only the following morning as the vultures descend over his body.

The fate of Aureliano will be the fate of all the Buendías, as of Macondo itself. Oblivion lies ahead for everything and everyone. For a time, the memory of Colonel Aureliano Buendía survives through a street which, on the anniversary of the ending of the civil wars, was named after him by the Conservative opponents he had fought for so long. However, even this meagre resource proves unreliable in the end. In the closing pages of the novel, we find one of the very last of the Aurelianos searching through the local archives in an attempt to trace his lineage; an arthritic priest, watching from his hammock, takes an interest and asks his name:

> 'Aureliano Buendía,' he said.
> 'Then don't wear yourself out with searching,' exclaimed the priest with unshakeable conviction. 'Many years ago there was a street here with that name, and at that time it was the custom for people to give their children the names of streets.'

Nothing that the people of Macondo can ever do will save them, for they are subject to the workings of an external world that remains resolutely independent of them. The Buendías have numerous failings and inadequacies, and often act from what seem to be the worst of motives. In the end, however, I think it is as victims, rather than villains, that they face condemnation to the ultimate solitude of extinction.

VI

Macondo – ii

A people without history is like the wind in
the buffalo grass.   (Sioux saying)

It is, of course, the arrival in Macondo of a United States banana
company that leads to the eventual disintegration of the town and its
inhabitants. Predictably, and in keeping with a pattern I have already
noted, the first signs of the coming invasion are clear enough to the
reader, but are lost on the local people. A faceless gringo, Mr
Herbert, who specializes in the captive balloon business, comes to
town. The people are unimpressed with his balloons, having seen far
more exciting inventions in the hands of the gypsies, and Mr Herbert
is preparing to go and ply his trade elsewhere when the Buendías
invite him to lunch. There he tastes the local bananas, and the rest
follows. The banana industry moves in, and Macondo, superficially,
at least, is now connected to the modern world. Electricity, the
telephone, the gramophone, and the cinema arrive at about this
time, while another faceless gringo, Mr Brown, brings in the first
motor car. Most of the people in Macondo are disorientated and
bewildered by the invasion, no longer sure of their position in the
town. Ferocious guard dogs appear, and the North Americans build a
separate enclosure for their own people, surrounded by an electric
fence. The banana company alters the course of the river, the magical
river 'with its white stones and icy currents', and it is placed out of
sight, behind the cemetery. The streets are suddenly full of brawling
adventurers and scandalous sexual behaviour, and the local police
are replaced by hired assassins armed with machetes. Eight months
after Mr Herbert's visit, the transformation of Macondo is complete:
' "Look at the mess we've got ourselves into", Colonel Aureliano
Buendía used to say at the time, "just for inviting a gringo to eat
bananas".'

Not everyone in Macondo feels this way, however. Aureliano Segundo and Úrsula, for example, are exhilarated by the rapid changes and the sudden influx of new people from a wider world. What took place in the early years of the twentieth century, in connexion with the development of the banana industry on Colombia's Atlantic coast, occurred in many other places in Latin America, and throughout the world, with foreign exploitation of a wide range of products: sugar cane, coffee, cotton, petroleum, and so on. The cycle is a familiar one: foreign investment in these industries creates boom conditions, leading to increases in local wages, and offers a seductive impression of progress and modernization. It produces new social conditions, suggests the possibility of something different, new and exciting. Even in the highly stratified social world of Macondo (and we should remember that such stratification long pre-dates the arrival of the banana company) there are Saturday dances where local people and newcomers mix; Meme Buendía makes friends with Mr Brown's daughter, learns to swim, to play tennis, and even to eat Virginia ham with slices of pineapple.

The damage which so often results from external involvement in developing national economies is not, however, always as immediately apparent as the glittering social and economic transformations that seem to be on offer. Foreign exploitation of natural resources has done much, for example, to inhibit the growth of strong national industries, and has worked to create ties of economic dependency, so that many countries of the developing world – not least, the much-derided 'banana republics' – have come to serve as little more than convenient repositories of raw materials. Foreign companies, quite naturally, have seldom shown much interest in genuinely modernizing or progressive measures, such as providing better housing, education, or health-care, or training for local personnel beyond a necessary minimum. Inevitably, corruption tends to follow upon the necessity of maintaining the free flow of profit. At both local and national levels, foreign companies have traditionally been adept at ensuring that their particular needs and interests are well represented and understood, either through informal systems of bribery, or through action to secure the passing of formal legislation beneficial to them. As García Márquez has pointed out, a worker on the plantations in the heady days of the banana boom might earn three times the wages of the local mayor or judge, so that justice was invariably for sale. The same has proved true in the circumstances of the recent marijuana and cocaine boom.

The banana industry in Colombia began to develop in the late 1880s. A necessary precondition for such development was the building of the Santa Marta railway, between 1882 and 1887. This railway ('the innocent yellow train that was to bring . . . so many delights and misfortunes, and so many changes, calamities and feelings of nostalgia to Macondo') initially linked the port of Santa Marta with the town of Ciénaga; it was later extended further south, reaching Aracataca in 1906. In García Márquez's account, in *One Hundred Years of Solitude*, it is one of the Buendías who initiates the building of the railway: Aureliano Triste conceives of the idea of linking Macondo with the outside world as a means of expanding his local ice-making business, and so, ironically, opens the way for the final destruction of his family and his town.

Historically, the dominant influence in the development of the banana industry in Colombia was the United Fruit Company. United Fruit, a conglomerate formed in 1899 through the merger of a number of US companies, began operations in the area around Santa Marta in the very first years of the twentieth century. By the 1930s, the company controlled some 60 per cent of the banana trade world-wide, and, according to a Colombian government report of 1938, at that time owned three-quarters of the banana-producing land in the department of Magdalena. In the mid-1960s, the company changed its name to United Brands.

The United Fruit Company has long attracted controversy, as a result of its methods and its successes. A lyrical account of its history and development is provided in a book by Stacy May and Galo Plaza entitled *The United Fruit Company in Latin America*. This is how they convey the atmosphere of the early years:

It is not a simple success story from the beginning; it is more than that. It is a story of dreams and ambitions, of struggle and despair, of misunderstanding and even of hatred, of trial and error . . . it is the saga of the rise of stout-hearted men, big as Ulysses in their achievements. It could be written as a romance, its pages bathed in the clean salt spray of the tropical seas as flying fish scatter before the bows of graceful Yankee clipper ships.

Others, of course, have felt rather differently about the company. In particular, it was the near-monopoly of the banana trade that opponents of United Fruit found alarming, for this allowed the company to leave large tracts of land uncultivated, as a means, among other things, of controlling the price of the fruit. Estimates suggest that, in some areas, up to 85 per cent of available land was left fallow, and, in countries where many families were permanently undernourished for want of enough land on which to grow food, such a policy, whatever its commercial attractions, was bound to appear provocative.

Moreover, the industrial power of United Fruit also enabled the company to acquire considerable political influence. Its role in 1954, for example, when it helped to bring to an end the only period of democratic government that Guatemala has ever enjoyed, is now well known. The details of that affair are carefully explored by Stephen Kinzer and Stephen Schlesinger in their book *Bitter Fruit: the Untold Story of the American Coup in Guatemala*, published in 1983.

Bananas have never constituted a high proportion of Colombia's principal exports, generally less than 10 per cent of the total, compared with figures of up to nearly 80 per cent for the contribution of coffee exports. So, in that sense, Colombia has never been a banana republic. However, the banana industry played a vital role in the economy of the Santa Marta area, where between twenty and thirty thousand workers were employed on the plantations. The promotion of the banana trade was also a key element of Colombian government policy in the period 1904–9, under the presidency of Rafael Reyes. This was the time of the real banana boom. Early in 1907, Reyes proposed, and Congress later approved, a measure which exempted the banana industry from all export taxes for eight years. Partly under the stimulus of such measures, Colombia's banana exports increased rapidly, from 787,244 bunches in 1904 to 3,222,152 bunches in 1909. There is, incidentally, a fine irony in the manner in which Reyes came to abandon the Colombian political scene. His presidency had come under increasing attack from both Conservative and Liberal groups, and, by the middle of 1909, his position had become impossible. In June of that year, he went to the banana zone on a presidential tour of inspection. On the evening of 13 June, he failed to appear at a reception in his honour, and secretly left the country on board a United Fruit banana boat bound for England.

After 1909, banana production in Colombia continued to increase, if at a less frenetic rate, reaching a peak in the 1920s. The latter decade was a time of generalized economic boom in Colombia known as the 'Dance of the Millions'. United States private investment in the country developed on a very large scale, leading to the establishment of important construction projects, which, in turn, led to a shortage of cheap labour, and it is in this context that the increasing evidence of working class militancy may be best understood. Paul Oquist notes that, between 1924 and 1927, the real wages of agricultural workers increased by 30 per cent. Other signs of the growing strength of organized labour were an increasing use of strike action, particularly directed against foreign business interests, and the formation of radical political groupings, such as the Revolutionary Socialist Party, founded in 1926. Over a period of some fifteen years, there were four major strikes against United Fruit in the banana zone; they took place in 1918, 1924, 1928, and 1934, and it is the third of these strikes that figures prominently in *One Hundred Years of Solitude*.

The organization of the 1928 strike began early in October, when a meeting of workers' delegates was called to formulate a series of demands to present to the company. There were nine demands in all, affecting such matters as housing, collective insurance, health-care, and education. In many ways, the most important demand was the apparently straightforward one that the United Fruit Company should recognize that it was indeed the legal employer of the workers it employed. The practice of the company at that time of hiring workers through small labour contractors was enabling it to bypass all existing Colombian labour legislation. As was customary policy, the company declined to negotiate over the list of demands, and a general strike was declared throughout the banana zone in the second week of November. The strike was a legal one, as an official government labour inspector, Alberto Martínez, confirmed. He issued a report favourable to the position of the workers, but the prevailing conditions were such that he simply found himself arrested as a result.

In fact, the Colombian government was itself in dispute with the United Fruit Company over two issues: the refusal of the company to allow the railway to be used to carry the bananas of independent Colombian producers, and the company's unwillingness to relinquish its unlimited control, which it had enjoyed since 1907, over the irrigation waters in the zone. For all that, the government, almost inevitably, felt obliged to side with the company and against the strikers. There may, as Paul Oquist suggests, have been a genuine fear that the United States would intervene militarily on behalf of the company; only a few months earlier, the US had conducted one of its periodic invasions of Nicaragua, in defence of 'American lives and property'. Whatever the motivation, the Colombian government sent its troops into the banana zone, under the command of General Carlos Cortés Vargas; over four hundred strikers were jailed, and violent resistance followed. The attitude of the strikers was scarcely made more flexible by the position adopted by a commission sent from the Ministry of Industry to settle the dispute. One member of that commission gave a speech, quoted in part in Miguel Urrutia's *The Development of the Colombian Labor Movement*, in which he said:

> The rural salaries in the banana zone are the highest in the republic, and the lack of organization and morality among workers in this region makes any wage increase useless . . . since any surplus over a subsistence wage will be spent by the workers on vices which are harmful to their health, and the wage increase will therefore not be translated into results truly beneficial to the working classes.

By 4 December, the company felt confident enough to try to resume full-scale production with the support of its strike-breaking workers and the army. This was bound to lead to further confrontation. On the night of 5 December, Cortés Vargas received a telegram informing him that the government had declared a state of siege in the banana zone. Cortés Vargas then issued a decree banning all meetings of more than three people. That same evening, a crowd of striking workers began to gather in the square by the railway station in Ciénaga. At 1.30 a.m. on 6 December, Cortés Vargas arrived in Ciénaga with an army detachment. The decree prohibiting gatherings in public places was read out, and the crowd ordered to disperse. When the strikers refused to move, Cortés Vargas gave the order to fire into the crowd, and a number of people − casualty figures vary widely, as we shall see – were killed. After that, the zone was in turbulence for months. The strikers reacted violently against company property and personnel, and the army responded with brutally repressive measures. Once again, the number of people killed remains uncertain.

In the aftermath of the massacre in Ciénaga, and the generalized reign of terror that followed, something like a conspiracy of silence developed over what had taken place. The Colombian government clearly had nothing to gain from a revelation of the truth, and the people living in the banana zone were understandably reluctant to expose themselves to further reprisals. It was in these circumstances that the young Colombian lawyer, Jorge Eliécer Gaitán, made his political reputation. Twenty years later, Gaitán would be the leader of the Colombian Liberal party, and it was his assassination in Bogotá, on 9 April 1948, that opened up the long period of the *violencia*. At the time of the massacre of the striking banana workers, Gaitán was in Europe. On his return to Colombia, he went to the zone and spent some days there, conducting his own unofficial enquiry. He collected written and oral testimony, and later, in September 1929, he took advantage of his recent election as a member of the Colombian Congress to denounce the government's conduct in a highly emotional debate. As Urrutia says: 'This was to be one of the most famous debates in Colombian parliamentary history.' The visitors' gallery was packed, and Gaitán's oratory quickly established his authority as one of the few effective populist politicians Colombia has yet produced. It is interesting that, early on in the debate, Gaitán read out a letter denouncing the barbarous conduct of the armed forces in the zone, written by the parish priest of Aracataca, Father Angarita.

García Márquez's account of the strike and the massacre in *One Hundred Years of Solitude* is clear, and, on most of the essential points, in rough accord with the known facts. What distinguishes his version from others is his deeply satirical presentation of the antics of the banana company, and a conscious exaggeration of detail. Fernanda is the first character in the novel to notice the signs of coming trouble, as she returns to Macondo, after committing her daughter to the convent, on a train guarded by armed police. The great strike begins two weeks later, and José Arcadio Segundo emerges as one of its leaders (' "That's all we needed," Fernanda said to herself, "an anarchist in the family" '). Cortés Vargas is mentioned by name in the course of the narrative, and, indeed, García Márquez has drawn quite closely on the account of the massacre which Cortés Vargas himself published in 1929. Readers of Spanish interested in the parallels between the two versions will find the relevant text in the books by either Lucila Inés Mena or Gustavo Alfaro. The two versions differ radically, however, over the question of casualties. In García Márquez's account, the dead number more than three thousand, and there are only two survivors, José Arcadio Segundo and a small child, neither of whom, significantly, will be believed when they try to tell the story of what they have seen. According to Cortés Vargas, on the other hand, only nine people were killed when he ordered his troops to fire on the crowd. Almost certainly, neither of these casualty figures is correct – though, for his part, García Márquez has frequently insisted that accuracy in this instance was never his primary consideration.

García Márquez seems to be concerned with three important issues in his reconstruction of the Ciénaga massacre. First, there is his natural sympathy with the position of the strikers, with their demands for better living and working conditions, with the general political dimension of the strike. Second, there is his desire to rescue from a continuing conspiracy of silence an important event in the history of Colombia. The fact that neither of those who witnessed the massacre is able to persuade others of the truth about what happened is a reflection both of the fear which later silenced so many of those who took part in the events of 1928, and of the unwillingness of the Colombian establishment to acknowledge its share of responsibility. This large-scale, collective repression of the past has potentially lethal consequences. For once you fail to admit the existence of something important in your past, you are close to denying the past any significance at all; and, from then on, it is easy to deprive the present and the future of all significance too. In their submission to a process of wilful forgetfulness, the people of Macondo are taking a road that leads towards the picture-postcard cliché of the endlessly backward, yet always happily smiling, group of natives, caught in the illusion of an eternal circularity, reduced to a passivity which only the intrusion of an historical perspective might work to disturb. This process of repression can be seen in the response of the woman whom José Arcadio Segundo meets as he escapes from the train that is carrying away the dead. The woman may well have lost members of her own family in the massacre; she must, at least, have some idea of what has occurred, but she says: 'There haven't been any dead here'; and she adds: 'Since the time of your uncle, the colonel, nothing has happened in Macondo.' That is precisely the attitude which the establishment seeks to create. A little later, as the leaders of the strike are being systematically rounded up by the military and killed, we have a confirmation of the 'official view'. Relatives of the dead and missing come in search of news, but the army officers tell them: 'You must have been dreaming . . . Nothing has happened in Macondo, nothing is happening, and nothing will ever happen. This is a happy town.'

García Márquez's third area of interest, in connexion with the Ciénaga massacre, relates to a question that recurs frequently in his writing: what can anyone legitimately seek to know about the 'truth' of an historical event? Something clearly happened in the square in Ciénaga, but what exactly? What is recoverable? We have the account by Cortés Vargas. He argues that, on the night of 5 December, the situation was extremely precarious. Large numbers of people who supported the strike were advancing towards Ciénaga; to have delayed would have been to risk much greater bloodshed. Furthermore, he says that he could not be sure of the loyalty of all his troops. Then we have an account by Alberto Castrillón, a prominent strike leader; we have Gaitán's retrospective and highly emotive version; we have contemporary newspaper reports, including the editorial published in the Liberal Santa Marta paper *El Estado*, on 5 December, which saw the whole social fabric of the zone under threat and the menace of Bolshevism in the air. We have, too, the text of a telegram sent by the Head of the US Legation in Colombia to the US Secretary of State on 16 December 1928, which reads, in part: 'I have the honor to report that the Bogotá representative of the United Fruit Company told me yesterday that the total number of strikers killed by the Colombian military exceed one thousand.' Lucila Inés Mena and Gustavo Alfaro have gathered together, in their respective books, a fascinating collection of accounts relating to the period, some of which fail to mention the massacre in Ciénaga at all, while others reveal radically differing attitudes in respect of the scale and ultimate importance of what took place, with widely differing casualty statistics to support their various positions. So García

Márquez's own account of the massacre, with its conscious exaggerations, is also a reminder that all versions of the past are incurably fictitious; and the reader is thus further prepared for the conclusion of the novel, with its deeply self-dramatizing conviction that literature can never bring the past back to life, and its clear challenge to recognize that what we have been reading has, of course, been a fiction all along.

Nevertheless, the massacre of the striking banana-plantation workers has not, in the end, been forgotten. García Márquez's novel is only one of a number of Colombian novels that have attempted to reconstruct the events of 1928. In Ciénaga itself, there is now a monument to those killed, the work of Rodrigo Arenas Betancurt. On 5 December 1978, the fiftieth anniversary of the massacre, some 8,000 people gathered in the Plaza de Santamaría in Bogotá to pay homage to the dead. Of considerable interest, too, is the series of articles by Carlos Low which were published in 1978, also in commemoration of the fiftieth anniversary of the events. The articles appeared in *Alternativa* (nos 187–191, November to December 1978), the magazine which García Márquez helped to found in 1974 precisely to serve as an alternative source of information about the history and politics of Latin America. The subsequent history of Colombia's banana zone has, however, been mixed. The great strike of 1934, the first successful strike against United Fruit in Colombia, did much to recover the ground lost by the banana workers in 1928, but United Fruit simply decided, as a result, to reduce exports from Colombia, and to increase its holdings in Ecuador and Central America instead. Between 1943 and 1946, United Fruit pulled out of the zone altogether: in 1944, production had fallen to 441,394 bunches, from a peak of 10,332,113 bunches in 1929. The company resumed operations after 1946, through a subsidiary, the Compañía Frutera de Sevilla, finally selling out, in 1966, to the Colombian government, on terms which many felt were unduly favourable to the company.

After the massacre of the plantation-workers in *One Hundred Years of Solitude*, the banana company takes it final revenge. The terrible Mr Brown calls down a storm upon Macondo. It rains for nearly five years, and, when the biblical flood ceases and people look at their world again, all has changed:

> Macondo was in ruins. In the marshy streets there were remains
> of broken furniture, animal skeletons covered with red lilies, the
> last reminders of the hordes of outsiders who had fled from
> Macondo as recklessly as they had arrived.

The banana company takes away everything it has brought, leaving
the people, somehow, with so much less than they had before. The
narrative is now increasingly coloured with images of decay, as the
influence of the outside world recedes, and Macondo returns to the
primitive chaos out of which it was first constructed. During the time
of the rains, Úrsula Buendía, who has tried to hold the family
together through a succession of generations and disasters, becomes
the mere plaything of the young Aureliano and Amaranta Úrsula, 'a
big broken-down doll that they carried about from one corner to
another'. She seems to have been so old for so long that she could
never die, and yet, after the rains, she does, mad and blind, one
morning just before Easter. Then Rebeca dies: she, conversely, has
been for so long out of reach, locked away in her voluntary exile, that
it is hard to believe she has not been dead for many years already.
Fernanda, too, dies, bringing to an end the aristocratic aspirations of
her impoverished highland family; and, as she nears death, she
achieves something of the humanity she never knew in life: 'She felt
so old, so worn out, so far away from the best moments of her life, that
she even yearned for those that she remembered as the worst . . .
She became more human in her solitude.'

There is a moment when, had this been a different sort of novel,
one might have looked forward to the possibility of an escape from
the unremitting process of decline. Amaranta Úrsula, who has
completed her education in Brussels, returns one day to Macondo
with Gaston, her newly acquired husband. Immediately, she sets
about putting the Buendía house in order:

> She scattered the red ants which had already taken possession of
> the veranda, brought the rose bushes back to life, uprooted the
> weeds, and planted ferns, marjoram, and begonias again in the
> flowerpots along the railing.

There follows a flurry of carpenters, locksmiths, and masons 'who
repaired the cracks in the floor, put doors and windows back on their

hinges, restored the furniture, and whitewashed the walls inside and out . . .' and the world when Macondo was young seems about to be re-lived through the impulse of a Buendía who, returning with a knowledge and perspective of the outside world, might finally break with the endlessly incestuous round of the Buendía family. However, this will never happen. Amaranta Úrsula's husband recognizes very early on that his wife's determination to go back to Macondo has been 'provoked by a mirage of nostalgia'. When they had first known each other, in Europe, 'she spoke to him of Macondo as the brightest and most peaceful town in the world, and of an enormous house, scented with marjoram, where she wished to live until old age with a loyal husband and two indomitable sons who would be called Rodrigo and Gonzalo, and never Aureliano and José Arcadio . . .' This nostalgia for an impossible Macondo, a Macondo whose peace was shattered many years before her birth, leads her relentlessly back into the depths of the familial circles from which there is no recall. Her children will never be called Rodrigo and Gonzalo (the names of García Márquez's own two sons). She is fated to fall in love with her nephew, the young Aureliano with whom she used to play as a child, and she will have only one son. He will be born out of her incestuous passion and will have the tail of a pig – the child feared and anticipated for so long by Úrsula. He will be given the name Aureliano, and it is with him that the Buendía line will come to an end.

The tone of the final sections of the novel is not, however, one of unrelieved gloom. There is a terrible sense of impending destruction, but there is also a very different strain in the narrative, a kind of self-conscious and very literary playfulness. García Márquez writes himself into the story as the character Gabriel, along with his friends Álvaro, Germán, and Alfonso (see above, p. 42), and then he writes his friends out of the book, sending Alvaro on a wildly evocative train-journey across the United States, and consigning the other two to instant oblivion. Gabriel stays on in Macondo, until he wins a trip to Paris as first prize in a contest run by a French magazine; then he, too, deserts Macondo, and leaves for Europe 'with two changes of clothing, a pair of shoes, and the complete works of Rabelais', a parody of García Márquez's departure from Colombia in 1955. In the concluding pages of the novel, the narrator also tells the mad story of Gaston's attempts to bring an airmail service to Macondo, a project which ends in failure when the plane he has ordered is delivered by mistake to the Makondos of Tanganyika; incidentally, the reference to 'a group of German aviators' who are in competition with Gaston vaguely links the episode to the time of the founding of the Colombian national airline, Avianca, in 1919. Avianca is the oldest airline company in South America, and there was prominent German involvement during its early years.

For all the playfulness, it is the sense of desolation and destruction which prevails, as the novel reaches towards a conclusion. When Amaranta Úrsula and Aureliano fall in love, they are no longer able to think of anything outside their passion, a passion which is complete, self-contained, and physical to a degree that surpasses everything else in the novel. Now it is clear that there will be no revival of the Buendía fortunes, and Amaranta Úrsula is content to give the house back to its natural predators, as long as she is left in peace to make love:

> In the bewilderment of passion, she saw the ants devastating the garden, satiating their prehistoric hunger on the timbers of the house, and she saw the torrent of living lava taking possession of the veranda once again, but she bothered to fight them only when she found them in her bedroom.

The couple's love is so real, so exclusive, so destructive, that they lose 'their sense of reality, the notion of time, the rhythm of daily habits', and their sexuality is so intense, that 'in a short time they did more damage than the red ants'. They close themselves to the world and become trapped in a fatal nostalgia, for 'the uncertainty of the future made them turn their hearts towards the past'. Then follows the sad irony of the birth of their child, who might have been a saviour, because he alone, of all the Buendías in the novel, has been born out of love:

> Through her tears, Amaranta Úrsula saw that he was one of the great Buendías, powerful and headstrong like the José Arcadios, with the open and clairvoyant eyes of the Aurelianos, and predisposed to begin the race again from the beginning and cleanse it of its pernicious vices and its solitary calling, for he was the only one in a century who had been engendered with love.

However, the reader knows well enough by now that this is not a book in which there are new starts. Amaranta Úrsula dies in a torrent of blood after the birth of her child. Aureliano wanders in grief through the wreck that Macondo has become, leaving his new-born son at the mercy of the devouring ants, and all that remains is the final, and long-anticipated, revelation enshrined in the manuscripts of Melquíades.

The reader has been aware, from very early on in the book, of the existence of Melquíades's manuscripts, but, until the last moment, their precise content and status remain obscure. Aureliano Segundo attempts to decipher the texts at a point about half way through the novel, but Melquíades tells him, in a visitation, that the manuscripts can only be understood when they have reached one hundred years of age; and this is the clue to the fact that what the parchments contain is Melquíades's account, written in advance and with full foreknowledge, of the one hundred years of the Buendía family that are also the subject of the novel we are reading. José Arcadio Segundo, in his turn, attempts a decipherment, and it is he who initiates the young Aureliano in the study of the texts. Aureliano will complete the decipherment, and, at that point, the novel will end. Aureliano shares a privileged relationship with the narrator, and is clearly designated as a source of knowledge within the book. It is he, alone of all the characters, who accepts what José Arcadio Segundo has to say about the massacre of the banana workers. It is he who discovers that the language of Melquíades's manuscripts is Sanskrit, and, in the final moments, it is he who finds the code which renders the texts intelligible.

The point at which everything becomes clear to Aureliano is the moment when he sees the body of his new-born son being dragged away by the ants. In an instant, he understands a key sentence in the manuscripts: '*The first of the line is tied to a tree and the last is being eaten by the ants.*' He realizes that the parchments contain a history of his own family, extending over seven generations, from the time of José Arcadio Buendía, who spent the last years of his life in madness, tied to a chestnut tree, down to the death of the final Buendía, his son Aureliano. He realizes, too, that his own destiny will be contained within the manuscripts, and so he withdraws from the world to complete their decipherment. As he reads, the great wind that will destroy Macondo begins to blow around him. He reads of the moment of his own conception, and of his place in the predetermined scheme of things. Everything, he discovers, has been known in advance, and can only end in the way that was foreseen. So that when, in 1595, the English pirate Francis Drake sacked Riohacha, which was then a tiny village of pearl-fishers, hardly bigger than the early Macondo, it was only so that the Buendía story could be set in motion, and so that, in the end, he, Aureliano, would fall in love with his aunt, Amaranta Úrsula, and that, through the intensity of their passion, they would destroy the race of the Buendías.

By now, 'Macondo was already a terrifying whirlwind of dust and rubble being spun about by the wrath of the biblical hurricane', and Aureliano moves on quickly, passionate to know the end. He reaches the point in the manuscripts where he is captured in the very act of deciphering them, a moment of intersection that is pure present, after which, for Aureliano, all is prophecy. He reads on, into the future, but he understands now that he will never leave the room in which he is reading; he has no future beyond the story in which he is a character, and the last sentence of the parchments can only be a sentence of death. On the final page, he discovers, in the words of Emir Rodríguez Monegal, that he is simply 'a ghost who has been dreamed by another man', just a fictional character, 'trapped in a labyrinth of words', and that his fate, completely conterminous with the Macondo that is dying, is to be annihilated so totally that not even a memory will remain.

One Hundred Years of Solitude works consistently on emotional and imaginative levels that are both highly personal and massively collective. For García Márquez himself, the book represented the culmination of a long-felt desire to write the story of Macondo, to bring the past into imaginative focus, as a means of trying to connect the cosmopolitan self he had acquired with a small Colombian town and a childhood world that now seemed inescapably magical. The book is thus about a search for an origin, for a way back, and that is why the narrator is so close to the Aureliano who, in the final pages of the novel, sets out to decode the mystery of his own past. In the end, the book accepts that the past is only recoverable as fiction, and implies that, once this inevitability is acknowledged, it may then, as pure fiction, be relegated to oblivion. Of course, the emotional tensions involved are far more complex than that, but, still, an important element of exorcism is attached to the character of Melquíades, his magic parchments, and the narrator's relationship to them.

So, *One Hundred Years of Solitude* is a contribution to a private demonology, a personal reflection on one of the great paradoxes of the past: that the past will not leave you alone, and yet it cannot be recovered in a way that will sustain you in the present, a paradox which some people experience as torture, and others, more softly, as an invitation to nostalgia. The story of Macondo is also, as we have seen, a highly self-conscious literary work. It is concerned with the function of writing generally, with the proper role of literature, its limits, illusions, and deceptions. One of the most problematical aspects of any narrative is that, by its very form, it can so easily work to undermine our sense of the utterly unrepeatable nature of experience. The past of a novel is always there to be recovered, by an effortless turning of the pages. As readers, we can always begin again, return to the time when Macondo is young, to the point where a favourite character is still alive. However, the world outside the book is different, and *One Hundred Years of Solitude*, like *The Autumn of the Patriarch*, calls on the reader to recognize that fundamental difference, with an affirmation of the absolute significance of the present, and a rejection of the labyrinths of nostalgia in which the imagination can so happily lose its way. Both novels, in the end, reach out towards a plane of total clarity, offering a truth which, when formally summarized, seems merely banal, and yet which, supported by a passionately creative conviction, attains the status almost of a revelation: that there is only one life, 'arduous and ephemeral', and that, divorced from the constant recognition that this is so, there can be nothing truly of value in the world.

One of García Márquez's greatest strengths, I think, lies in his intuitive understanding of both the infinite possibilities and the inherent limitations of the creative imagination. He knows all about the power of nostalgia, and he never loses sight of the need to resist it. He could have made a simple tragedy out of the story of the Buendías, and sometimes we come close to feeling that *One Hundred Years of Solitude* is, indeed, a tragedy. But the novel is never allowed to remain on that level, for, if it is a story about the failure of a dream, it is about a dream that was flawed and irrelevant from the start. The desire to remake the world from the beginning, to found a new identity, whether personal, tribal, or continental, and to found it in freedom, divorced from all contaminating or degrading influences, is a compelling fantasy. Yet neither the past nor the present of Latin America allow for an honest myth of a lost paradise. When the Spanish arrived on the island of Hispaniola in the late fifteenth century, the indigenous population numbered a quarter of a million people. Forty years later, their numbers had been reduced to fewer than five hundred, largely through torture and forced labour, while today, in Haiti, which shares the island of Hispaniola with the Dominican Republic, people are old at forty, almost 80 per cent of the population is illiterate, and the overwhelming majority earn less than $150 a year.

The past is merely a dead weight on our shoulders, until we can learn from it. The Buendías are never given that chance, never allowed to comprehend the forces that are shaping their lives. So they live out their hundred years in an apparently timeless circularity, from which all notion of progress or development is absent. Nothing can be done for them, for they belong already to the past, a past which, like the Aracataca of childhood, is finished, unalterable, and which must be accepted as such, in all lucidity, and without self-deception. The great solitude of the dead will always lie beyond human understanding or power of action. Only in a present free from nostalgia is there a possibility of change; and, at the point where change appears as the only conceivable response to the unbearable solitude of the past, literature, as García Márquez has always recognized, must give way before the claims of other modes of thought and other forms of action.

Select Bibliography

AUTHOR'S NOTE

This book is primarily intended for readers who do not know Spanish, and, for that reason, I have translated all Spanish passages into English. Where the text concerned is taken from one of García Márquez's novels, I have naturally looked at the published translations by Gregory Rabassa and J.S. Bernstein, and, in the case of *One Hundred Years of Solitude*, I have also made use of the French translation by Claude and Carmen Durand, *Cent ans de solitude*, Paris, 1968. I willingly acknowledge a debt to these translations, although my own are generally more literal, less consciously literary.

The standard bibliography is *Gabriel García Márquez: an Annotated Bibliography, 1947–1979*, compiled by M.E. Fau, Westport, Connecticut, and London, 1980. This work contains a great deal of valuable reference material, but the annotations are, in general, unhelpful, and some of the summaries of individual items wildly inaccurate.

The best general book on García Márquez is by the Peruvian novelist Mario Vargas Llosa, *García Márquez: historia de un deicidio*, Barcelona, 1971. Inevitably, given its date, it excludes consideration of García Márquez's later works. The book is a very long one, and, for various reasons, unlikely to appear in English translation.

The best general books in English are G.R. McMurray, *Gabriel García Márquez*, New York, 1977, and R.L. Williams, *Gabriel García Márquez*, Boston, 1984. Also of interest are: R. Janes, *Gabriel García Márquez: Revolutions in Wonderland*, Columbia, Missouri, and London, 1981, and R.L. Sims, *The Evolution of Myth in Gabriel García Márquez from 'La hojarasca' to 'Cien años de soledad'*, Miami, 1981.

I list below the sources I have used in writing the present book.

I COLOMBIA

C.W. Bergquist, *Coffee and Conflict in Colombia, 1886–1910*, Durham, North Carolina, 1978

R.H. Dix, *Colombia: the Political Dimensions of Change*, New Haven, Connecticut, and London, 1967

R. Dumont and M.F. Mottin, *Le Mal-développement en Amérique latine: Mexique, Colombie, Brésil*, Paris, 1981

Enciclopedia de Colombia, 7 vols, Editorial Nueva Granada, Bogotá, 1977

G. García Márquez, 'Sólo para menores de 30 años', *Alternativa*, no. 114, 16–21 May 1977

—— 'Los idus de marzo de la oligarquía', *Alternativa*, no. 128, 15–22 August 1977

—— 'La literatura colombiana, un fraude a la nación', *Eco*, 33, no. 5, September 1978, 1200–06. This article first appeared in *Acción Liberal*, Bogotá, no. 2, April 1960. It is reprinted in vol. 4 of García Márquez, *Obra periodística*, ed. Jacques Gilard (see bibliography for chapter II below)

P. Gilhodes, *Politique et violence: la question agraire en Colombie, 1958–1971*, Paris, 1974

E. González Bermejo, *Cosas de escritores*, Montevideo, 1971

C. Harding, 'Colombia: New Beginning?', *Index on Censorship*, 11, no. 4, August 1982

A.E. Havens and W.L. Flinn (eds), *Internal Colonialism and Structural Change in Colombia*, New York, 1970

T. Jenkins, 'Drug Traffic', *New Statesman*, 29 October 1982

L.I. Mena, 'Bibliografía anotada sobre el ciclo de la violencia en la literatura colombiana', *Latin American Research Review*, 13, no. 3, 1978, 95–107

NACLA Report on the Americas, 17, no. 3, May–June 1983. Special number on Colombia

P. Oquist, *Violence, Conflict, and Politics in Colombia*, New York and London, 1980. An exceptionally fine analytical study

A. Orlov and R. Ueda, 'Central and South Americans', *Harvard Encyclopedia of American Ethnic Groups*, ed. S. Thernstrom, Cambridge, Massachusetts, and London, 1980

J.L. Payne, *Patterns of Conflict in Colombia*, New Haven, Connecticut, and London, 1968

R.W. Ramsey, *Survey and Bibliography of La Violencia in Colombia*, Gainesville, Florida, 1974

E. Santa, *Rafael Uribe Uribe: semblanza de un gran patriota*, Bogotá, 1959

—— *Nos duele Colombia: ensayos de sociología política*, Bogotá, 1962

J.M. Valdeblánquez, *Historia del Departamento del Magdalena y del territorio de La Guajira, desde el año de 1895 hasta el de 1963*, Santa Marta, 1964

R.S. Weinert, 'Violence in Pre-Modern Societies: Rural Colombia', *American Political Science Review*, 60, 1966, 340–7

World Development Report 1982, Oxford University Press, for the World Bank

II GABRIEL GARCÍA MÁRQUEZ

Alternativa, no. 194, 25 December 1978–22 January 1979, on the foundation of the human rights organization *Habeas*

J. Benson, 'García Márquez en *Alternativa* (1974–79): una bibliografía comentada', *Chasqui*, 8, no. 3, May 1979, 69–81

—— 'García Márquez en *Alternativa* (1979–80): una bibliografía comentada', *Chasqui*, 10, nos 2 and 3, February–May 1981, 41–6

D.W. Foster, 'Latin American Documentary Narrative', *PMLA*, 99, 1984, 41–55

G. García Márquez, *Relato de un náufrago: que estuvo diez días a la deriva en una balsa sin comer ni beber* . . . Barcelona, 1974
—— in *Alternativa*, no. 29, 25 March–10 April 1975. An important article on the evolution of his political beliefs
—— 'No se me ocurre ningún título', *Casa de las Américas*, 16, no. 100, January–February 1977, 84–9
—— in *Alternativa*, no. 124, 25 July–1 August 1977, the article on Rodolfo Walsh
—— *De viaje por los países socialistas: 90 días en la 'Cortina de Hierro'*, Bogotá, 1978
—— *Periodismo militante*, Bogotá, 1978
—— *García Márquez habla de García Márquez*, ed. A. Rentería Mantilla, Bogotá, 1979
—— 'Fantasía y creación artística en América Latina y el Caribe', *Texto Crítico*, 14, July–September 1979, 3–8
—— *Obra periodística*, 4 vols, ed. J. Gilard, Barcelona, 1981–3. García Márquez's journalistic writings 1948–1960. The introductions to these volumes contain much important information
—— 'The Last and Bad News of Haroldo Conti', *Index on Censorship*, 10, no. 6, December 1981
—— *'El olor de la guayaba': conversaciones con Plinio Apuleyo Mendoza*, Bogotá, 1982. English translation, *The Fragrance of Guava*, London, 1983
—— 'The Solitude of Latin America', *Granta*, 9, 1983, 56–60. The Nobel Prize acceptance speech, translated from the Spanish by Marina Castañeda
—— 'Mystery Without End', *Granta*, 11, 1984, 158–69. On the disappearance of Jaime Bateman Cayón, translated from the Spanish by Margaret Jull Costa
J. Gilard, 'El grupo de Barranquilla', *Revista Iberoamericana*, 50, nos 128–9, July–December 1984, 905–35
G.R. McMurray, 'García Márquez Interview and Legal Problems in Colombia', *Hispania*, 58, no. 3, September 1975, 553
K. Müller-Bergh, *'Relato de un náufrago*: Gabriel García Márquez's Tale of Shipwreck and Survival at Sea', *Books Abroad*, 47, no. 3, 1973, 460–6
R.M. Nixon, *Six Crises*, Garden City, New York, 1962
H.D. Oberhelman, 'Gabriel Eligio García habla de Gabito', *Hispania*, 61, 1978, 541–2. An interview with García Márquez's father, reprinted in *Gabriel García Márquez*, ed. P.G. Earle, Madrid, 1981
—— *The Presence of Faulkner in the Writings of García Márquez*, Lubbock, Texas, 1980. Of more general interest than the title implies
V. Rodríguez Núñez, ' "La peregrinación de la Jirafa"; García Márquez: su periodismo costeño', *Casa de las Américas*, no. 137, March–April 1983, 27–39
E. Santos Calderón, 'Alternativa: 6 años de compromiso', *Alternativa*, no. 257, 27 March 1980. A retrospective view of *Alternativa*, published in the final issue of the magazine
M. Simons, article on García Márquez in the *New York Times Book Review*, 5 December 1982

III   TWO STORIES OF THE *VIOLENCIA*

L.I. Bedoya and A. Escobar, *La novela de la violencia en Colombia: 'La mala hora' de Gabriel García Márquez, ficción y realidad*, Medellín, Colombia, 1980
V. Bollettino, *Breve estudio de la novelística de García Márquez*, Madrid, 1973
R.H. Dix, *Colombia: the Political Dimensions of Change*, New Haven, Connecticut, and London, 1967

A. Dorfman, 'La muerte como acto imaginativo en "Cien años de soledad" ', *Homenaje a G. García Márquez*, ed. H.F. Giacoman, Long Island City, New York, 1972, 107–39

P.G. Earle, 'El futuro como espejismo', *Gabriel García Márquez*, ed. P.G. Earle, Madrid, 1981, 81–90

G. García Márquez, *El coronel no tiene quien le escriba*, ed. G. Pontiero, Manchester, 1981

—— 'La Poésie à la portée de tous', *Magazine Littéraire*, no. 178, November 1981, 31

D. Kadir (ed.), *Triple espera: novelas cortas de Hispanoamérica*, New York, 1976. Contains the Spanish text of *No One Writes to the Colonel*

P. Oquist, *Violence, Conflict, and Politics in Colombia*, New York and London, 1980

G. and A. Reichel-Dolmatoff, *The People of Aritama: the Cultural Personality of a Colombian Mestizo Village*, Chicago, 1961

M. Vargas Llosa, *García Márquez: historia de un deicidio*, Barcelona, 1971

IV   AFTER SUCCESS: *THE AUTUMN OF THE PATRIARCH*; *CHRONICLE OF A DEATH FORETOLD*; and *EL AMOR EN LOS TIEMPOS DEL CÓLERA*

P.L. Ávila, 'Una lectura de *Crónica de una muerte anunciada*', *Casa de las Américas*, 24, no. 140, September–October 1983, 28–40

J.A. Booth, *The End and the Beginning: The Nicaraguan Revolution*, Boulder, Colorado, 1982

G. Brotherston, 'García Márquez and the Secrets of Saturno Santos', *Forum for Modern Language Studies*, 15, 1979, 144–9

—— (ed.), *Spanish American Modernist Poets*, Oxford, 1968

J.M. Cohen (ed.), *The Four Voyages of Christopher Columbus*, Harmondsworth, 1969. The passage dealing with the arrival of Columbus in the New World is on pp. 51–6

R. Debray, 'Cinco maneras de abordar lo inabordable o algunas consideraciones a propósito de *El otoño del patriarca*', *Nueva política*, 1, 1976, 253–60

J.H. Elliott, *The Old World and the New, 1492–1650*, Cambridge, 1970

J. Franco, *Spanish American Literature Since Independence*, London and New York, 1973

G. García Márquez, '. . . Mucho de lo que he contado es la primera vez que lo digo . . .', *América Latina*, Moscow, 25, no. 1, 1980, 79–105

—— 'Le Récit du récit', *Magazine Littéraire*, no. 178, November 1981, 33–5. See also the interview on 20–5 of the same issue

—— '*El olor de la guayaba*': conversaciones con Plinio Apuleyo Mendoza*, Bogotá, 1982

E. González Bermejo, *Cosas de escritores*, Montevideo, 1971

A. Kapcia, 'Revolution, the Intellectual and a Cuban Identity: The Long Tradition', *Bulletin of Latin American Research*, 1, 1982, 63–78

G.R. McMurray, *Gabriel García Márquez*, New York, 1977

S. Menton, 'Ver para no creer: *El otoño del patriarca*', *Gabriel García Márquez*, ed. P.G. Earle, Madrid, 1981, 189–209

J. Ortega, '*El otoño del patriarca*: texto y cultura', *Gabriel García Márquez*, ed. P.G. Earle, Madrid, 1981, 214–35

J.M. Oviedo, 'García Márquez: la novela como taumaturgia', *Gabriel García Márquez*, ed. P.G. Earle, Madrid, 1981, 171–88

G. Palau de Nemes, review of *The Autumn of the Patriarch*, in *Hispamérica*, 11–12, December 1975, 173–83. (In Spanish)

M. Palencia-Roth, *Gabriel García Márquez: la línea, el círculo y las metamorfosis del mito*, Madrid, 1983

L. Pavieso, '*El otoño del patriarca*: il romanzo della dittatura centenaria', *Gabriel García Márquez*, ed. P.L. Crovetto, Genoa, 1979, 159–73. A very interesting article

M. Pelling, *Cholera, Fever and English Medicine, 1825–65*, Oxford, 1978

Playboy, February 1983, interview with García Márquez

O. Prego, 'García Márquez o la memoria de la realidad', *Cuadernos de Marcha*, 2, no. 13, May–June 1981, 91–5

—— 'Conversaciones con Gabriel García Márquez', *Cuadernos de Marcha*, 3, no. 15, September–October 1981, 69–77

Time, 7 March 1983, on *Chronicle of a Death Foretold*

M. Tirado, 'Conversando con José Coronel Urtecho', *Nicaráuac*, 9, April 1983, 81–99

E. Torres, *La dramática vida de Rubén Darío*, 4th edition, Barcelona, 1966

J. Valle-Castillo, 'Rubén Darío: poeta y ciudadano de su tiempo', *Casa de las Américas*, 24, no. 142, January–February 1984, 155–66. An exceptionally informative article

C.D. Watland, *Poet-Errant: A Biography of Rubén Darío*, New York, 1965

R.L. Williams, 'The Dynamic Structure of García Márquez's *El otoño del patriarca*', *Symposium*, 32, no. 1, 1978, 56–75

V and VI   MACONDO (i and ii)

G. Alfaro, *Constante de la historia de latinoamérica en García Márquez*, Cali, Colombia, 1979

Alternativa, nos 187–91, November–December 1978. Series of articles entitled 'La masacre de las bananeras', commemorating the fiftieth anniversary of the Ciénaga massacre

C. Arnau, *El mundo mítico de Gabriel García Márquez*, Barcelona, 1971

C.W. Bergquist, *Coffee and Conflict in Colombia, 1886–1910*, Durham, North Carolina, 1978

E. Burgos-Debray (ed.), *I . . . Rigoberta Menchú: an Indian Woman in Guatemala*, London, 1984. Translated from the Spanish by Ann Wright. First Spanish edition, 1983

R.H. Dix, *Colombia: the Political Dimensions of Change*, New Haven, Connecticut, and London, 1967

J. Fernández, 'La ética del trabajo y la acumulación de la riqueza en *Cien años de soledad*', *Hispamérica*, 37, April 1984, 73–9

V.L. Fluharty, *Dance of the Millions: Military Rule and the Social Revolution in Colombia, 1930–1956*, Pittsburgh, 1957

R. Forgues, 'Le Printemps des peuples', *Silex*, 11, 1979, 125–31

J. Franco, *Spanish American Literature Since Independence*, London and New York, 1973. In particular, the introduction: 'The Colonised Imagination', 1–15

—— 'Les Limites de l'imagination libérale: à propos de *Nostromo* de Joseph Conrad et de *Cent ans de solitude*', *Silex*, 11, 1979, 65–71

D.P. Gallagher, *Modern Latin American Literature*, London, 1973

R. González Echevarría, '*Cien años de soledad*: the Novel as Myth and Archive', *MLN*, 99, no. 2, March 1984, 358–80

G. de Granda, 'Un afortunado fitónimo bantú: "Macondo" ', *Thesaurus* [Boletín del Instituto Caro y Cuervo], 26, no. 3, September–December 1971, 485–94

R. Jara and J. Mejía, *Las claves del mito en Gabriel García Márquez*, Valparaíso, Chile, 1972

J.B. Jelinski, 'Memory and the Remembered Structure of *Cien años de soledad*', *Revista de Estudios Hispánicos*, 18, no. 3, October 1984, 323–33

D. Kadir, 'The Architectonic Principle of *Cien años de soledad* and the Vichian Theory of History', *Kentucky Romance Quarterly*, 24, 1977, 251–61

J. Ludmer, *Cien años de soledad: una interpretación*, Buenos Aires, 1972

W.P. McGreevey, *An Economic History of Colombia: 1845–1930*, Cambridge, 1971

S. May and G. Plaza, *The United Fruit Company in Latin America*, Washington, 1958

L.I. Mena, *La función de la historia en 'Cien años de soledad'*, Barcelona, 1979

P. Oquist, *Violence, Conflict, and Politics in Colombia*, New York and London, 1980

J.A. Osorio Lizarazo, *Gaitán: vida, muerte y permanente presencia*, Buenos Aires, 1952

R. Paoli, *Invito alla lettura di García Márquez*, Milan, 1981

A.M. Penuel, 'Death and the Maiden: Demythologization of Virginity in García Márquez's *Cien años de soledad*', *Hispania*, 66, 1983, 552–60

G. and A. Reichel-Dolmatoff, *The People of Aritama: the Cultural Personality of a Colombian Mestizo Village*, Chicago, 1961

G. Reichel-Dolmatoff, *Colombia*, London, 1965

J.F. Rippy, *The Capitalists and Colombia*, New York, 1931

E. Rodríguez Monegal, '*One Hundred Years of Solitude*: the Last Three Pages', *Books Abroad*, 47, no. 3, 1973, 485–9

D. Saldivar, 'De dónde y cómo nació *Cien años de soledad*', *Explicación de 'Cien años de soledad*', ed. F.E. Porrata and F. Avendaño, Sacramento, California, 1976, 283–97

A.M. Taylor, '*Cien años de soledad*: History and the Novel', *Latin American Perspectives*, 2, no. 3, 1975, 96–112. An excellent article

A.M. Teja, 'El tiempo en *Cien años de soledad*', *Chasqui*, 3, no. 3, May 1974, 26–39

M. Urrutia, *The Development of the Colombian Labor Movement*, New Haven, Connecticut, and London, 1969

M. Vargas Llosa, *García Márquez: historia de un deicidio*, Barcelona, 1971

ADDENDUM

Inevitably, I missed a number of interesting items when I was preparing this book, while others appeared too late for me to make use of them. Here is a brief selection of such items: Evangelina Simón de Poggia, 'Anotaciones de antroponimia en *Cien años de soledad*', *García Márquez: lecturas críticas*, Rosario, Argentina, 1972, 59–87, an article on the etymological significance of proper names in *One Hundred Years of Solitude*; Gene Dilmore, '*One Hundred Years of Solitude*: Some Translation Corrections', *Journal of Modern Literature*, 11, no. 2, July 1984, 311–14, a brief, and partial, listing of translation errors in the published text of *One Hundred Years of Solitude*; Gabriel Fonnegra, *Bananeras: testimonio vivo de una epopeya*, Bogotá, 1980, about the 1928 massacre on the Colombian banana plantations; and

Cien años de soledad, ed. Jacques Joset, Madrid, 1984, a first, and very useful, annotated edition of the Spanish text of *One Hundred Years of Solitude*, with a good bibliography. García Márquez's account of the Velasco affair (see above, p. 47) has recently appeared in English: *The Story of a Shipwrecked Sailor*, translated by Randolph Hogan, New York and London, 1986; and there are some interesting first thoughts on *El amor en los tiempos del cólera* by Antonio Caballero in the Bogotá magazine *Semana*, 3–9 December 1985.

Index